❖ ❖ ❖

Uncoverings 1992

Volume 13 of the Research Papers of the
American Quilt Study Group

edited by Laurel Horton

Copyright © 1993 by the
American Quilt Study Group.
All Rights Reserved.

Copyright note: This is a collective work.
AQSG holds the copyright to this volume and
any reproduction of it in whole. Rights to individual
articles are held by the authors. Requests for
permission to quote or reproduce material from
any article should be addressed to the author.

Published by the American Quilt Study Group
660 Mission Street, Suite 400
San Francisco CA 94105-4007
Manufactured in the United States
Uncoverings is indexed by
America: History and Life
ARTbibliographies
BHA (Bibliography of the History of Art)
Clothing and Textile Arts Index
Historical Abstracts
MLA International Bibliography
Sociological Abstracts

ISBN 1-877859-06-0
ISSN 0227-0628
Library of Congress catalog card number:
81-649486

Cover: *News Reports*, by Teresa Cooper Jacobs, 1990.
Photograph by Mark Frey.
Cover courtesy of
In the Beginning
and
Teresa Cooper Jacobs

Contents

Cover Artist's Statement	5
Preface	7

RESEARCH PAPERS

Nancy Cameron Armstrong: *Quilts of the Gulf War, Desert Storm—Participation or Protest?*	9
Barbara Brackman: *Quiltmaking on the Overland Trails: Evidence from Women's Writing*	45
Dorothy Cozart: *The Handwork of Women of One Southern Family*	61
JaneE Hindman: *Quilt Talk: Verbal Performance Among a Group of African-American Quilters*	85
Carolyn Krone and Thomas M. Horner: *Quilting and Bereavement: Her Grief in the Quilt*	109
Kristin M. Langellier: *Show-and-Tell as a Performance Event: Oppositional Practice in Contemporary Quiltmaking Culture*	127
Margaret T. Ordoñez: *Ink Damage on Nineteenth-Century Cotton Signature Quilts*	148
Kari Ronning: *Quilting in Webster County, Nebraska, 1880-1920*	169

SPECIAL PRESENTATION

Virginia Gunn: *From Myth to Maturity: The Evolution of Quilt Scholarship*	192
Contributors	207
Index	209

Cover Artist's Statement:
News Reports

Teresa Cooper Jacobs

During the Gulf War I immersed myself in public radio news broadcasts and national call-in shows. I was feeling deep concern, indignation, and a sense of urgency to respond to blatant, deceptive manipulation of words and symbols regarding the nature of an escalating conflict and the need for, as well as the effects of, a military offensive in the Middle East. In retrospect I see that I had begun a personal quest to find out *What is really going on here? What am I experiencing?* and *What does any of this have to do with me?*

I did not find a sense of orientation nor a satisfying mechanism for response through the media, and so I began to discuss the news, its effects, and response options with just about anyone I encountered and everyone I could reach. I felt disheartened as many expressed a sense of isolation, and professed a belief that "I do not really matter and cannot really influence public policy nor hope to influence the course of events because 'they' will just do what they want anyway." So many expressed such a belief that it seemed to be functioning as a myth, a cultural myth which also seemed to prescribe or at least justify the general practice of disregarding the news, despite revelations of circumstances which directly and indirectly threaten our lives and the lives of our children and grandchildren and all life on Earth. Many people expressed denial, confusion, frustration, guilt, and above all, resignation.

My response was to create a quilt which I've titled *News Reports* (1991, 44" X 35"). It depicts my dizzying sense of riding in an airplane which is moving into a tail spin, a situation that only concise and efficient action can remedy. It shows a vortex pulling down life, fish, children, and the claws and jaws of the monster which even devours itself. It displays puffed up roosters which symbolize the cultural preponderance of the masculine perspective, male domination in positions of cultural power and the disproportionate misuse of trust, power, resources, words, symbols, and information by men. The quilt and the roosters represent the effects of our current gender/power imbalance rather than anything inherently negative about the masculine or men. Noticeably missing in this quilt is any overt representation of the feminine, that which is yet to be more fully explored, expressed, and integrated.

Preface

Although the papers for *Uncoverings* are selected on the basis of individual merit, when taken as a group they often share common themes or concerns. This year all of the papers, in one way or another, discuss forms of communication.

Communication takes place among quiltmakers and their families. Groups of quilters, both large and small, share particular modes of communication. Quiltmakers express themselves verbally, in writing, or through their works, and others interpret the meanings of what is said or not said. Both the text and the context, or, if you will, the medium and the message, are laden with information.

Nancy Armstrong's exploration of the creation of numerous Desert Storm quilts provides a timely look at the motivations of contemporary quiltmakers. For many of these artists, the opportunity to share strong and sometimes ambiguous feelings found an outlet through Nancy's research.

Kristin Langellier examines one of modern quiltmaking's most valued practices, quilters' Show and Tell. She finds that this deceptively simple communication ritual holds rich and complex meaning for the participating quilters, both locally and nationally.

JaneE Hindman reports from her experience as a participant/observer in a predominantly African-American quilting group. She analyzes different modes of verbal communication among members of this single small group in relation to other works on African-American quilts and forms of expression.

Carolyn Krone and Tom Horner provide perspectives from the healing professions on the ways traditional quiltmaking can serve as a largely non-verbal process to facilitate the mourning process following a loss. They use historic and fictional sources to support what they have found in their own counseling.

Several papers serve as conduits to the world of nineteenth century quiltmakers. Dorothy Cozart correlates the letters of the Caldwell women with their surviving artifacts to provide an insightful look into needlework traditions of earlier generations. Her paper helps us realize that quiltmaking was not an isolated form of handwork.

Margaret Ordoñez, a textile chemist, examines an ironic phenomenon: Signature quilts, intended to immortalize their makers and signers, have been damaged by the ink in the signatures. Further, she suggests how these important historic documents may best be preserved.

Barbara Brackman has examined the writings of women on the overland trails to present data which punctures yet another myth of American quiltmaking. In this case, the lack of quilt-related entries in written communications provides important negative evidence.

Kari Ronning looks at the quiltmaking context of turn-of-the-century Nebraska through the filter of contemporary newspaper accounts. Not only does her work bring to light important information during an understudied period of American quiltmaking, but it demonstrates the potential for research in many other local areas.

Finally, Virginia Gunn presents a thoughtful re-evaluation of early twentieth-century quilt scholarship, including the misinformation we once accepted as fact. She provides a perspective through which we can understand the creation and functions of these myths.

Together, these writers seek to communicate their explorations and experiences to readers, both present and future. Each such act of communication adds a piece to our as yet incomplete understanding of the whole picture of American quiltmaking. These writers also build upon the work of other researchers. The references cited by the authors of this volume include many of the articles published in the previous twelve volumes of *Uncoverings*.

Quilts of the Gulf War, Desert Storm—Participation or Protest?

Nancy Cameron Armstrong

*Having familiarity with a number of quilts made during previous wars and sensing something different at work, I hypothesized that "the motivations and feelings of the makers of quilts made in reaction to the Gulf War differed from the motivations and feelings of the makers of quilts made during previous wars." I developed a set of nineteen open-ended, primarily affective-domain questions. Participants responded to notices placed in quilting periodicals. Questionnaires were sent to quilters who contacted me; additional quilters were contacted directly as I learned of their quilts. One hundred and eighty-one quilters, aged late twenties to seventies, from seven countries and one sheikdom each included one or more visuals of her quilt with question responses which were analyzed using a Microsoft Works Database. The quilts/responses represent a continuum from anti-war/pro-peace to pro-war or pro the **necessity** for **this** war and expressions of patriotism. The majority, while supportive of the troops, were neutral or in opposition to the war. The most consistent response related to "doing something positive." While creation of a quilt was not **necessarily** intended to be cathartic, most experienced some form of catharsis upon completion. The extensive television coverage of the war caused great concern. The complex responses support the value of artists' statements to illuminate the intent of a work. Although patriotic quilts and quilts for worthy causes continue to be made, a large number of quilts easily recognized as anti-war and an even larger number described as anti-war contrasts sharply with the known quilts of previous wars.*

From August 1990 and the beginning of Desert Shield, until February 1991 and the end of Desert Storm, the attention of the world was riveted on the conflict in the Middle East precipitated by the invasion of Kuwait by Iraq in August 1990. My first letter from a quilter friend about what came to be known as the Gulf War "having a profound effect" on her quiltmaking came as early as March 16, 1991. After two more experiences with quilters referring with great feeling to their Gulf War quilts, I formulated a hypothesis, that "the motivations and feelings of the makers of quilts made in reaction to the Gulf War differed from the motivations and feelings of the makers of quilts made during previous wars."[1] To test this hypothesis I developed a questionnaire that was sent out to quilters whom I reached primarily through notices in a large number of quilting periodicals and newsletters.

Much is known and has been written about quilts of previous wars. American Quilt Study Group seminars have included papers by Horton on South Carolina Civil War quilts, Gunn on the Union quilts and U.S. Sanitary Commission of the Civil War, and Rowley on World War I Red Cross quilts.[2] Cozart's 1987 paper considered fundraising quilts from the Civil War and both World Wars.[3] Benberry, in *Nimble Needle Treasures* and *Quilters' Journal* in the 1970s, researched World War II patriotic quilts, including the Hatfield-McCoy *Victory Quilt* owned by the Ohio Historical Society.[4]

Starting in the 1980s, many statewide and regional projects have been designed and implemented by groups wanting to understand their quilt heritage. As each of these projects comes to fruition additional war-related quilts, most previously unknown or little known outside the family circle, are added to the public knowledge. Mary Conroy, in *300 Years of Canada's Quilts*, and Margaret Rolfe, in *Patchwork Quilts in Australia*, have documented quilting efforts of Canadian and Australian women during the two World Wars, and heritage projects in Canada and the United Kingdom, similar to those in the United States, are contributing to the world history of quilts made during war-times.[5] From war after war, we have examples of quilts that appear to be patriotic and, therefore, made by quiltmakers widely assumed to be supportive of the war efforts. (Figure 1.)

Much is known about the quilts—far less about the intimate thoughts of the quilters. Present day owners and project interviewers are pleased when a quilter's name, birth and death dates, ethnic

Figure 1. *Wings Over All* was an original Mountain Mist World War II pattern "honoring the Army Air Corps." Photo courtesy of The Stearns Technical Textiles Co.

origin, places lived, and similar information is known with a degree of certainty. Letters, diaries, and documents that provide insight into the patriotic, pro-war, anti-war, pacifist, or ambivalent feelings and motivations of the quilters are another matter. Statements made by quilters as specific as that of "A Southern Woman" in 1862, that "were she a man, she would be in the harness of the soldier and grasping the firelock," cited by Henley, may be limited in number and located infrequently for a number of historical reasons.[6] The dearth of such written materials has led in the past to the "phony thoughts historians frequently impose on quiltmakers" Benberry referred to in discussing documentation of living quiltmakers.[7]

In recording Gulf War quilt history, suppositions would be indefensible; as Benberry pointed out, "now quiltmakers can speak for themselves." At the AQSG Seminar in 1991, in Cincinnati, Debbie Hall spoke for herself eloquently and passionately about a *Wedding Quilt*. She described her glorious, loving friendship gift as "an affirmation of life and hope for the future," while at the same time she said it was a Gulf War quilt made at "a time of death and destruction."[8] My study includes a detailed response from Debbie and from 180

Figure 2. The Wytheville, Virginia *Support America Rally* was held February 10, 1991 at the George Wythe High School to honor the 128 women and men from Wythe County, Virginia serving in the Middle East. Roll Call was called by Army personnel. Photo courtesy of June Oxer Kerss.

other quilters about quilts started during the time period, Fall 1990–Spring 1991; in the quilters' eyes, they are Desert Storm quilts even when, to uninformed viewers, they lack apparent war connections. The questionnaire included nineteen primarily affective-domain questions. By July 31, 1991, 181—or 80% of the 227 quilters originally contacted—returned their questionnaires in time to be included in the first analysis of the study.[9] I received responses from thirty-six states; there are as few as one reply from thirteen states, and as many as forty-five, or 25%, from California. Of the remaining responses 6% are from Washington, 5% from Pennsylvania, 4% from each of four states: Massachusetts, New York, Ohio, and Texas. Four Canadian provinces account for 8%. Overseas responses from Denmark, England, the Federal Republic of Germany, Saudi Arabia, the United Arab Emirates, and the Sheikdom of Bahrain account for 4%. The replies from Saudi Arabia, the UAE, and Germany are from Americans and should not be considered as international replies although the vantage points do affect the responses. The reply from Bahrain is similarly from an English woman. Although each reply is from one quiltmaker, because of friendship and signature blocks, group quiltmaking, and class projects, several hundred individuals are involved. Information to amplify responses came from letters from military family members, newspaper clippings, an exhibition videotape, an audiotape of a *Support America Rally* and other secondary sources. (Figure 2.)

Only 1% of the makers are in their twenties, 17% are in their thirties, and 3% are in their seventies. Supporting Langellier's study of quilters in Maine that suggests "that quiltmaking is most easily accommodated when women's other responsibilities . . . diminish," 36% are in their forties and 33% are in their fifties; a total of 57% are forty-five or older.[10] The quilts were divided into three size categories. Small quilts with neither dimension exceeding 45" account for 29%. Medium quilts with neither dimension less than 45" nor larger than 69" account for 31%. Large quilts with at least one dimension larger than 70" account for 40%. That one larger dimension may be, as in the *Rally Quilt*, as large as 19 1/2 feet!

"Years from now, quilt collectors will know when these quilts were made."

The quilts were classified into four design categories. The first, and largest category, original quilts (57%), was further subdivided into three groups: non-representational (33%), pictorial (18%), and flags (6%). The second category, traditional or contemporary pattern modifications, an original/traditional middle ground, accounted for 14%. The third category, traditional quilts (25%), was also subdivided into three groups: exclusively or primarily traditional patterns (14%), friendship (7%), and signature (4%). A small number (4%) were grouped as class patterns, kits, or printed panels.

As the quilter's written description expressed her conscious intent, author-defined categories which classified quilts by emotional content were based on written responses rather than visuals. To avoid weighting responses, I assigned each quilt by dominant content to one of eleven categories on a continuum from patriotic, pro-war or pro the necessity for the Gulf War, through pro-peace/anti-war. The categories, the percentage of quilts in each category, a definition of the category, and an illustrative example of each category follow.

Patriotic (15%)—appealing to devoted love, support, and defense of country and its interests; the color selection and content are war related. The quilter describes herself as in support of the war and/or its necessity. Mary Andrews' stars, including her son Tony, in *Stars and Pride Forever* are four generations of family who served in the military from World War II to the present.[11]

Commemorative (28%)—serving as a memorial or reminder; content is war related. The quilter may or may not support the war, but recognizes it as a historical event of which note should be taken. Dottie Abendroth decided "to immortalize on *Salute to Operation Desert Storm* some of what I was seeing and hearing . . . people and events . . . quotes and phrases . . . military equipment."[12]

Supportive/Welcome Home (9%)—providing sympathy or encouragement to sustain mind, spirit, and courage under trial. The quilter may be undecided, supportive, or opposed to the war but has no ambivalence over supporting the troops. Betty McKinney noted that the quilt for her son, *Kevin's Yellow Ribbon Quilt*, was "made in anticipation of his safe return and with the illogical idea that the sooner the quilt was done the sooner he would be home. His safety had been my selfish, narrow and overriding concern—I leave it to others to reflect a more global view."[13]

Friendship (2%)—showing feelings of affection or personal regard; the color selection and/or content may be war related. Norma Coe was "reminded of the importance of friendships and those we love" when making *Hands Across the Sea—A Tribute to Friendship, Love and the United States Postal Service*.[14]

Neutral (5%)—relating to the war through time of making; the color selection may be war related. Trudy Jewell wrote that her Marine son "Steven always enjoyed my flower garden" and that *Wind-blown Tulips* "kept my mind busy instead of fretting over events I could not control."[15]

Pro-active/Celebrating Life/Hope/Healing (8%)—appealing to a state of mutual harmony among peoples. The quilter believes visualizing the desired situation as if it were present reality will have power to make it so. Susan Shie's Green Quilt project is the model for this category.[16] Linnea Nielsen, from Denmark, wrote that *Hope* has "no political message, only a prayer that humanity will grow so strong and wise, that peaceful stars and not explosives will be the lights in the dark nights in the future all over the world."[17]

Pro-peace (4%)—appealing to ending of hostilities, fighting, and warring among nations. In California, January 1991, before the annual quilting retreat held at Point Bonita, more than forty women decided "we've got to do something." Their signature *Peace Quilt* is one of the 23% of the 181 that involved a group. The sentiments are diverse—angry, humorous, serious—from "let peace begin with me" to "read MY lips, George, no more war."[18]

Mourning (8%)—expressing sorrow or grief over death, loss, or anything regretted. The quilter's concern lies not with the right or wrong of the Gulf War, but the irretrievable losses. Sandra Donabed made *Purple Hearts, Broken Hearts* with each "heart in some form broken, wounded or not whole." The heart with the five gold stars is Mrs. Sullivan who lost all five of her sons in the sinking of one ship in World War II; the purple heart with the silver star is Sandra's only brother, Gary, killed in Vietnam in 1968. She said, "the senselessness of war eats at me today—almost twenty-five years later."[19]

Pro-active/Confrontational (1%)—appealing to aggressive, defiant opposition. The quilter's intent is to move the viewer to action. Stephanie Randall Cooper, with daughters eight and ten, feels an urgency for involvement in the process of government; her quilt, *Inaction*, "the American flag, backwards and dripping with inequality, apathy, and lack of compassion challenges viewers to think about their responsibilities to the world."[20]

Environmental Protest (2%)—objecting to polluting the air, water, animals, plants, and other natural resources. In colors of sand, smoke, soot, and fire, *Desert Stormy Weather* records Katherine Knauer's feelings about "the deliberate eco-vandalism of Kuwait" and her "horror at the ceaseless barbaric behavior of mankind."[21]

Anti-War (18%)—objecting to use of force of arms among nations. Terrie Mangat wrote "I wanted so badly to feel completely patriotic, but in the back of my mind I kept thinking that if we had spent the money on solar energy research instead of war tools, we would not have had to get embroiled in this war, and our loved ones could have stayed safely home."[22]

Arranged from most frequent to least frequent in terms of emotional content, the distribution of quilts made over the eleven categories is: Commemorative (28%), Anti-war (18%), Patriotic (15%),

Supportive/Welcome Home (9%), Mourning (9%), Pro-active/Celebrating Life (8%), Neutral (5%), Pro-peace (4%), Friendship (2%), Environmental Protest (2%), and Pro-active/Confrontational (1%).

"If quilting rules exist, I definitely broke some with this piece."

In an analysis of construction techniques 52% are pieced, 30% are pieced with appliqué added, and 17% are primarily appliquéd. There is only one crazy quilt. Eileen Thompson Lehner chose "the crazy style to make an ironic political/moral statement in contrast to the title, *New World Order?* She wrote that crazy "fit the mood of chaos" she was trying to convey and hopes that the viewer will "feel the emotional dichotomy that was and remains present in my mind."[23]

When asked "What did you do differently with this quilt than you would have done if there had not been the war," 27% said the quilt was made as a direct result of the war. Colors other than they use generally were selected by 21%, and an additional 16% referred specifically to using atypical red, white, and blue and/or yellow. Construction techniques were not those used ordinarily by 9%, 5% varied their typical fabric choices, and 4% described a variety of approaches new to them. Comments in response to this question included the following: "beading was a major change," "the designing took an unexpected direction," and "for the first time I used words in the quilting."

Analysis of construction techniques places these quilts firmly in the late twentieth century, less, perhaps for innovative techniques than for the high percentage of quilters using both traditional and innovative techniques. Names, dates, and/or messages in one or more of several methods, including quilting, appear either on the top or the back of at least 42%. (Figure 3.) Since a question about inclusion of names or other words was not asked directly, a physical examination of the quilts might find the percentage who included them even higher than the 42% who volunteered the information. When asked if there was anything significant about the back of the quilt, 46% said yes. Labels, most of these having a large amount of detail, were specifically referred to by 28%. Beyond having something of interest on the back, 6% described their quilts as two-sided. Mary Langeloh gave each side of her quilt a name. *Letters in the Sand* has nine envelopes with possible pen-pal addresses; while on the other side, *Consumed by CNN* is a written record of events, impressions, and even terrible jokes of the period.[24]

Using a variety of photo transfer processes, 5% of the quiltmakers included photos on the quilt top; even more have placed photos on the back. Embellishments or embroidery appear on 31% of the quilts, and 17% include camouflage fabric. Satisfying for future quilt historians, 14% of those have the camouflage fabric designed specifically for the Gulf War, "Day Desert"—screen-printed early enough in 1990 to find its way into a 1991 book of textile designs.[25]

Two percent include signatures of prominent public, political, and military figures. The Department of Defense confirmed that although no detailed records were kept concerning which of the hundreds of requests General Powell received for autographs were for quilts, informally, they were aware of at least eleven instances where he signed a quilt panel.[26] General Schwarzkopf's executive assistant noted that both the General and his wife had "been asked to sign numerous quilt squares, some of which were to be used for fund-raising events."[27] (Figure 4.)

"I have never used so much symbolism before."

Traditional or contemporary patterns such as *Arabic Lattice, Arab Tent, Storm at Sea, Washington's Puzzle,* and *Judy in Arabia* were selected since their names could be associated with the Gulf War. Patterns were also selected for symbolic reasons. Nell Clinton-Moynihan's pattern for *Where Have All the Flowers Gone?* reminded her "of a whirlpool sucking the beauty out of the world."[28]

Symbolism has a long tradition in needlework.[29] Treschel's 1989 study of mourning quilts examined pictorial symbolism from as early as the eighteenth century to as recently as the quilts made following the 1986 Challenger disaster and the NAMES project begun in 1987.[30] Kathleen Francis, whose Challenger quilt is to hang in the Challenger Center in Washington, D.C., is one of the 41% of the Gulf War quilters who made reference to the symbolic use of ob-

Figure 3. A *Time for* . . ., by Margarita Wilcox, is one of the 23 quilts completed by the Online Quilters—Chapter II. Margarita says there is "a time for war, for peace, to love, and to mourn." Her poppy seed quilting pattern is a hope for a lasting peace. Photo courtesy of Margarita Wilcox.

jects. Her stone in *The Flower that Shattered the Stone* represents the power of weapons, shattered by the fragile beauty of the poppy. Jeanne Benson's poppies are *Poppies in the Sand* with no two flowers alike, blowing in the breeze, and lined up in rows—as the crosses at Arlington National Cemetery.[31] Poppies appeared symbolically on many quilts, as did olive branches, pine trees, and oak trees. Other symbolic representations include the full panoply of religious symbols; hearts and hands; yellow ribbons, flags, bunting, shields, and stars; ships, tanks, and planes; bombs and missiles; oil, flames, fire, and

Figure 4. Roxanne Rentzel's *Desert Storm* Double Irish Chain (92" x 83") "preserved history" on the plain alternate blocks with signatures of her brother's colleagues at Command Center, as well as signatures of Generals Schwarzkopf and Powell, Dick Cheyney, and Mrs. Bush and Mrs. Quayle. Detail photo courtesy of Roxanne Rentzel.

smoke; doves, eagles, and oil-drenched birds; blood, bodies, and coffins.

Yellow is not a color used frequently or comfortably by many quilters, yet yellow ribbons appear along with flags and eagles as the most ubiquitous symbols on the quilts, just as they may have been throughout the community where the tradition of using yellow ribbons to remember loved ones away from home flourished for many months. Mildred Edwards "never would have chosen yellow." *Yellow Ribbons* resulted only when guild friends surprised her with blocks for her daughter, a military police headquarters commander. Cedar Heights Baptist Church members, under Helen Carr's leadership, tied yellow ribbons through a cross-stitched prayer list which hung in the church entrance in Cedar Hill, Texas. Appliquéd ribbons are

Figure 5. Yvonne Porcella's *February* (60" x 46") "reflects the love she felt in the country during Desert Storm." Photo by Sharon Riesdorph.

"our promise to remember the troops in thought and prayer" on *Welcome Home American Heroes . . . who fought in the desert* **and** *in the jungle*. Each star, rose, oak leaf, acorn, dove, and olive branch is included for its symbolic meaning. In the title, Linda Cockrell added "a long, over due welcome home" to the Vietnam vets. Yvonne Porcella thought about using yellow ribbons to decorate *February*, but "did not want to make a blatant message"; yellow ribbons became a simple yellow binding.[32] (Figure 5.)

Yellow in any form was usually identified as relating to yellow ribbons; Janet Vavloukis' yellow ribbons on *Time of War* progressed to black to symbolize the increase in casualties as a war lengthens. Gayle Soles did not include yellow fabric in any of her work during the war; using a pattern designed for a class project, *Bows and Glory*, Gayle changed the name to *Bows and Glory: a Mourning Quilt* and the prescribed yellow ribbon fabric to black to represent her objections to U.S. actions and to mourn the dead Americans and allied personnel, the thousands of dead Iraqi soldiers and civilians, and the injured of all countries.[33]

Coalition flags—particularly the Kuwait flag—were included on many quilts, more frequently on the back than the top, but U.S. flags waved on the tops and the backs in the fabric, the piecing, and the appliqué, and in the symbolic red, white, and blues of quilts in each of the eleven categories. From a soldier's grave in Ohio, an American flag, "which the wind had whipped off its standard," appeared on the back of Lois Ide's *Thanks to and in Honor of*. . . . In California, on *I Love America*, "real American flags were used for the roofs of houses." Carol Steiner hoped "it wasn't illegal!"[34]

A step away from real flags, the eleven original flag quilts are as diverse in emotional content and construction as quilts in any category. *Non incende signum nostrum, Burn Not Our Flag*, by Michelle Fitch, was inspired by the Yakima Valley Museum quilt, made in Illinois in 1886 to commemorate the Civil War battles in which Emma Van Fleet's husband fought. Michelle looked up the figures on lives lost following the flag into battle. She wrote, "I was amazed at the reverence in handling this quilt demanded. I could not place it on the floor next to my chair when interrupted while quilting. It was always folded and placed gently in a protected location." Adding her yellow ribbon in the black eagle's talon completed her project. (Figure 6.) Shirley Grear's *Bits and Pieces of America* "had to appear to be flying because patriotism must be active." Her symbolic colors included "purple mountains' majesty and amber waves of grain," from the song *America the Beautiful*, as the quilt "represents not the war, but the peace for which it was being fought."[35]

Figure 6. Michelle G. Fitch made *Non Incende Signum Rostrum* (42" x 59") "in protest, and so that someday, after I'm long gone, someone will know how I felt." Photo by Nancilu B. Burdick.

Appliquéd and quilted camels appeared frequently on the quilts, just as live camels appeared frequently on the television screen. Linda McFarland's *War and Peace in the Middle East*, made with black fabric for death and dried-blood mauve, included quilted camels "for a very small bit of humor in such a serious, depressing quilt." The camel Betty McKinney quilted on Kevin's quilt resulted from his Holloman Air Force Base group naming their tent city "Camelot." Through Emily Owens' ironic *Good-bye Cruel World . . . I'm Off to Join the Circus, or the Gulf War from the Camel's Point of View*, she "was able to pour herself into making something while we as a country destroyed so much."[36]

Color symbolism appeared most frequently in the use of yellow, and of red, white, and blue, but examples were various and extensive: "red blood leaks into the sand," "mottled blue and red for sky and fire," "blue grids for the high technology," and "black for emptiness and finality." Black, when not symbolizing death and mourning, usually represented oil and/or smoke. Pam Wareham used Navy blue, nurse white, and watery blues for *From Sea to Shining Sea* which went in her friend Nancy's duffel bag to Saudi Arabia where it hung in her tent. Nancy, a Navy nurse reservist with two daughters and one son, was activated shortly before her fortieth birthday.[37]

"It feels too personal to part with."

Langellier found that 62% of Maine quilters most often give their quilts away; Woods, in Canada, found that around 80% of the objects made are for family members, 15% are for friends, and that a large majority of quilters have helped to produce quilts for charity.[38] Desert Storm quilters more closely resemble Wood's findings since 75% are keeping the quilts typically "to be passed down as a record of our family interests and history" and 22% were gifts, mostly to family. Two percent of family gifts were to husbands, 7% to children or grandchildren, 4% to more distant family members. Gifts to friends accounted for 6%, and 3% were given to institutions. Of the balance, 2% were sold, and 1% were made for raffles. Executive Assistant Lynn Williams was not sure of the exact number of mostly red, white, and blue quilts General Schwarzkopf has received; she guesses about a dozen. Several are displayed in the Schwarzkopf guest bedroom; "the others are packed and stored, as they plan on passing them on to their children."[39]

"I envied those people who knew exactly how they felt."

Although 51% of the quilters knew one or more people who participated directly in the war, only 12% had husbands, brothers, daughters, or sons in the Gulf. Another 8% had more distantly related family members; 32% reported a range of close friends to distant acquaintances. Two percent corresponded with pen pals. The impression, supported by statistics and detailed responses, was that conservatively 75% had no one close to them involved in the war. Mary Mashuta noted, "I was interested to see how pro-war my niece was until her female roommate was called up and put on stand-by." Mary observed, "the war was no longer an abstract issue for her."[40]

When asked if they had a different reaction to this war than to previous wars, 85% answered yes. Many replies were couched in terminology connected with moral and political thinking of "just war" theory (*justa bella*).[41] Reasons for the positive response were as divided as the Congressional debates that preceded the war, with 4% happy about the positive coming together of the country, but 5% distressed about excessive patriotism and the suppression of dissent. Another 5% said yes because they believed it was a necessary war, while 7% said yes because they believed it was an avoidable war. Many of those who admitted a different reaction to this war were quite young or much involved with young families in previous wars; these 10% said yes because they were more mature during this war. Because they were now mothers of young children 8% said yes, and another 8% because they had children of military age for whose lives they feared. Because they had family serving in the military 10% said yes, they definitely had a different reaction to this war. The largest number of yeses had to do with involvement; 17% described themselves as feeling more involved, but not always understanding why. With some of this group, television was only one of several reasons they gave for feeling involved, however, 16% attributed feeling involved directly to intensive TV coverage.

"Glued to the TV watching CNN"

Television was both praised and vilified with 34% referring to watching much television, primarily CNN. (Figure 7.) Time and again, responses to half of the nineteen questions were related to "the TV war." Television imagery became quilt imagery; "the brilliant green tracers over Baghdad" appeared on several quilts. Judy Jolly wrote from England, "during the news bulletin I saw how Bedouins on camels were sharing the desert with all sorts of war-fare. It was only a shot of plus or minus a second, but got stuck in my mind as being so strange." Canadian Billy Reid, living in Florida, noted that the Gulf War happening before her eyes was "frightening and deadly serious and at the same time it seemed like a Hollywood production." Janet Vavloukis saw "an intense media event that seemed to focus on our impressive array of sophisticated weaponry and an almost carnival atmosphere."[42]

Dottie Abendroth described herself as "a Gulf War junkie. I felt so drawn to it that I didn't want it to end. In fact, I think I went into a mild depression when it was over." Wendy Lewington-Coulter, from Canada, expressed her concern about this seductive aspect of TV through her quilt's design. *Watch It* is about the "manufacturing of consent through television" and "our ability to compartmentalize information, to see the world as . . . images made for our viewing pleasure." Coulter concluded, "If we don't like the picture, we simply change the channel. Choice of programs takes the place of significant political choice."[43]

"I found myself crying for the world."

Answers to several questions resulted in responses that related to the costs of war—costs that have been publicized widely since the ceasefire. Some were "torn between being proud of what we could do with our weapons and our strategy and being horrified at the destruction of life of all forms, human and the environment."

In disagreement over the idea that this was a war fought for oil, there was no disagreement that the oil fires were catastrophic. Whether fully or reluctantly in support, or totally opposed to this war and even all wars, reply after reply spoke to feeling "pain for all the innocent people, especially the helpless little children, left maimed and scarred for life."[44] (Figure 8.)

Not only the Israeli, Iraqi, and Kurdish women and children were of concern. Oilen Duncan's World War II experiences sneaking food past Japanese sentries to British POWs fifty years ago in Penang flashed back to her with the first women POWs in January, 1991; her compassion led to thirteen guild members making twenty-six wall-hangings for returning POWs and two infants whose father was killed in action.[45]

Quilts of the Gulf War

Figure 7. Sharon K. Lyman "used high tech construction methods" for *War Is Hell, Man* (72" x 57") since Desert Storm was a "high tech war." The quilt is wrapped in barbed wire. Photo courtesy of Sharon K. Lyman.

"Vietnam was prolonged, wasted, and abandoned."

Oilen Duncan was one of the 46% who lived through World War II. All of the respondents lived through "the undeclared Vietnam War." Many made reference to the treatment of the Vietnam fighting forces after they returned home. Janet Vavloukis' view was that "the immediate reaction to this war was an intense wave of patriotism, that may have sprung from guilt and other complex emotions associated with the Vietnam War." Patricia Andersen is twice divorced. She feels her husbands' "personalities were badly affected by their Vietnam experiences" which contributed, "in both cases, to marriage difficulties." Linda Cockrell's account of having "many classmates from high school killed in Vietnam" was an experience shared by others; equally as many did "not remember much about the Vietnam War." They were busy mothers involved with small children and family or, as Pam Dolan, young and looking at "everything through rose-colored glasses." Dolan commented "how different my daughters were with Desert Storm. At ages ten and eleven they watched the news nightly. Both girls began writing to servicemen hoping to brighten their day."[46]

"Women made a life choice where this result was a possibility."

Much was made of "our women in the Gulf." The facts are that 32,250, roughly 6%, of the force of 540,000 were women.[47] When

Figure 8. Making *Iraqi Woman Buying Vegetables* (29" x 24") helped a Jewish quilter, Sima Elizabeth Shefrin, remember "that we were terrorizing and killing countless numbers of ordinary Iraqi people . . . and that was, of course, completely unacceptable." Photo by Brenda Hemsing.

asked if women "at the front" affected their feelings about the war, 48% said, simply, no. Eight percent said no, women have always been at the front, "they just weren't acknowledged or legitimized."

Two percent indicated ambivalence; "I found it difficult to integrate the two roles these women face—that of nurturers and that of protector/soldier." Eleven percent said yes, with no further explanation. Four percent said yes, they were proud of them. Twelve percent said yes, they were "distressed that women with children at home had to go off to war with personal death as a very real potential." Several expressed even greater concern "for families where both parents were deployed and young children were without either parent." Two percent of the replies were similar to "I don't believe women should go to war; seeing women over there really bothered me." Five percent saw it as a betrayal that "now women are buying into this military stupidity."

Two of the study participants, a reserve Army nurse and a regular Army anesthetist, were also participants in the war. On returning to civilian life, Marca Davies made *During the Storm* using the friendship blocks made for her at a quilting retreat. Marca is a pacifist, but joined the reserve because as a nurse she had skills to contribute. Her response to the war was "intense fear, confusion over being involved with a war I did not believe in and strange about all of the fuss and flag waving of people at home." Caryl Gaubatz, made *Storm Windows* while living in tents in Saudi Arabia and Iraq because "she wanted something positive to come out of the experience." Her involvement in the war from November 1990 until April 1991 ultimately led her, at the age of 47, to request Army reassignment. Her last patient in the Gulf was a forty-two-year-old Iraqi civilian who, as the result of an Iraqi land mine, lost his kidney and his spleen, required a colostomy, an iliostomy, and arm and leg surgery. Sometime in the middle of the night, during the seven hours of surgery, Caryl began to ask herself if making life and death decisions was what she really wanted to be doing for the rest of her life.[48]

Direct results of the Gulf War were a change in duty assignment for one participant and a change in approach to quilting for many. When asked, "How did others react to your quilt," 74% reported favorably, and 8% experienced mixed reactions—typically positive from friends and family and negative from strangers. Eight percent reported that others experienced a release for their own emotions and an opening for sharing them. Seven percent were pleased their message was understood, and 2% were unhappy they were misunderstood.

"No one said much."

Langellier provided statistics about the importance of Show and Tell, for many quilters the single most important aspect of guild and other meetings. Sociability and personal support were ranked second and third to inspiration as reasons to quilt and to belong to a quilting group. Of the Maine quilters, 62.1% said personal support was an important or very important reason for being part of a group. When asked by Woods to rank the reasons that they quilted, Canadian quilters rated creativity and personal satisfaction 4.2, on a scale of 1 to 5, "very unimportant" to "very important." Woods noted the importance of Show and Tell as an affirmation of that creativity and satisfaction. Not surprisingly, the 7% of the Desert Storm quiltmakers who were met with "a curious silence" about their quilts were distressed, felt rejected, or at least wondered "if people were afraid to comment."[49]

Charlotte Yde, from Denmark, lecturing about contemporary quilters in Europe shared *Blue Rituals 2, the Gulf*. Yde commented, "I don't think there was any reaction at all," and further observed that "most middle-aged Danish women get quite embarrassed about political or emotional statements." A Massachusetts quilter, Sandra Donabed, noted a similar reaction to *Purple Hearts, Broken Hearts*. "During a talk last spring to the New England Quilter's Guild I showed it to 650 women. The reaction was complete silence." From Indiana, Penny Sisto wrote of people withdrawing from both of her Desert Storm quilts and that "their withdrawing makes me feel a little more isolated in my antipathy to war." Californian Gayle Soles wrote, "I chose those who saw my quilt," and where it hangs in her house is farther than the "usual visitor would come." Another Californian, Betty Sampson, said, "It was a way to find out who agreed

Figure 9. Teresa Cooper Jacobs, through *News Reports* (44" x 35"), expressed her concerns "about our collective future if we do not make important environmental, economic and social changes soon." Photo by Mark Frey.

with me and dared to say so." A forbearing observation was made by a Nebraska quilter that "perhaps the bottom line is that people are uncomfortable with messages."⁵⁰

If silence is difficult, overt rejection may be worse. Teresa Cooper Jacobs shared her complex, symbolically laden, and anti-war *News Reports* with one of her relatives who expressed "ferocious displeasure and condemnation." Teresa was asked to take away her relative's favorite quilt and to leave. She wrote that "it took a long time . . . to find the courage to write about my experiences and to share the quilt again."⁵¹ (Figure 9.)

"I also repainted my dining room and cleaned a lot."

Answers to the questions about possible catharsis and emotions in making the quilt were the most difficult to analyze. No catharsis was intended by 48%. While 22% said a catharsis was intended and achieved, a further 22% said that a catharsis was never experienced. Although a catharsis was not intended, 24% were aware of one after completing the quilt. Results from adding the two groups, and a few qualified responses, are that 48% said yes, making the quilt was cathartic.

The replies were lengthy and generally related to far more than emotions. The most consistent reply was from the 38% who referred to doing something positive, the "feeling that it was somehow soothing to be putting something together while the world seemed to be falling apart." While 33% said yes, their quiltmaking was a participation in the war in the tradition of the Sanitary Commission and Red Cross quilts and women "doing their part," 51% said no. Heather Urquhart was one of the 13% who said definitely not a participation, but a protest.

She described *Don't Make the War So Beautiful* as "my contribution to the history of dissent." Most surprising were the 27% who said something similar to "I could barely stand to leave the quilt alone until it was finished. When the last stitch went in I felt drained and relieved."⁵² They felt an urgency, a demand, even an obsession to complete this particular quilt; 14% mentioned a date with special war-related significance as coinciding with the completion of the top, the quilting, or the entire quilt.

"No idea how healing it could be to work on it."

Many made clear that the quilt provided catharsis for more than emotions and feelings engendered by the Gulf War or unfinished business with the Vietnam War. During the Desert Storm invasion, Carol Johnson planned her pictorial wall hanging of the Monument Valley while she was tending two young grandchildren. Her son's wife was undergoing surgery; the cancer was found to be inoperable. A month after Kayoko's death, *Desert Storm* was donated to raise funds for research at a Latter Day Saints Hospital. Carol dedicated the quilt to the beauty of this earth and to her daughter-in-law for her great courage. Karen Bovard's largely black *Quilt for the Unknown Civilians* mourns many "cultures which have suffered massive civilian losses through the ages . . . in the African slave trade, the genocide of Native Americans, the Holocaust, Hiroshima, Cambodia, and the Middle East.[53] (Figure 10.)

"I could make a statement through my quilts."

When asked to describe their emotions in the making of their quilts replies included such terms as anxious, confused, depressed, fearful, helpless, hopeless, and powerless. Nonetheless, quilts were started and finished, and many quiltmakers discovered something about their own abilities and strengths in the process. Asked if the reactions of others to their quilts had a further effect on their feelings, 54% said yes. In the 1990s the word "empowerment" may become a cliché from overuse; but 13% included such ideas. "It was quite a departure for me, . . . the extra push I needed to extend my creativity. It was less safe." "I had always made pretty quilts before. I now hope to make only quilts that express something and create reactions in the viewer." "Being a novice quilter, I had never previously thought of making a quilt in response to an event that was extraneous to my personal life. I am generally not daring. I now realize a quilt can be as plausible as any other art form."[54]

Conclusions

Is this group of quilts a representative sample of quilts made in reaction to the Gulf War? Perhaps not. One of the 20% who did not complete her questionnaire wrote briefly, "I did not respond when I saw the depth behind your questions, since my small piece was not made with deep emotional involvement." Elinor Czarnecki, a professional quilter with both sons serving in the Gulf War, designed *Salute to America*. "Spouses and mothers of servicemen and women" who sent Elinor "a photograph of their loved one in uniform with the service person's name, and a fifty-cent U.S. stamp" could receive the pattern free. Elinor gave away over 2,000 patterns. Nothing stated here reveals the feelings and motivations of any of the recipients of the 2,000 patterns, the makers of any of the quilts that may have been made following patterns included in nearly every popular quilting magazine of the time, or any other Desert Storm quilts that may have been made.[55] My conclusions refer to a particular 181 quilts and their self-selected makers, who may or who may not be statistically representative, and their responses to questions, several of which proved to be extremely volatile and generated complex replies.

The high percentage (71%) of medium-to-large size quilts was a surprise, as was the large number of original quilts or quilts which were modifications of traditional designs. A not unreasonable opinion, drawn from the responses, is that deeply felt convictions about a major event require a large canvas and an expression of a personal point of view. The high percentage of professional and/or art quilters in the database is another possible reason for both large and original quilts.

The large number of articles about labeling and documenting quilts that have appeared in popular publications, and the consciousness-raising influence of the heritage projects is reflected in a high percentage of quilters taking credit for their art with labels and artist's statements.[56]

Figure 10. Karen Bovard's *Quilt for the Unknown Civilians* (50 1/2" x 41"), "titled to stand in balance with the tradition of the tomb of the unknown soldiers," is quilted with a variety of symbols including Islamic stars, a menorah, Stars of David, and African calabash motifs for forgiveness, security and home. Photo by Bill Burt.

The quilts made by the 51% of the sample who knew someone, whether a close relative or a distant acquaintance are: Friendship, 100%; Supportive/Welcome Home, 75%; Neutral, 75%; Mourning, 60%; Commemorative, 57%; Patriotic, 46%; Pro-active/Celebrating Life, 36%; Environmental Protest, 33%; Pro-peace, 29%; and Anti-war, 25%. Those who knew someone made approximately twice as many Friendship quilts, one half again as many Supportive and Neutral, and less than half as many Anti-war as might be expected statistically.

Three of the five women with husbands serving in the Gulf and two of the three with military daughters made friendship quilts. Ellen Crockett, made one of the twenty-six quilts from the GEnie Online computer group block swap. About *With a Little Help from My Friends* she said, "If not for the war, I would not have done anything remotely like this. I don't usually like sampler quilts, and don't ever work in red, white, and blue." What was important and "got her through" the eight months her Battalion Commander husband was in Saudi Arabia was her friends' support. Barb Eikmeier described working with her Kansas guild while her husband was in Saudi Arabia. Designing their 1991 raffle *Eagle Quilt* was a way to relieve her anxiety. The design is "reflective of supporting the troops" but, she added, "the care and support I felt from members . . . would be difficult to attach a symbol to."[57]

Maureen McGee's husband was not deployed, but many dear friends were. *Desert Storm* was made to commemorate the event. She "purposely did not use any overt symbols of patriotism . . . the heavy use of red fabric was in anticipation of a much larger fatality rate." Of the twenty-two quilts made by those with the closest relatives in the war, only three were in the Patriotic category. McGee wrote, "although I have always supported my husband's career as a military officer, I have always dreaded the time when armed conflict would occur. Although casualties were mercifully light, they were dreadful and tragic for the families and friends involved. The men and women . . . were not just unknown strangers to me."[58]

Twenty-three participants or 13% in the study were aged fifty-eight or older and could be expected to have memories of World War II, the Korean War, Vietnam, and the large number of other wars and conflicts to which they referred. Comparing only the quilts they made: twelve were Commemorative, five were Anti-war, three were Supportive, two were Pro-active/Celebrating Life. This older group of quilters made only one Patriotic quilt.

A greater number of Anti-war quilts than Patriotic was not anticipated. Trying to identify a commonality in the makers of these thirty-two quilts, I made a data entry on an item of information many gave voluntarily. Sixty-four or 36% of the 181 respondents made reference to themselves as quilting teachers, artists, and/or professionals. Quilts made by this self-identified group were: Pro-active/Confrontational, 100%; Mourning, 71%; Anti-war, 69%; Environmental Protest, 67%; Pro-active/Celebrating Life, 40%; Pro-peace, 33%; Commemorative, 19%; Patriotic, 19%; Supportive, 13%; and Neutral, 1%. The professional quilters made twice as many Mourning and Anti-war quilts, half as many Commemorative and Patriotic, and less than half as many Supportive as might be expected statistically.

Analyzed in a variety of ways, these 181 quilts and the written responses seem to support the hypothesis "that the motivations and feelings of the makers of quilts made in reaction to the Gulf War differed from the motivations and feelings of the makers of quilts made during previous wars." A large number of mourning quilts, a large number of quilts easily recognized as anti-war, and an even larger number described as intended to be anti-war contrast sharply with quilts of wars prior to Desert Storm. Quilts relating to previous wars, quilts celebrating peace, quilts reproaching the government, and quilts protesting environmental and civilian atrocities are all concerned with emotional content not present in the known quilts of previous wars. Perhaps the most important difference about these particular war quilts is the opportunity to learn from the makers why and how they were made.

Most of the quilters expressed gratitude for the opportunity the study provided to express their feelings. "Thanks for giving us a voice," and "I feel as if somebody is still listening" were typical responses. Nancy Vase wrote, "instead of someone doing a study long after we are all dead, it's nice to know our actual intentions are being sought while we can still put them on paper ourselves instead of having someone second guess us." Gloria Harries, whose Navy son Eric asked her, with the permission of his chief, for a quilt to take to war on his bunk, wrote: "I did not realize how important to me these quilts were, until your study woke me up."[59]

A large number commented on the cathartic possibilities not only of the quilt, but of the questionnaire. From Quebec: "putting my thoughts down with regards to the Gulf War has been a coming to terms with what happened, but, as yet, not an understanding of why." From California: "you've helped me to see my quilt from an historical perspective." From Michigan: "I discovered feelings that I probably wasn't aware of at the time, because I never put my thoughts to words on paper. Maybe I should do this with all my quilts."[60]

Nell Clinton-Moynihan observed that the questionnaire helped her to reflect on why her quilt was important, but that "it also affirmed . . . the value of a journal . . . to go back to what I had written at the time of the war . . . to report . . . what my real feelings were, rather than what I remembered them to be." Langellier and Woods documented this willingness of contemporary quiltmakers to participate in building the history of the ongoing late twentieth century quilt movement.[61]

Each of us is the sum of our experiences. Feelings about events and the motivations for actions come from who we are—a truism no less true for a member of the Ladies' Union Aid Society in 1864 or a modish 1918 reader of *Modern Pricilla* than it was for the quiltmakers of 1991. There are a number of Gulf War quilts whose messages might be understood easily and correctly visually, without benefit of the makers' words. However, when asked how they felt about artists' statements 48% of the respondents said they are desirable and helpful; 21% that they always like them; 11% that they should be required; 11% that they should be available, but not directly next to the quilt in exhibits. Six percent would prefer they not be pretentious; but only 3% said no, they do not like them ever. Most quilters want to speak for themselves. What would quilters of previous wars have said about their apparently patriotic quilts, if they had had the opportunity to reply to a questionnaire or make an artist's statement?

These quilts represent the total spectrum of political belief. In an exhibition, juxtaposition with all points of view is a welcome idea; with the Gulf War quilts, a selection of diversity is essential to create a balanced perspective for the viewers. It was necessary to have the approval of the makers; not one withheld authorization. Karen Andreasen wrote "I find it hard to appreciate some of the more gruesome quilts that the war produced. However, I do respect what those quilts tell us and will tell others in the future." Cheryl Nelson's Navy Reservist husband was called to active duty for seven months. Her philosophical reply was that "the maker of the anti-war quilt has the country's best interest at heart. If she didn't care about the country she wouldn't have made the quilt statement; ergo, the anti-war quilt is equally as patriotic and possibly even more so than the pro-war quilt . . . it comes down to one's perception of protest and rebellion." Lee Conklin's son-in-law was deployed to Saudi Arabia while her son was marching in peace rallies in New York City; she added, "both guys are friends and understood each other's feelings." Across the country, Deanna Davis' son marched in San Francisco's peace rallies; the Great Seal's *E Pluribus Unum*, many from one, became *Peace is Patriotic* on Deanna's quilt. In a pluralistic society citizens expect that there will be room for expression of all points of view.[62]

Two of the quiltmakers' responses and their two-sided quilts pull together every aspect of the study. In 1992, Mary Mashuta included the camouflage fabric from Vietnam and the Gulf War on the top of *Lessons Learned*. Mary commented, "Americans again had strong controversy among themselves about whether or not we should be involved in the Persian Gulf War. However, after years of seeing what had happened to the Vietnam vets, Americans decided as a whole to support the troops whether or not they as individuals agreed with decisions made in Washington." The waving hands on the back of the quilt are for "the cheering or protesting crowds—viewer's choice." The yellow and black hands symbolize the yellow ribbons seen everywhere, the black spots the oil that figured so prominently.[63]

The pattern for the top of Mary Lou Ficarra's *Desert Storm, a Mother's Reflections* symbolizes her feelings about the war, "fighting windmills." The yellows represent the ribbons; the reds, whites, and blues—patriotism; the olives and khakis—our sons and daughters. One moment she felt proud of her son and all the troops; the next, resentful they had to be there at all. One side of the quilt is pride and the other fear. With two sons of war age, she was "terrified of losing one of them and of seeing a loss of innocence to a war over oil and power." On the back, the six cotton scarves, symbols of the country's enthusiastic, flag-waving endorsement of the war, reminded her of the silk campaign scarves on the back of antique political quilts. The back sashing represents a bloodied flag, and the inscription which inspired the quilt is a powerful 1915 anti-war song Mary Lou heard sung by an old woman being interviewed in a nursing home.

> I didn't raise my son to be a soldier,
> I brought him up to be my pride and joy.
> Who dares to place a musket on his shoulder,
> To shoot some other mother's darling boy?

Mary Lou has been upset when people seem to see only one side of the quilt. She feels "there are two sides to every story."[64]

An exhibition, *Women in the Eye of the Storm*, during November 5–8, 1992, at the International Quilt Festival in Houston, Texas brought together twenty-seven of these quilts for the first time. The correspondence provided far more than the answer to a theory. This is not the final chapter of the study, but the preface. There are indeed "stories that need to be told" in more detail than is possible here.

Acknowledgments

I wish to thank the hundreds of gracious women around the world who are united by a common concern for the human implications of war and who have freely shared with me their intimate thoughts about these concerns. I am indebted to each of them.

The American Quilt Study Group wishes to thank the Northwest Quilting Connection, Fraser Valley Quilters of British Columbia, and Hazel Hynds for their generous donations toward the publication of Nancy Armstrong's paper.

Notes and References

1. Nina Lea Mussellam, letter to author about *Fireworks Over the Gulf*, March 16, 1991; Kathleen Bisset shared *Godspeed* at Show and Tell in Calgary, Alberta, September 21, 1991; Debbie Hall shared a *Wedding Quilt* October 12, 1991.

2. Laurel Horton, "South Carolina Quilts and the Civil War," in *Uncoverings 1985*, ed. Sally Garoutte (Mill Valley, CA: American Quilt Study Group), 53–69; Virginia Gunn, "Quilts for Union Soldiers in the Civil War," in *Uncoverings 1985*, ed. Sally Garoutte (Mill Valley, CA: American Quilt Study Group), 95–121; Nancy J. Rowley, "Red Cross Quilts for the Great War," in *Uncoverings 1982*, ed. Sally Garoutte (Mill Valley, CA: American Quilt Study Group 1983), 43–51.
3. Dorothy Cozart, "The Role and Look of Fundraising Quilts 1850–1930," in *Pieced by Mother: Over 100 Years of Quiltmaking Traditions*, ed. Jeannette Lasansky (Lewisburg, PA: Oral Traditions Project, 1987), 87–94.
4. Cuesta Benberry, "Victory Quilts," *Nimble Needle Treasures* (September 1970): 4–5; "More Patriotic Quilts of the World War II Era," *Nimble Needle Treasures* (December 1970): 4–5; "Hatfield-McCoy Victory Quilt," *Quilters' Journal* (Fall 1979): 6–7; *Quilters' Journal* (Spring 1981): 8, includes photo of Hatfield-McCoy women making the Victory Quilt.
5. Mary Conroy, *300 Years of Canada's Quilts* (Toronto: Griffin House, 1976), 83–85, 94–96; Margaret Rolfe, *Patchwork Quilts in Australia* (Richmond Victoria, Australia: Greenhouse Publications, 1987), 100–6, 114–20. Not as widely known as heritage projects completed and ongoing in the United States, projects have also been undertaken in Canada (AB, BC, ON, MB, PE, and PQ) and in the United Kingdom (British Quilt Heritage Project and Ulster Quilt Survey.)
6. Bryding A. Henley, "Alabama Gunboat Quilts," in *Uncoverings 1987*, ed. Laurel Horton and Sally Garoutte, (San Francisco, CA: American Quilt Study Group, 1989), 11.
7. Cuesta Benberry, "Letter to the Editor," *Quilter's Newsletter Magazine* (March 1991): 70.
8. Debbie Hall, letter to author, November 1991.
9. The project is ongoing and now includes 250 quilters from thirty-nine states, eleven countries, and Bahrain. Items of correspondence with participants and non-participants to complete the project exceed 1,500. For reliable comparisons, it was necessary to have replies to the same nineteen questions from each participant. Further, although twenty-six, or 14%, of the original 181 made more than one quilt, to eliminate undesirable weighting, analysis was limited to one quilt per quilter. All questions were open-ended to avoid restricting responses or creating a mindset or anticipated reply as participants described their quilts, their emotions about wars and quiltmaking, and the relationship of the two.
10. Kristin M. Langellier, "Contemporary Quiltmaking in Maine: Re-fashion-

ing Femininity," in *Uncoverings 1990*, ed. Laurel Horton (San Francisco, CA: American Quilt Study Group, 1991), 32.
11. Mary Andrews, letter to author, June 15, 1992.
12. Dottie Abendroth, letter to author, June 1992.
13. Betty McKinney, letter to author, April 1992.
14. Norma Coe, letter to author, April 24, 1992.
15. Trudy Jewell, letter to author, April 1992.
16. Susan Shie, *Green Quilts Update*, 2612 Armstrong Dr., Wooster, OH 44691.
17. Linnea Nielsen, letter to author, March 1992.
18. Lauré Campbell, letter to author, March 14, 1992.
19. Sandra Donabed, letter to author, February 3, 1992.
20. Stephanie Randall Cooper, letter to author, February 15, 1992.
21. Katherine Knauer, letter to author, November 15, 1991.
22. Terrie Hancock Mangat, letter to author, December 13, 1991.
23. Eileen Thompson Lehner, letter to author, February 22, 1992.
24. Mary Jane Langeloh, letter to author, March 28, 1992.
25. Susan Meller and Joost Elffers, *Textile Designs; Two Hundred Years of European and American Patterns*, (New York: Harry N. Abrams, 1991), 264.
26. James P. Terry, letter to author, July 23, 1992.
27. Following tradition, most provided "cream-colored muslin fabric." Lynn Williams, letter to author, July 31, 1992. *Newsweek* (September 28 1992): 1, photograph includes red, white, and blue quilts and Day Desert teddy bears. "Schwarzkopf at home with patriotic memorabilia."
28. Nell Clinton-Moynihan, letter to author, January 24, 1992.
29. Patsy Orlofsky and Myron Orlofsky, *Quilts in America*, (New York: McGraw-Hill, 1974), 227–29, 236, 250, 253, 260.
30. Gail Andrews Treschel, "Mourning Quilts in America," in *Uncoverings 1989*, ed. Laurel Horton (San Francisco, CA: American Quilt Study Group).
31. Letters to author: Kathleen W. Francis, April 12, 1992; Jeanne Benson, May 8, 1992.
32. Mary Coyne Penders, *Color and Cloth*, (San Francisco: The Quilt Digest Press, 1989). Color theory helps quilters understand the power of yellow and why many find it difficult to use effectively. Bonnie Leman, "The Needle's Eye," *Quilter's Newsletter Magazine* (May 1991), 4; letters to author: Mildred Edwards, May 23, 1992; Helen Carr, April 1992; Linda Ribal Cockrell, May 1992; Yvonne Porcella, January 14, 1992.
33. Letters to author: Janet Vavloukis, May 11, 1992; Gayle Garrity Soles, April 1, 1992.
34. Letters to author: Lois Ide, April 24, 1992; Carole Steiner, April 20, 1992.

35. Letters to author: Michelle Fitch, April 7, 1992; Shirley Grear, December 21, 1991.
36. Letters to author: Linda McFarland, July 18, 1992; McKinney; Emily Owens, June 16, 1992.
37. Pam Wareham, letter to author, April 24, 1992.
38. Langellier, 37; Mary Lou Woods, "A Sociologist Looks at an Old Craft in Contemporary Canadian Life," Paper presented at the Biennial Seminar of the Canadian Quilt Study Group, Thunder Bay, Ontario, (June 2, 1992).
39. Williams letter.
40. Mary Mashuta, letter to author, April 13, 1992.
41. Jean Bethke Elshtain, "Just War as Politics: What the Gulf War Told Us About Contemporary American Life," in *But Was It Just?: Reflections On the Morality Of the Persian Gulf War*, ed. David E. Decosse (New York: Doubleday, 1992), 44.
42. Letters to author: Judy Jolly, December 29, 1991; Billie Reid, February 16, 1992; Vavloukis.
43. Letters to author: Abendroth; Wendy Lewington-Coulter, April 13, 1992.
44. "The Day We Stopped the War," *Newsweek* (January 20, 1992): 16–25; Decosse, 124; Letters to author: Sherri Young Dunbar, April 19, 1992; Diane Covitz, February 23, 1992.
45. Oilen Duncan, letter to author, April 12, 1992.
46. Bob Greene, *Homecoming: When the Soldiers Returned from Vietnam*, (New York: G.P. Putnam's Sons, 1988); Letters to author: Vavloukis; Patricia Andersen, April 7, 1992; Cockrell; Pam Dolan, February 12, 1992.
47. Elshtain, 56.
48. Letters to author: Marca Davies, March 12, 1992; Caryl Gaubatz, February 3, 1992.
49. Langellier, 45–46; Woods; Einstein.
50. Letters to author: Charlotte Yde, April 21, 1992; Donabed; Penny Sisto, January, 1991; Betty Sampson, May 13, 1992.
51. Teresa Cooper Jacobs, letter to author, May 20, 1992.
52. Letters to author: Heather Urquhart, February 24, 1991; Karen Andreasen, June 24, 1992.
53. Letters to author: Carol Johnson, February 10, 1992; Karen Bovard, April 6, 1992.
54. Letters to author: Joni Black, April 2, 1992; Urquhart; Vavloukis.
55. Letters to author: Pat Halls, April 1, 1992; Elinor Czarnecki, July 20, 1992; "Yellow Ribbons," *Quilter's Newsletter Magazine* (May 1991): 46–48; Elinor Czarnecki, "The Old Stars and Stripes" and Vou Best, "Desert Shield," *Stitch 'N Sew Quilts* (July/August 1991): 10–12, 50–51; Vou Best, "Desert

Storm," *Stitch 'N Sew Quilts* (November/December 1991): 46–47, 52–53; B. Suzanne Cosmo, "Remembering," *Traditional Quilter* (February 1992): 2, 16–17.

56. Jean Ray Laury, "Talking It Over," *Quilter's Newsletter Magazine* (January 1990): 20, 61; Marie Shirer, "Writing a Record of Your Quilt," *Quilter's Newsletter Magazine* (September 1986): 48.
57. Thousands of quilters participate via computers, modems, and telephones in block swaps, pattern exchanges, and an unending variety of networking and support for each other. Sarah Saville Shaffer, "With a Little Help from My Friends," *Ladies Circle Patchwork Quilts* (December 1992): 66–67; "With a Little Help from My Friends," *Quilting International* (September 1992): 43; Letters to author: Ellen Crockett, July 16, 1992; Barb Eikmeier, May 4, 1992.
58. Maureen McGee, letter to author, April 10, 1992.
59. Letters to author: Nancy Vase, May 2, 1992; Gloria Harries, April 28, 1992.
60. Letters to author: Joni Black, April 28, 1992; Judy Cohen, March 6, 1992; Mary Andrews, June 15, 1992.
61. Clinton-Moynihan; Langellier, 53; Woods.
62. Letters to author: Andreasen; Cheryl Nelson, April 1, 1992; Lee Conklin, April 1992; Deanna Davis, February 25, 1991.
63. Rhonda Cornum, *She Went to War*, (Novato, CA: Presidio, 1992), 180; Mashuta.
64. Marilou Ficarra, letter to author, June 30, 1992.

Quiltmaking On The Overland Trails

Barbara Brackman

Popular myth imagines quiltmaking to be one of the activities that occupied women and children traveling along the Oregon/California Trails between 1840 and 1870. To examine the myth I read seventy-nine firsthand accounts of life en route. While reading these published diaries, letters, and memoirs, I noted any mention of fabric, quilts, sewing, or other handwork. I found few references to sewing of any kind, and none to patchwork or quilting. One might conclude that such sewing was commonplace and not worth mentioning in accounts of daily work, but some women who laid over for extended periods of time mentioned sewing extensively once they were somewhat settled. After noting complaints about the labor-filled journeys and the scarcity of materials, I have concluded that quiltmaking was impractical in transit due to a dearth of time and fabric. Analysis of the seventy-nine accounts indicates that daily tasks of frontier women differed from those in the lives they left in the east.

One quarter of a million people crossed North America on the California/Oregon Trails between 1841 and 1866. Travelers often kept diaries of their journeys. Merrill J. Mattes, the primary chronicler of what he calls the Great Platte River Road, has published an annotated bibliography of over 2,000 narratives, of which 274 are women's accounts.[1] From the documents left by men, women, and children, we know much about their adventures.

When immigrant traffic on the trail began 150 years ago, the United States extended as far west as Iowa and Missouri. Beyond that line, the area that is now called Kansas and Nebraska was "Indian Territory," reserved for tribes native to the region and those who had been forcibly relocated from eastern states. West of Indian Territory was unplatted wilderness across the plains and over the Rocky Mountains to California and Oregon (including what is now Washington). These coastal territories attracted adventurers with the promise of fertile land, easily taken from the natives. After 1849, California gold beckoned many.

A typical cross-country trip began in the eastern states. People often traveled in the company of extended families and friends from their hometowns. They first journeyed in boats and trains, on rivers and roads that brought them to "jumping-off places" such as Independence, Westport, and St. Joseph, Missouri, and Council Bluffs, Iowa (once known as Kanesville). Boxes and trunks were loaded onto Conestoga wagons or spring wagons led by teams of oxen purchased in these outfitting centers. Travelers left Missouri and Iowa in late April or early May, when the grass had sprouted enough to provide fodder for oxen, horses, and cattle. Anyone who stayed too long in St. Joe or Westport risked being caught in early winter snows in the western mountains. Consequently, each spring turned the outposts on the Missouri River into boom towns.

"I could not begin to tell you how many there are in St. Joseph that are going to Oregon and California, but thousands of them," wrote Mary M. Colby to her family in 1850. "It is a sight to see the tents and wagons on the banks of the river and through the country. They are as thick as camp meeting tents twenty or thirty miles and some say for fifty miles."[2]

In the jumping-off places, travelers bought supplies and equipment they had not carried with them. Their planning was aided by several published guides to the trails, which not only explained the safest routes but also advised travelers what to take. Space was scarce because wagons carried food for up to seven months. Rudolph B. Marcy's guidebook was typical in telling travelers to pack light. "I once traveled with a party of New Yorkers en route to California. They were perfectly ignorant of everything related to this kind of campaigning, and had overloaded their wagons with almost everything except the very articles most necessary. . . . They soon learned that champagne, East India sweetmeats, olives, etc., etc., were not the most useful articles for a prairie tour." Articles that Marcy and

Figure 1. The general route of the Oregon-California trails.

other guide-writers considered necessary included bedding. "The bedding for each person should consist of two blankets, a comforter, and a pillow, and a gutta percha or painted canvas cloth to spread beneath the bed upon the ground and to contain it when rolled up for transportation."[3]

Nancy Osborne Jacobs recalled the items her family considered important. "In our prairie schooner we carried all of our provisions for the six months trip, father's chest of tools, a box of books, mostly histories of Greece and Rome, etc., Bibles, a few miscellaneous ones and all of our clothes, bedding and household equipment."[4]

The length of the trip varied. Efficient travelers blessed by clear weather and good health might arrive in Oregon in late summer; unlucky parties might have to winter in Salt Lake City with the Mormons and arrive at their destinations the following spring. Diarists often detailed their daily mileage. Elizabeth Dixon Smith, traveling in 1848, noted from two to twenty miles per day, with most days ranging between fifteen and eighteen.[5] Others might make thirty miles per day.

Popular myth imagines quiltmaking as one of the activities that occupied women and children on the trail. A recent work of children's fiction, for example, describes a child stitching *The Josefina Story Quilt* as she moves west with her family.[6] However, few examples of quilts survive with reliable evidence that they were patched or quilted on the trail. An appliqué quilt made by Elizabeth Currier is believed to have been made by her on an overland trip in 1846.[7] The California Heritage Quilt Project uncovered one that commemorated a family's trip. Inscriptions include: "Left Illinois for California, April 15, 1859;" "Pieces cut out in the winter of 1859 by Grandma," "Seven months on the road. Arrived in Columbia. October 28, 1859." The blocks presumably were stitched on the trail by the children in the family, but the inscriptions look to have been added later and the setting fabrics date from the last thirty years of the century when railroads were carrying people west.[8]

It is surprising to find so little material evidence of quiltmaking on the trail, because the years between 1840 and 1865 were prime decades of quiltmaking's popularity. By 1832, quilts were so established a part of household textile production that a woman living in Delaware could confess to her diary: "Lydia Sims . . . assisted me in putting in my first quilt. Cry shame! to think that I have been married and a housekeeper for more than fourteen years and never before was thus occupied."[9] The antebellum years were the peak time for appliquéd and album quilts in the eastern states.[10]

Could it be that the all quilts made en route to the west were used and used up upon arrival? To examine the question from another perspective, that of the women's memories, I read seventy-nine first-hand accounts of life on overland trails, written between 1843 and 1869.[11] As I read the diaries, letters, and memoirs, I noted any references to fabric, quilts, sewing, or other handwork. In all these references, I found no first-hand accounts of sewing patchwork or quilting while in transit.

In fact, any kind of sewing other than mending seemed to me

uncommon in the women's writings. My observations about sewing contradicted other students of women's lives on the trails. Sandra Myres, who has edited several diaries, concluded that "sewing was a favorite pastime."[12] To obtain some idea of how often sewing may have occurred, I chose three volumes of written records from Kenneth L. Holmes's series Covered Wagon Women, (Volume 2 included records from 1850, Volume 4 from 1852 and Volume 9 from 1864–1868) and reread them, counting any references to sewing. Of the seventeen women, nine never mentioned sewing, six mentioned it once, and two mentioned it more than ten times.

The majority of the references I found were to general sewing of clothing, especially mending and patching (I assume from the context that "patching" meant patching clothes rather than making patchwork for quilts). There are two possible reasons for the dearth of entries describing sewing or quiltmaking while on the trails. The first is that travelers did little sewing; the second is that they did much (as they did in their permanent homes), but that the activities were so commonplace they were not worth the mention.

I believe that travelers did very little quiltmaking and little sewing aside from necessary mending. Reasons include a lack of time to sew, a lack of fabric with which to sew, and an abundance of bedding, which gave the women no incentive to make quilts for their new homes in the west.

A persistent component in the myth of western immigration is the image of women sewing while riding in the wagons. Most healthy immigrants walked or rode horseback to conserve the strength of their draft animals, so far fewer women rode in the wagons than myth recalls. John Mack Faragher, after reading eighty-seven women's diaries, letters, and memoirs, writes that riding was not common, but "when they did choose to ride, women busied themselves with mending or knitting."[13] Knitting, which can be accomplished on a bumpy ride, under low light and other adverse conditions, is the most likely type of handcraft done while riding.[14] Riding inside the wagons was rough enough that sewing of any kind was difficult. Helen Carpenter, early in her 1857 trip, complained in her diary: "It has been too cold for sewing and the road has been so rough and uneven that I accomplished but little with the needle." Lucy Rutledge

Figure 2. Kansas artist Henry Worrall recorded a wagon train between 1860 and 1875. Courtesy of the Kansas State Historical Society.

Cooke, on the other hand, did manage to sew at least once while she rode. "Yes, we were sewing as we rode along. I have made Sis a little sun bonnet today." But she later complained that she was at a loss as to how to amuse herself, for, although she had sewing to do, it was "what I cannot do well while riding. I might knit but have only red yarn which I bought for Sis but it is too near summer to commence woolen socks."[15]

The most likely time for handwork was in nightly camp or daytime rest stops. Some wagon trains rested for hours midday, especially when temperatures exceeded one hundred degrees (a common summer event). Susan Shelby Magoffin wrote in her diary on the Santa Fe Trail: "I have opened a regular mantuamaker's [dressmaker's] shop on the Plains. I am sewing on a dress everyday at noon and will finish it soon." Magoffin had an advantage over the women on the immigrant trails along the Platte. As the lone woman in a trade caravan, she was required to do little cooking, laundry, or other family maintenance. The more typical women on the California/Oregon trails describe little leisure time in camp. Tamsen Donner cataloged her time when the wagons were not rolling: "I botanize and read some, but cook a 'heap' more."[16] Mary Louisa Black wrote, "I finished a letter home yesterday which occupied all the leisure I could get."[17] Sarah Davis wrote, "We . . . nooned and the men all went in a swimming and I sew and wash."[18]

Agnes Sengstacken in recalling her 1851 trip years later, wrote that the women often knitted around the campfire at night while the men talked. After a tornado hit nearby, an older woman complimented her friends on their coolness. "You just sit there with your sewing or your knitting just as though nothing had happened."[19] Like noontime camps, evening camps were busy times for women and no mention of any needlework but mending or knitting was made.

Many parties laid over at camps every Sunday due to religious objections to traveling on the Sabbath. Winton U. Solberg read sixty-five diaries of men and women who made the trip in the 1850s and found that one-third kept the Sabbath as they could.[20] Catherine Haun mentioned one Sunday when a member of the party acted as minister, preaching "in the center of the corral, while we all kept on with our work. There was no disrespect intended but there was little time for leisure or what the weary pilgrim could call his own."[21] For women who had time to spare from livestock and household maintenance, Sundays might have provided hours to stitch, but keeping the Sabbath extended to a ban on handwork, too. Louisa Cook regretted after a Sunday of traveling that the only sign of the Sabbath was "the ladies have laid by their knitting and sewing, etc." Rebecca Ketcham customarily did not do handwork on the Sabbath, with one exception, which she noted on a Sunday night. "This morning I so entirely forgot the day I took my knitting and sat down to work."[22]

Yardage for clothes and scrapbags for patchwork were no more a necessity than champagne and olives. The diarists and letter writers rarely mention packing fabric. One exception was Lucy Rutledge Cooke, who brought calico to make into a dress, but never got a chance to sew it and finally traded it in Salt Lake City for more valuable wool alpaca dress fabric. Margaret Frink in her 1897 memoirs recalled packing a full supply of clothing and a "trunk full of dress goods not yet made up."[23]

Several travelers mentioned buying material at outposts. Mary Ringo bought fabric for a dress in Kearney City, Nebraska Territory, in 1864, and noted "we find the goods about as cheap as they are in the states."[24] Helen Carpenter found fabric in Lawrence, Kansas Territory, in 1859, but a few days later near Fort Riley was disappointed to find "the store contained but little in the way of dress goods. The best I could do was to buy some brown and black chequered cotton pants cloth to make a jacket."[25] Even Salt Lake City, the biggest settlement of European-Americans on the trail, did not stock everything the traveler needed. Back on the road after a winter in Salt Lake City, Lucy Cooke mentioned her longing for fabric. "If only I had some muslin. How nicely I could be preparing our underclothes for we are all quite destitute."[26] There is one intriguing record of a traveling fabric shop. "Two enterprising women purchased a supply of cloth and other dry goods which they sold from the back of their spring wagon to pay expenses on the way to California," wrote Robert Beeching in 1849.[27] These women, unfortunately, did not leave a diary.

Once in California or the Oregon Territory, some women had access to fabric brought around South America's Cape Horn on ships.

Figure 3. Family and a covered wagon. Johnson County, Kansas, 1908. This horse-drawn wagon was probably used for shorter trips at the turn of the century. Courtesy of the Kansas State Historical Society.

However, those who settled in isolated areas continued to find fabric scarce. Remembering her first year in Oregon, a woman described it as "the most unhappy period of my life . . . simply for want of something to do. I had no yarn to knit, nothing to sew, not even rags to make patches. One day Mrs. Parrish gave me a sack full of rags and I never received a present before nor since that I so highly appreciated as I did those rags."[28]

The lack of fabric and time precluded sewing, but there was another factor in the absence of quiltmaking on the overland trails. People brought ample bedding with them and thus had no need to make quilts for warmth en route or for their new homes. Because quilts have both functional and symbolic meaning, they were a likely choice for bedding for mid-century travel. Many quilts survive in the west with family stories that they were brought across the plains in covered wagons. In addition to the evidence of material culture and family histories, there is ample written evidence that quilts were in good supply in the luggage of westering Americans.

Rebecca Ketcham inventoried bedding after her first night sleeping on the ground outside Westport. "How would you who have so many comforts at home, like to have an India-rubber cloth spread on the ground, then a quilt or blanket, and with your carpet bag and clothes for a pillow lay yourself down to sleep, while your only protection from the cold night air was a cloth tent? Over our bed clothes we have an India-rubber cloth which protects us from the dampness which comes through the tent."[29] Ellen Tootle, on her first day on the road, described a typical wagon home. "We are not as comfortable today as we expect to be. Things were just put in every way. The inside of the wagon is filled nearly to the top with boxes, trunks, comfortables, blankets, guns, a mattress, all the etc. of camp life."[30]

Quilts, comforts, and comfortables were mentioned in many different contexts in the women's writings. Aside from several references to quilts as bedding, I found two references to trading quilts to the Native Americans for moccasins, one to having quilts stolen during the night, one to burying the dead in quilts, and one to protecting a wagon from attack with quilts. One of the very few references to actual quiltmaking was near Fort Laramie, in what is now

Wyoming, where a traveler peeked into a tent and saw several Native American women working. "One was making patch work."[31]

One might argue that although women wrote about quilts as objects, they did not mention their quiltmaking or most other types of sewing because it was so much a part of daily life, on or off the trail, that it did not merit mention in letters, diaries, or memoirs. To examine this argument I looked at the writings of two women who kept accounts while on the trail and while temporarily settled.

Ruth Shackleford left two diaries. She traveled to California along the Oregon/California trail in 1865 and, dissatisfied with California, returned east in 1868 along the Butterfield Overland Mail Route through Arizona and Texas. After the Shacklefords left California for Missouri in 1868 they lived for five weeks in Hood County, Texas, considering whether to settle there. A faithful diary keeper, Shackleford wrote an entry every day of both trips. The diaries stop toward the end of the second trip, and we must assume a volume has been lost. In the 189 entries of her six-month trip in 1865, she mentioned sewing five times between April 8 and September 7: "patching," doing some patching," "patching my old dress," "trying to patch his pants," and "making Mary a sunbonnet." On the return trip, while on the road, she wrote 120 entries, including only two references to sewing.

During the thirty-five days she lived in a house or camped in her wagon in Hood County, she mentioned sewing eleven times. Not only did the frequency of her sewing increase while she was settled, its character changed. Her first reference in Hood County was to patching, the functional clothing repair most women did while on the trail. Three days later "Mrs. Kirkland came down and stayed all day with me. We have been sewing." The next day she began "stitching shirt bosoms for Mrs. Ledbetter, finishing four for which I got twenty-five cents apiece." The rest of her accounts in Hood County mention sewing shirts, sacks [dresses], and handkerchiefs for sale. Sewing became her business there.[32]

Ruth Shackleford is only one of thousands of travelers, and a rather late example, yet her diaries offer an excellent view of the contrasting role of sewing in her life on the road and in camp. While travel-

Figure 4. A family photographed outside their wagon in Johnson County, Kansas, about 1900. By this time the days of the cross country trails were past, but the photo gives us a glimpse of life in a wagon. Courtesy of the Kansas State Historical Society.

ing she mentioned sewing 7 days out of 309 (about 2 percent); while temporarily settled, she mentioned it 11 out of 35 (32 percent). If Shackleford thought sewing too mundane to mention on the road, why did she record it while settled? It is doubtful that her attitude about recording her daily work changed; it is more likely that the content of her daily work changed.

The records of Lucy Rutledge Cooke, a series of letters to her sister, are not as easy to quantify. She only occasionally gave accounts of sewing as her daily work, but she more often mentioned it as an account of work already done or to be done in the future. She discussed in detail clothing she planned to sew, had finished sewing or wished she had time or fabric to accomplish. During her winter in Salt Lake City, her references to sewing and fabric increased. It appears that she, like Ruth Shackleford, found more fabric and more time to sew while settled, even temporarily.[33]

My examination of the role of quiltmaking on the overland trails was begun as part of my work on the Kansas Quilt Project, in which I focused on quilts made on the frontier, the edge of European-American culture. To my surprise, I found precious little evidence of any quiltmaking in Kansas in its early days as a territory or as a state.[34] I also found sparse indications of the making of friendship quilts in Kansas or other western states in the mid-nineteenth century when it was so popular in the eastern states.[35] And with this paper, I find little evidence of quilts made on the trails across the plains and mountains. My conclusions corroborate historian Rachel Maines's thesis that quiltmaking requires an abundance of fabric rather than a scarcity.[36]

These findings dispute the widespread American myth of quiltmaking as a frontier craft, done by women in sod houses and ox-drawn wagons. Today's historians are working to construct a new history of the west and of the first European-American women to settle there. It is evident from the scarcity of quiltmaking that the daily life of frontier women differed from the lives they left in the east.

Acknowledgments

The American Quilt Study Group wishes to thank the Kansas Quilt Project for their generous donation toward the publication of Barbara Brackman's paper.

Notes and References

1. Merrill J. Mattes, *Platte River Road Narratives* (Urbana, IL: University of Illinois Press, 1988).
2. Mary M. Colby, "We Live in a Log Cabin," in *Covered Wagon Women: Diaries and Letters from the Western Trails 1840–1890*, vol. 2, ed. Kenneth L. Holmes (Glendale, CA: Arthur H. Clarke, 1983), 48. Excerpts from diaries and letters have been edited for grammar, spelling, and punctuation in this paper.
3. Rudolph B. Marcy, *The Prairie Traveler: A Handbook for Overland Expeditions* (New York: Harper and Brothers, 1859), 36–37.
4. Nancy Osborne Jacobs, "Incidents of Early Western History, as Related by Nancy Osborne Jacobs, A Survivor of the Whitman Massacre," in *Told by the Pioneers*, vol. 1 (Olympia. WA: Washington Pioneer Project, 1937), 78–86.
5. Elizabeth Dixon Smith, "Diary of Elizabeth Dixon Smith," in Holmes, vol. 1, (1983), 111–156.
6. Eleanor Coerr, *The Josefina Story Quilt* (New York: Harper and Row, 1986).
7. Jeanna Kimball, *Red and Green: An AppliqueTradition* (Bothell, WA: That Patchwork Place, 1990), 19.
8. Jean Ray Laury and the California Heritage Quilt Project, *Ho for California: Pioneer Women and Their Quilts* (New York: Dutton, 1990), 44.
9. W. Emerson Wilson ed., "Phoebe George Bradford Diaries," *Delaware History* 16 (April 1974): 11.
10. Barbara Brackman, "Signature Quilts: Nineteenth Century Trends" in *Uncoverings 1989*, ed. Laurel Horton (San Francisco, CA: American Quilt Study Group), 25–37.
11. The Kenneth Holmes series contains unedited diaries and letters from sixty-eight women in volumes 1–9. (Volume 10 covers material written after my cutoff date of 1869.) I read five complete diaries in Sandra Myres, ed., *Ho for California: Women's Diaries From the Huntington Library* (San Marino, CA: Huntington Library, 1980). I read six other complete diaries and mem-

oirs, totaling seventy-nine. I have also read excerpts from numerous diaries in anthologies. Although I quote from the excerpted diaries, I have not counted them because I have not read the complete writings and do not know if the woman ever mentioned quilting.
12. Myres, 133.
13. John Mack Faragher, *Women and Men on the Overland Trail* (New Haven, CT: Yale University Press, 1979), 83.
14. For a discussion of knitting on the trails see Anne L. MacDonald, *No Idle Hands: A Social History of Knitting* (New York: Ballantine Books, 1988).
15. Helen Carpenter, "Kansas to California," in Myres, 100; Lucy Rutledge Cooke, "Letters on the Way to California," in Holmes, vol. 4 (1985), 233, 294.
16. Stella M. Drumm, ed., *Down The Santa Fe Trail and Into Mexico: The Diary of Susan Shelby Magoffin* (Lincoln, NE: University of Nebraska Press, 1982), 156. Tamsen Donner, "The Donner Party Letters," in Holmes, vol. 1, (1983), 72.
17. Mary Louisa Black, "Seven Months on the Oregon Trail, 1864," in Holmes, vol. 9 (1990), 79.
18. Sarah Davis, "Diary from Missouri to California, 1850," in Holmes, vol. 2 (1983), 189.
19. Agnes Sengstacken, *Destination West: A Pioneer Woman on the Oregon Trail* (Portland, OR: Binfords and Mort, 1942) 46, 51.
20. Winton U. Solberg, "The Sabbath on the Overland Trail to California," *Church History* 59, no. 3 (1990): 340–55.
21. Catherine M. Haun, *A Woman's Trip Across the Plains in 1849*, quoted in Solberg, 350.
22. Louisa Cook, "Letters from the Oregon Trail 1862–1863," in Holmes, vol. 8 (1989), 31; Leo M. Kaiser and Priscilla Knuth, eds., "From Ithaca to Clatsop Plains: Miss Ketcham's Journal of Travel, " *Oregon Historical Quarterly* 62 (September and December 1961): 380.
23. Lucy Rutledge Cooke, 256; Margaret A. Frink, "Adventures of a Party of Goldseekers," in Holmes, vol. 2, (1983), 59.
24. Mary Ringo, "Diary of Mary Ringo," in Holmes, vol. 8 (1989), 211.
25. Helen Carpenter, 100.
26. Lucy Rutledge Cooke, 294.
27. Robert Beeching, quoted in Sandra Myres, *Westering Women and the Frontier Experience 1800–1915*, (Albuquerque, NM: University of New Mexico Press, 1982), 263.
28. MacDonald, 85.
29. Kaiser and Knuth, 251.

30. Ellen Tootle, "A Trip to the Colorado Mines in 1862," in Holmes, vol. 8 (1989), 63.
31. Juanita Brookes, ed., *Not By Bread Alone: The Journal of Martha Spence Heywood* (Salt Lake City, UT: Utah State Historical Society, 1978), 18.
32. Ruth Shackleford, "To California by the Mormon Trail, 1865" and "California to Texas in 1868" in Holmes, vol. 9 (1990), 87–150.
33. Lucy Rutledge Cooke, 209–95.
34. Barbara Brackman, "Quilts on the Kansas Frontier," *Kansas History* 13 (Spring 1990), 13–22; Barbara Brackman, "The Rocky Road to Kansas," in *Kansas Quilts and Quiltmakers* (Lawrence, KS: University Press of Kansas, in press).
35. Brackman, "Signature Quilts."
36. Rachel Maines, "Paradigms of Scarcity and Abundance: The Quilt as an Artifact of the Industrial Revolution," in *In the Heart of Pennsylvania: Symposium Papers*, ed. Jeannette Lasansky (Lewisburg: PA: Oral Traditions Project, 1986), 84–9

The Handwork of the Women of One Southern Family

Dorothy Cozart

This article examines what the author believes to be typical roles of the women of a mid-nineteenth century Southern family in the production of clothing and decorative household articles. Using family letters written during the years 1846–1863, the author quotes excerpts which indicate such things as the kind of handwork being done, the women's attitudes toward the handwork, and how those attitudes were being transmitted to their children. In addition, she uses extant family artifacts which remain in two collections, one in the home of a descendant who lives in Oklahoma and one in a small college in Georgia, to illustrate the family's production. She concludes with an evaluation of the women's roles and their reaction to these roles.

In 1935, my father-in-law's Aunt Hattie sent him a large group of items that had belonged to his relatives in Georgia and Tennessee. She had already given some things to her brother's family in Columbus, Georgia, and to Wesleyan College in Macon, Georgia. She wanted her nephew, Hugh Holman Cozart, to have some of the possessions, and, at the same time, she gave additional items to a nephew's family in Canada. In the Cozart Collection [as the items given to Hugh Holman Cozart will subsequently be called] were, among other things, an accumulation of papers, covering a time span of about sixty years, from 1840 to 1900. Among the papers were Family Letters [as they will subsequently be called], some written as early as 1845, but most written during the years 1850 to 1863. Another large group of items consisted of pieces of clothing and other handmade articles, along with the tools used in their production.

When I became a member of the Cozart family, I was fascinated by the letters and other papers and by the wealth of handwork that had apparently been done by three generations of women, members and descendants of one Caldwell family. They had first lived in Georgia, but most of them later moved to Tennessee.

In my research I have contacted all the recipients, or their descendants, given items by Hattie Cozart Gates. I corresponded with the granddaughter of one of the principal letter-writers. Mary Cozart Burns was very interested in the family genealogy, as I was, but remembered virtually nothing about the handwork. I also contacted members of the nephew's family in Canada, but they knew little about the articles given to that family.

Fortunately, an article had appeared in *The Wesleyan Alumnae* in 1930, telling of "The Arrival of a Treasure Chest."[1] Most of the items given to Wesleyan College [which will hereafter be referred to as the Wesleyan Collection] were described in the article. It also explained that the reason for the gift was that the mother and aunt of the donor had both attended Wesleyan College in its early years. In 1987, after attending the AQSG Seminar in Gatlinburg, Tennessee, my husband Hugh and I visited Wesleyan College and saw all the articles that remain there. The bulk of the research material used herein is based on the contents of the Cozart and Wesleyan Collections.

Mary Walker and Charles Young Caldwell were married, probably in Putnam County, Georgia, a few years before the 1821 land lottery. They received a grant in that lottery and moved to their new home in Houston County soon afterward. Two daughters, Harriet and Elizabeth, were born in Putnam County prior to their move, and four other children, Samuel, Mary, Martha, and Julia, were born after their move, in the decade of the 1820s. Charles Caldwell was what could be considered a small plantation owner, a planter. He owned fewer than ten slaves, and cotton was the main crop on his plantation.

During the 1830s Caldwell prospered, and, in 1836, he helped found the Georgia Female College, later called Wesleyan College, in Macon, Georgia.[2] Family tradition states that he contributed money to its foundation.[3] By 1836 Harriet, the oldest daughter, had married Dr. John Strother, a physician. Elizabeth, or Lizzie, as she is called in the Family Letters,[4] had married Robert Owsley, a teacher. Martha attended Georgia Female College in 1839, and Mary graduated from there in 1841. In 1845, Martha married Robert Nelson, and Samuel also married that year.

With the scattering of the family members, letters became an important way of keeping in touch, and the first of the Family Letters were written shortly after the death of Mary Walker Caldwell in August 1846. By the time of her death, Mary had, in addition to five daughters, four granddaughters who would carry on the tradition of producing all the family clothing and making domestic articles popular at the time. (Figure 1). What emerges from an examination of the Family Letters and the extant articles in the Cozart and Wesleyan Collections may be a very typical example of the handwork being done in other southern homes at the same time.

Most of the Family Letters were written by four of the sisters, Harriet, Mary, Martha, and Julia. There is only one letter from Lizzie, who must have been a semi-invalid most of her life. She died at age thirtyeight, of "chronic bronchitis."[5] The oldest, Harriet, wrote frequent, long, and descriptive letters. She undoubtedly felt responsible for her siblings after the death of her mother and often offered advice or sympathy as she felt it was needed.[6] After her sisters had children, she often made clothing for them. For example, on May 9, 1857, she wrote to Martha: "Will you send me a measure of David and Abner—the length of their arms & waists? You can notch some paper & write at the notches. I would like to do something if I could for them."[7] Mary Ellen, her only daughter, was the oldest of the next generation. She often stayed in the Caldwell home and had a close relationship with her aunts. There are a number of communications from her in the Family Letters.

Mary, the third sister, was literally the family's teacher. Because she did not marry, she lived in her sisters' homes after the death of their father in 1854, and there she taught nieces and nephews, as well as cousins and neighbor children. Mary probably studied painting at Georgia Female College, and the theorem paintings mentioned

Figure 1. Relationship of Family Members

Charles Young Caldwell m. Mary Walker

Harriet	Elizabeth (Lizzie)	Samuel	Mary	Martha		Julia
m.	m.	m.		m.1	m.2	m.
John Strother	Robert Owsley	Susan Lesuesur		Robert Nelson	Abram Cozart	Abram Cozart
Mary Ellen	Joanna	Ellen		Charles Young Caldwell	Hattie	Mattie
m.					m.	
Cyrus Sneed	Newday	Julia			Josiah Gates	Joseph
						Hugh Holman
						Joseph Hugh (husband of author)

(Each of Charles Young and Mary Walker Caldwell's married children also had sons, but they are not given here as they are not referred to in this article.)

in *The Wesleyan Alumnae* may have been done there.[8] Her niece and grandniece both considered her a "wonderful artist."[9]

Julia, the youngest, was, according to Harriet, "alternately indulged or neglected as such children generally are."[10] In 1846, when Julia was seventeen years old, Abram Cozart, from Harrodsburg, Kentucky, came to her father's plantation, probably selling horses. He had been driving hogs, or horses and mules, from Kentucky to Georgia for at least three years. Sometime before December 1, 1846, Abram asked Julia to marry him, and they were married the following March. Joseph Henry Cozart, their oldest child, and my husband's grandfather, was born in 1848. In 1853, shortly before the birth of Julia's fourth child, the Cozarts moved to Philadelphia, Tennessee, where Abram became a merchant and commission buyer. On August 24, 1854, Julia died of cholera. Julia's last letter reads, in part: "I am shirt making. Don't you feel for me some days & don't think I am obliged to lay my work down more than one thousand times, and you know if I get off that well. I will in the course of time, if I live, to finish my shirts."[11]

Fortunately, Martha, who was two years older than Julia, was able to go to Tennessee to help Abram with the children. It is not surprising that she and Abram were married in December of the same year. Martha had been married previously, but she and Robert Nelson did not live together very long. Martha's granddaughter, Mary Cozart Burns, said that he was a "ne'er-do-well," according to Martha's daughter Hattie.[12] In 1851, Martha was granted a divorce by the Georgia Senate, and the surnames of both her and her son, Charles, were changed to her maiden name: Caldwell.[13] After Martha married Abram, Charles became a part of the family in Tennessee, and the Cozarts were to have six more children. Of the eleven children, only two were girls: Mattie, Julia's daughter; and Hattie, Martha's daughter. It was Martha, and later Hattie, who saved the papers and other family memorabilia.

In the Cozart and Wesleyan Collections are approximately one hundred handmade items. Most are clothing, but also included are domestic articles made with netting, crocheting, candlewicking, and teneriffe lace. There are enough hair flowers to make a large wreath, and many more articles.

Figure 2. Two of the three samplers in the Cozart Collection. The larger one was made by Harriet Caldwell and the smaller one by her sister, Mary Walker Caldwell. Each contains their maker's initials, and the smaller one also has the name "Mary" on it. Only the "1" and the "8" remain of the date on the smaller one. Photo by Jim Nay.

Few of the items in either Collection can be designated as having been made by a particular member of the Caldwell family. However, by careful examination, the makers of a few items can be deduced. For example, there are three samplers in the Cozart Collection.[14] The largest bears the initials, "H. C.," which could stand for Harriet Caldwell. (Figure 2). There are no initials on a smaller one, but the smallest contains the strongest evidence as to the makers of all three. Not only are the initials "M. W. C." on the piece, but the name "Mary" is also there. This sampler was certainly made by Mary Walker Caldwell, the third sister. The largest one was then surely made by Harriet, and the one without initials must have been made by Lizzie, who was between Harriet and Mary in age. The three are all done on the same even-weave linen and use the same colored thread. Mary's is the same width as Harriet's. Lizzie's is rectangular and measures approximately seven by nine inches. There is part of a date at the top of Mary's; the "1" and "8" are clearly visible, but she had trouble with the last two numbers, and only holes remain. Therefore it is impossible to assign a date to their making. However, if it is assumed that Martha and Julia were too young to make samplers when these were done, then they may have been made in the early 1830s.[15]

The Cozart Collection includes a beaded bag. (Figure 3). In the handsewn lining, just below the opening, are the initials "M. G. N." There can be little doubt that it was made by Martha Glenn Nelson, and because she was married in 1845 and regained her maiden name after her divorce in 1851, it would have been made between those years.

Probably a more tenuous attribution has been made for what is labeled on the reverse side as "A. W. Cozart's Note Case." The case has a series of handsewn pockets with letters of the alphabet on each pocket, and, at one end, wider pockets for "Accounts," "Orders," and "Receipts." A careful comparison of the script letters and words on the case to the many handwritten letters of Martha, his second wife, has led me to the conclusion that she was the one who made the case for Abram Whitenack Cozart.

The only item whose maker was clearly identified was originally in the Wesleyan Collection: "a glazed chintz quilt made by the mother of Mary and Martha Caldwell . . . made for the huge four-posters of a century ago and [the] tiny stitches must number millions."[16] Regrettably, the quilt is no longer in the Collection. The only extant material proof that the Caldwell women made quilts is a tattered remnant of an antique quilt which remains in the Cozart Collection. However, there is evidence in the Family Letters that they did, indeed make quilts. Martha wrote to Julia in 1853: "I have

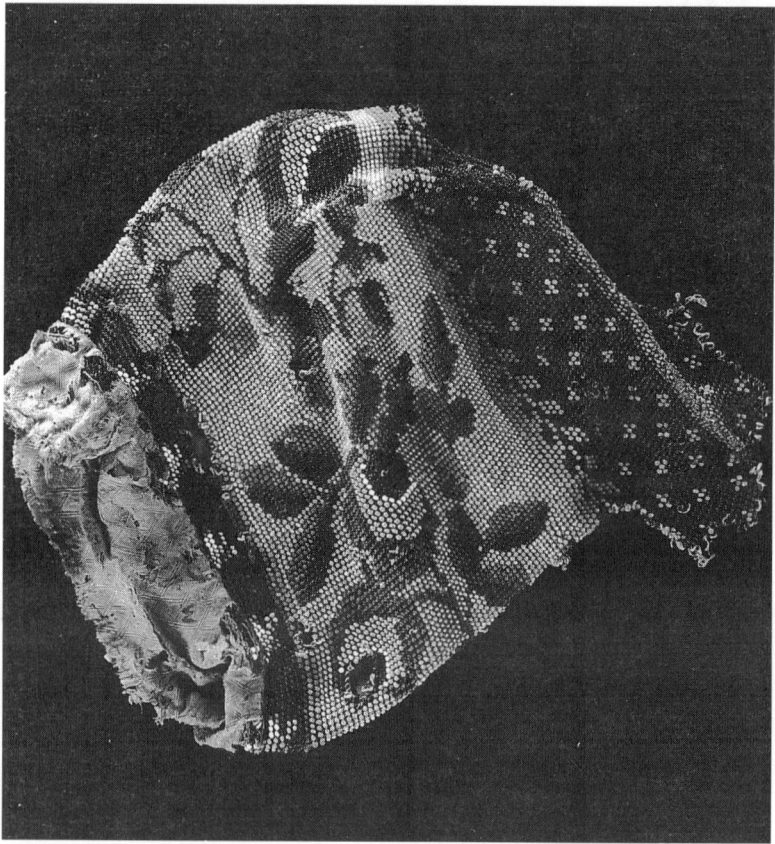

Figure 3. Part of a hand beaded bag made in the mid-nineteenth century by Martha Caldwell. Initials on the lining (shown at the top of bag) identifies the maker. Photo by Jim Nay.

trimmed your quilt pieces ready for putting together."[17] Mary Ellen, Harriet's daughter, obviously learned to make quilts at home, since soon after she was married, she wrote: "I shall have to make me some quilts &c. I have commenced one quilt, have two ready to quilt. It feels very odd for me to have to go off & depend on myself but that time generally comes to us all."[18]

In addition, the Caldwell sisters must have attended quiltings in their neighborhood whenever they were held. Mary wrote about some social events while Martha was visiting Julia in Tennessee.

> Since I wrote you I attended a quilting up at Mrs. Turner's. . . . Everyone else around here was there. . . . The quilt was a plain one & finished soon after dinner. Papa seemed to favor my going though he & our baby [Martha's Charlie was staying with them.] were alone, but Sammy went after me about 4 o'clock & I did not go very early. Many others went later. It was a very pleasant company. Later in the evening the grand Party came off & Mrs. Buck N. told me a great deal of rude playing. I enjoyed the first of the party well enough & I never liked these plays.[19]

About twenty years earlier, "A Lady" had cautioned readers of *The Young Lady's Friend* about joining in "any rude plays that will subject you to being kissed or handled in any way by young gentlemen."[20]

Mary continues in the same letter: "Mrs. Scott had sent me word that she would come to see us that day Tuesday. . . . She was making a <u>Tulip Quilt</u>, tolerably pretty. The other ladies were sewing on calico dresses for the little girls. They seemed to enjoy their visits &, of course, I did."[21]

The earliest Family Letters mention weaving a number of times, and it is evident that it had been an important activity in the Caldwell home. It is virtually certain that all the sisters learned to card wool, to spin, and to dye wool and cotton thread, as well as to weave. In addition, the Cozart Collection includes a four-yard length of handwoven linen. In the selvage, at the end where the weaving was finished, are the initials "H. C." These initials could stand for Harriet Caldwell. There are also four weaving drafts in the Cozart Collection.

It is clear, however, that about the time the Letters began, in 1846, the family weaving was being done by women in the neighborhood, and, in one letter, Mary says that she may not be able to get the "counterpains" woven, as there were not many weavers around.[22] Later, Harriet found someone near her home to do the weaving. "You may send your thread when Major [a slave] comes or when our cart comes up—Mrs. Newton says she will weave the Virginia Beauty at 12 1/2¢ a yard.[23] Since two white cotton counterpanes are included in the Wesleyan Collection, (Figure 4), it may well be that the Virginia Beauty was white cotton. Indications that this is true are Mary's use of the word "counterpane" and Harriet's use of "thread." The Caldwell women apparently made distinctions between white cotton counterpanes and colored wool coverlets and between cotton thread and wool yarn in much the same way that we do today.

Further proof of this is Mary's use of the word "coverlid" when she writes of planning to have one made for Julia soon after her move to Tennessee. Mary writes: "Does Julia want her Blanket woven after the Orange Quarter pattern."[24] One of the weaving drafts in the Cozart Collection is for that pattern, and it must have been well-liked by the family. However, when Julia's coverlet was finished it was "brown wool woven . . . after the pattern of what we call the double bow knot."[25] In the Wesleyan Collection is a brown and white wool coverlet, which I had hoped would be either the Double Bow Knot, or even the Orange Quarter pattern. However, its pattern has been identified as Nine Snowballs.[26] When Julia received her coverlet, she wrote her appreciation. "I am thankful to Mary for having the blanket wove. I am proud to think there is one in this wide world that think of me and my pleasure. . . . I feel very thankful for such favors that I may never be able to return.[27]

By 1853 the loom room at the Caldwell home was being used as a smoke house.[28] And, in addition to the weaving, the carding and dyeing, at least with indigo, were also being done outside the home. That year Mary wrote about washing their wool and having it carded at Mathew's Mill.[29] In the same letter she says she has completed the supervision of the spinning of the wool and was considering hiring a Mrs. Aiden to dye it blue. Note that Mary was supervising the

Figure 4. One of a pair of handwoven pillow shams in the Wesleyan Collection. They match one of the two white cotton counterpanes in the Collection. Photo by Jim Nay.

spinning. This is the only mention of any handwork activities being done by the family's slaves.

During the Civil War, the women spun cotton and carded and spun wool, and the letters mention the necessity for spinning because thread was so expensive.[30] Also, cards became very scarce, and Harriet notes: "I could have got them in the summer at $1.00 but they are all gone now. I have one pr. only."[31]

Most of the thread made was probably used for knitting; however, at least one of the sisters, Martha, started weaving again. After Harriet visited a fair in Macon in 1860, she wrote Martha. "I hope that the next fair you will show everything except your children—your flannel, cabbage, cows and all.[32] One letter to Tennessee notes: "I was glad to hear about your homespun dresses . . . the new linsey is very pretty."[33]

The Caldwell women who had children spent much time sewing clothing for them. (Figure 5). And, in fact, most of the references in the Letters concern garment construction. When Martha was expecting Charlie, her first child, Harriet wrote: "I have just finished the muslin dress, two nice little caps & sent them & your thimble & an untrimmed cap."[34] In the Cozart Collection are two baby's dresses and several netted embroidery caps, for adults as well as children. (Figure 6). When Charlie was small, his mother called him "Buddy." In August 1848, Martha wrote to Harriet, describing a dress she had

Figure 5. A linen jacket made for one of the children of the Caldwell women. It is fully lined and has buttonholes on the waist band so that it could be buttoned onto trousers. Photo by Jim Nay.

made for him. "I have finished Buddy's Linen dress. It was sent for by the time it was finished by the Vineville ladies for a pattern. It is worked in bright colors."[35] Most items of the children's clothing in both Collections are embellished with hemstitching or embroidery or other decoration, as was Buddy's linen dress. As Martha's family grew, her relatives made many garments for her children. In 1857, when Martha had a new baby, Mary Ellen wrote: "I felt very much mortified that Ma sent that unfinished dress for the baby.... I knew you had work enough of your own to do & it was no favor to send you half finished tedious work."[36]

During the Civil War stockings had to be knitted by hand. In

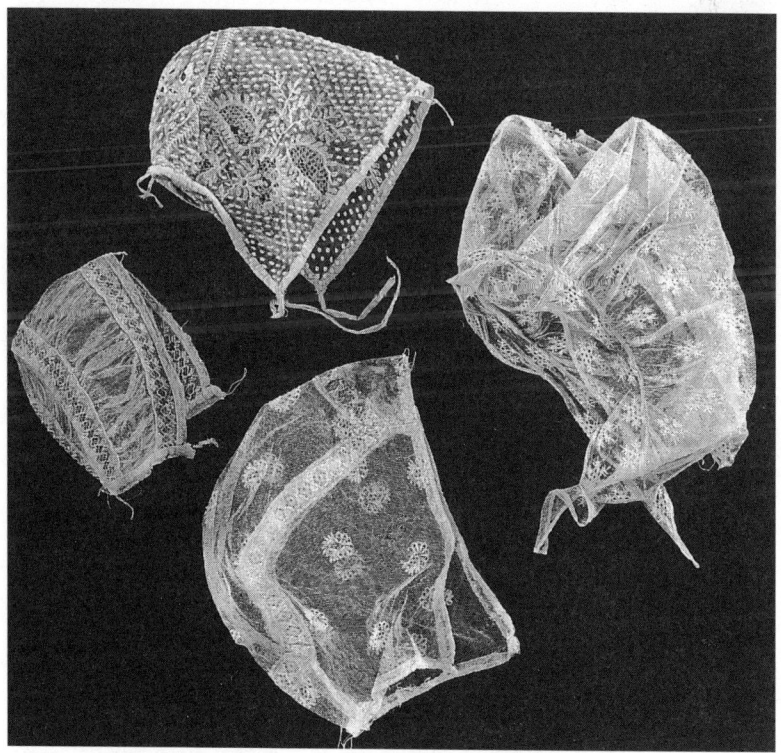

Figure 6. Netted embroidery caps in the Cozart Collection. One is for a newborn baby and another is for a small child. Two must have been made for adults. Photo by Jim Nay.

January, 1862, Mary Ellen wrote: "I have knit Hattie some little Rail Road Stockings but will send them next time with some other things."[37] The stockings were knitted in the railroad stitch, which made a pattern resembling railroad tracks.[38] Emma Tyler Blaylock, who lived in Barnesville, Georgia, at the same time as Harriet and Mary Ellen, later wrote in her memories of the war the following: "Our hosery was pretty, but a lot of trouble. Knitting was the fancy work of the period. Railroad, open work and clock and leaf patterns were the favorites."[39]

Frequent advice was given to the girls in the family about their manners, or about perfecting their handwork skills. Mary Ellen wrote to twelve-year-old Mattie in August 1863. "I am glad to learn that you can sew so nicely & that you needlework too."[40] The Caldwell family must have made this distinction between plain and fancy needlework. Mary was staying with Harriet and Mary Ellen when the letter above was written. She wrote to Samuel's daughter, Cattie, whose family was living in Tennessee with Martha and Abram. She had knitted stockings for Cattie's sister, Julia: "Tell her they are to remind her to be good, mind her sister, spell pretty, wear bonnet and be a little lady. Teach her to knit or sew, which ever she does best, but not keep her too long confined at one thing."[41] Earlier Harriet had given similar advice to Mattie's mother, Julia. "Tell Mattie that a wax doll of [Mary] Ellens is put away for her. She must make Pa and Joe [her brother] a heap of shirts & socks & learn to spell by the time Ellen goes to see her & carry the doll.[42] Mattie was three at that time, and about ten years later Harriet complimented Mattie on her knitting. "Tell Mattie we are proud of her socks she has finished for David [another brother]."[43]

Often samples of the fabrics being used for clothing were sent in the Letters, and some of them remain. When Mary Ellen married Dr. Cyrus Sneed, Harriet not only included a scrap of the wedding dress, a pink and purple plaid taffeta (Figure 7), she also described it. "It has flowing sleeves with two ruffles, one falling over the other at the bottom—plain waist with lapels going up from the belt out on the shoulders with fancy ribbon quilled at the outer edge."[44] The makers may have copied a style seen in a magazine. It is known that the Caldwell women had access to some magazines, as a bound volume of *Peterson's*, 1860, is in the Cozart collection.

Figure 7. Some of the fabric scraps sent by the Caldwell women in their Letters. The lower one is the purple and pink plaid taffeta used in Mary Ellen Strother Sneed's wedding dress. Photo by Jim Nay.

The women frequently described the clothing they were making for themselves. Soon after Julia and Abram moved to Tennessee, Mary teased Julia about two new dresses, which had obviously been described in a previous letter. "I congratulate Mrs. C. on having 2 new dresses. But I thought the Ladies wore Cashmere up there in the region of snow. But she is preparing them for the time she returns to this climate."[45] Shortly thereafter Martha described her new undersleeves to Julia. "I have just finished for myself a pair of Jaconit undersleeves with the insertion bands and ruffled.[46] One of a pair of similar undersleeves is in the Cozart Collection except that the ruffles are edged with intricate *broderie anglaise*. (Figure 8). A yard of jaconette is listed on a bill of sale for goods purchased by the Caldwells at about the same time. It cost thirty-three cents.[47]

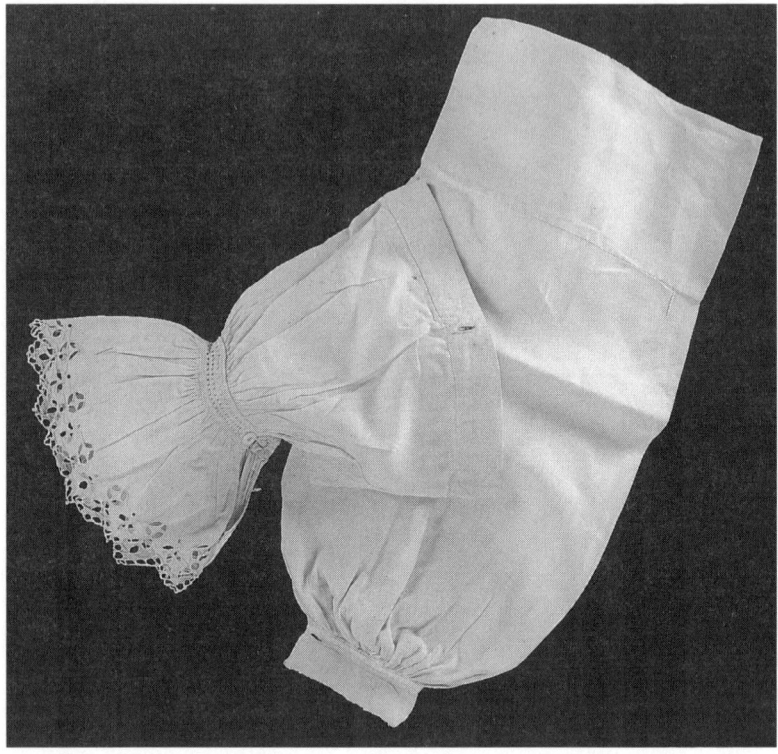

Figure 8. Two undersleeves from the Cozart Collection. The one on the left is similar to one described by Martha Caldwell in a Family Letter. Photo by Jim Nay.

Some of the garments in both Collections were made using a sewing machine. And, although there is no mention of a purchase of one in the Letters, examination of some of the clothing has revealed that one may have been purchased by Martha and Abram shortly before the Civil War. The most concrete evidence is that three small boy's caps in the Wesleyan Collection have machine stitching. The different sizes would probably fit boys from about ages two to seven. Three of the Cozart sons were born in 1853, 1855, and 1857, and they could have worn the caps in about 1860. Two garments, a girl's long white dress, made for a child about a year old, and an apron which might fit a two or three-year-old, may have been made for

Hattie, who was born in 1860. (Figure 9). Since there were only two girls in the Cozart family, and since Mattie was ten years older than Hattie, it is fairly safe to assume that both pieces were made for the younger daughter.

A large group of patterns, used from about 1850 to 1900 are in the Cozart Collection, including three late nineteenth-century commercial blouse patterns. Most, however, are not for clothing, but for embroidery. (Figure 10). Harriet and Mary Ellen were apparently particularly adept at making patterns. One is inscribed: "Mrs. M. G.

Figure 9. One of the garments made using a sewing machine. It is representative of the decorative detail used by the Caldwell women. The decoration on the bib, pockets, ends of the ties and around the skirt were done by cutting out small circles of a red and white checked fabric. The circles were then applied with a buttonhole stitch around the edge of each circle. Photo by Jim Nay.

Cozart from M. E. S. [Mary Ellen Sneed] (November 1859.)" [parentheses hers]. Some of the patterns have numerous needle holes in them, indicating that they were used again and again, being sewn to the fabric each time. And a piece of white cambric is still attached to one pattern, unfinished.

The Cozart Collection also contains various handwork tools. Perhaps the hand-wrought scissors are the same ones that Julia left in Georgia after her visit in February 1853. "Penny [a slave] found Julia's little scissors . . . in that box in the kitchen which has Lizzie's things

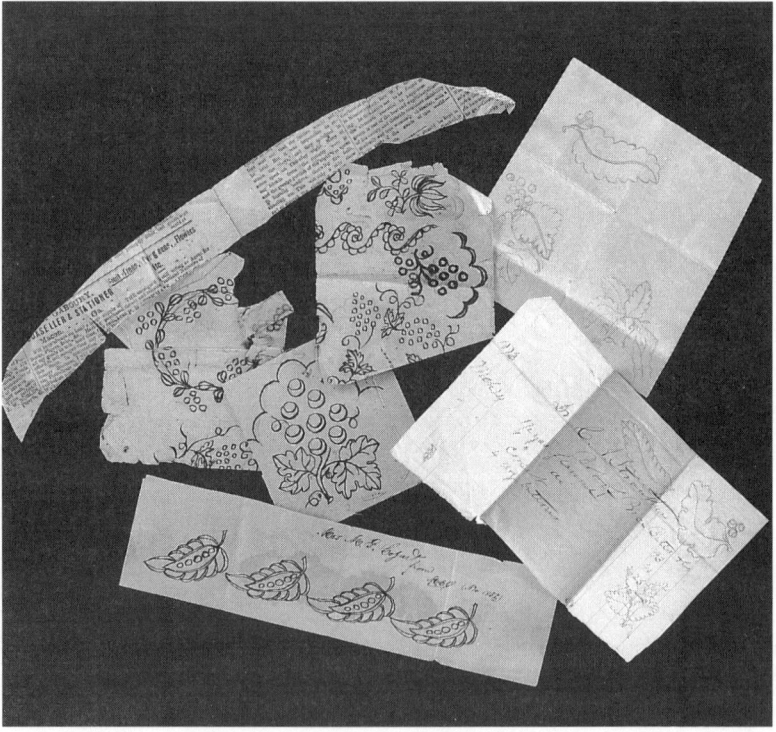

Figure 10. Some of the many patterns in the Cozart Collection. A collar pattern has been cut from a Macon, Georgia, newspaper, and some patterns have been sketched on a bill for sewing supplies. Another pattern was done for Martha Cozart by Mary Ellen Sneed and is dated 1859. Photo by Jim Nay.

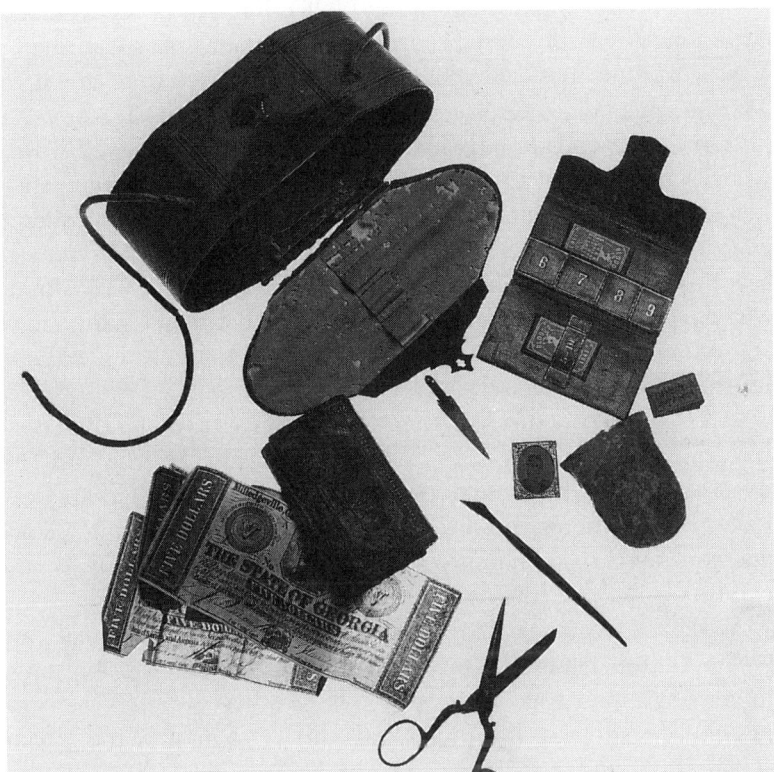

Figure 11. A sewing case owned by one of the Caldwell women. All of the articles were still in the case when it was sent to Oklahoma as a part of the Cozart Collection. Photo by Jim Nay.

in it. Said she happened to think Miss Martha was cutting & pressing that day & might have let them fall in the box."[48] A leather-covered sewing case that could also be used as a purse still contains a stiletto, a needle case with packages of various-sized needles, and a chamois-skin thimble bag. Also in the case is an unidentified photograph and a wallet containing twenty-five dollars in Georgia Confederate five-dollar bills. (Figure 11). Other handwork tools in the Collection include knitting needles, crochet hooks, and several hairpin lace implements, some of which were purchased, some homemade.

There are no thimbles in either Collection, but, since thimbles have long been considered special gifts for young girls learning to sew, it is quite possible that the family thimbles were given to Martha's granddaughers, some of whom lived in Georgia.

The Letters end abruptly with three written November 29, 1863. Mary, who was staying with Harriet in Barnesville, Georgia, ends her letter: "If communication keeps up, I hope to see you one of these days."[49] The letters were to be taken to Philadelphia, Tennessee, by a Mr. Ballard. Since the three letters are in the Collection, Mr. Ballard must have made it, although the Battle of Chattanooga started on November 23. Communication did not keep up, and after that battle Tennessee was in Union hands.

All of the family survived the war. Martha and Abram then outlived all the other members of their generation. Martha and her daughter Hattie, the woman responsible for sending the Cozart Collection to Oklahoma and the Wesleyan Collection to Macon, Georgia, continued to do handwork, and pieces of their later work are extant.

When, in December 1860, Harriet visited the First Annual Fair of the Cotton Planters' Convention in Macon, she wrote a long, interesting letter to her "Friends/Kinfolks Brothers & Sisters" in Tennessee. She wrote of the increasing scarcity of money, the gloom apparent during the Christmas season, and the impending election of delegates to the Georgia State Convention, held the day after the letter was written. She also wrote enthusiastically about the beautiful and unusual things she had seen at the fair—the "<u>very pretty</u>" embroidery, the unusual crochet work, and the "simple and <u>showy</u> parlor ornaments." She had entered some of her work. "By tomorrow night I hope to see the reports of Premiums."[50] The premium lists in Macon newspapers do not reveal that she won any awards,[51] and, due to the war, there was no second annual fair.

Harriet's letter exemplifies some of the conclusions that can be reached about this family and their handwork. The artifacts in the Cozart and Wesleyan Collections reveal that the Caldwell women were skilled needlewomen, proud of their sewing accomplishments. The variety shows that the women were aware of fashion trends both in clothing styles and in domestic decorations. They enjoyed doing handwork and must have been challenged to experiment with popular methods and new techniques. In addition the Family Letters display the pleasure the women shared in creating useful and stylish wearing apparel for themselves and their loved ones. Their frustrations are also apparent.

They were not unique.[52] And, although there is little literature on this subject at present, they were probably very typical in their time and place. The study of family collections like this will lead to a better understanding of how women of the nineteenth century made quilts and did other handwork in spite of the complexities of everyday life.

Acknowledgments

The American Quilt Study Group wishes to thank the Central Oklahoma Quilters Guild and the Prairie Quilt Guild for their generous donations toward the publication of Dorthy Cozart's paper.

Notes and References

1. "The Arrival of a Treasure Chest," *The Wesleyan Alumnae* 6 (November 1930): 158–59.
2. Samuel Lutterell Akers, *The First Hundred Years of Wesleyan College 1836–1936* (Macon, GA: Produced by Beehive Press; printed by Stinehour Press, 1976), 45.
3. Hattie Cozart Gates to Hugh Holman Cozart, August 15, 1935.
4. This name is spelled variously, "Lizza" and "Lizzy," as well as "Lizzie," in the Family Letters. It has been regularized to "Lizzie" herein, as have the other names, "Mattie," "Hattie," and "Cattie," which have variant spellings. Other spelling and punctuation in the Family Letters have also been regularized where necessary for clarity.
5. *Rose Hill Internment Book* (Macon, Georgia) 69.
6. Harriet Caldwell Strother to Martha Caldwell, April 25, 1852. This letter consoles Martha concerning the gossip following her divorce.
7. Harriet Caldwell Strother to Martha Caldwell Cozart, May 9, 1857.
8. Akers, *The First Hundred Years*, 28. Painting was taught during the time Mary was attending there. "Treasure Chest," 159.
9. Mary Cozart Burns to Dorothy Cozart, July 13, 1973.

10. Harriet Caldwell Strother to Abram Cozart, December 12, 1846.
11. Julia Caldwell Cozart to Martha and Mary Caldwell, June 13, 1854.
12. Mary Cozart Burns to Dorothy Cozart, July 8, 1972.
13. Georgia, *House Journal* (1851), 191.
14. Pamela Wagner, *Hidden Heritage: Recent Discoveries In Georgia Decorative Arts, 1733–1915* (Atlanta: High Museum of Art, 1990), 21. Guest curator Pamela Wagner states that Georgia-made samplers are extremely rare. "A dozen were documented for the Georgia Decorative Arts Survey, most of which have embroidered upper and lower case alphabets followed by the numbers zero to nine."
15. Little has been written about samplers made in the South. Other regions have been well documented, however. Those sources, such as Glee F. Krueger, New England *Samplers to 1840* (Sturbridge, MA: Old Sturbridge Village, 1956), and Gayle A. Rettew, *Behold the Labour of My Tender Age, 1780–1850* (Rochester: Rochester Museum and Science Center, 1983), and also Tandy and Charles Hersh, *Samplers of the Pennsylvania Germans* (Birdsboro, PA: German Society, 1993) agree that samplers were being made by girls elsewhere in the United States during the years I have assigned to the Caldwell samplers.
16. "Treasure Chest," 159.
17. Martha Caldwell to Julia Caldwell Cozart and Abram Cozart, July 24, 1853.
18. Mary Ellen Strother Sneed to Martha Caldwell Cozart and Mary Caldwell, January [undated], 1856.
19. Mary Caldwell to Martha Caldwell, Julia Caldwell Cozart, and Abram Cozart, March 2, 1853.
20. A Lady [Eliza Ware Farrar], *The Young Lady's Friend* (Boston, American Stationers' Co., 1837), 283.
21. Mary Caldwell to Martha Caldwell, Julia Caldwell Cozart, and Abram Cozart, March 2, 1853.
22. Mary Caldwell to Julia Caldwell Cozart and Abram Cozart, July 22, 1847.
23. Harriet Caldwell Strother to Mary Caldwell and Martha Caldwell Nelson, January 1, 1847.
24. Mary Caldwell to Martha Caldwell, Julia Caldwell Cozart, and Abram Cozart, March 30, 1853.
25. Mary Caldwell to Julia Caldwell Cozart and Abram Cozart, July 18, 1853.
26. Jim Liles to Dorothy Cozart, May 11, 1988. He had sent a photograph of the coverlet to Sadye Wilson, author of *Of Coverlets* and she identified it.
27. Julia Caldwell Cozart to Mary and Martha Caldwell, July 25, 1853.
28. Martha Caldwell to Julia Caldwell Cozart and Abram Cozart, July 18, 1853.
29. Mary Caldwell to Martha Caldwell, Julia Caldwell Cozart and Abram

Cozart, March 30, 1853. Jim Liles to Dorothy Cozart, January 24, 1988. "If a carding mill existed in the neighborhood, it would have been used unless the cost was prohibitive." Liles also wrote that indigo dyeing was usually done by a "blue" dyer because the dye pot stunk so much.
30. Mary Ellen Strother Sneed to Cattie Caldwell, January 28, 1862.
31. Harriet Caldwell Strother to Samuel Caldwell, January 29, 1862.
32. Harriet Caldwell Strother to Martha Caldwell Cozart, January 1, 1861.
33. Mary Ellen Strother Sneed to Cattie Caldwell, January 28, 1862.
34. Harriet Caldwell Strother to Martha Caldwell Nelson and Mary Caldwell, January 1, 1847.
35. Martha Caldwell Nelson to Harriet Caldwell Strother, August [undated], 1848.
36. Mary Ellen Strother Sneed to Martha Caldwell Cozart, July 15, 1856.
37. Mary Ellen Strother Sneed to Cattie Caldwell, January 28, 1862.
38. Anne L. McDonald, *No Idle Hands: The Social History of American Knitting* (New York: Ballantine Books, 1988), 173.
39. Emma Tyler Blalock, "War Memories," *The History of Lamar County*, ed. Mrs. August Lambdin (Barnesville, Georgia: *The Barnesville News-Gazette*, 1932), 239.
40. Mary Ellen Strother Sneed to Mattie Cozart, August 1, 1863.
41. Mary Caldwell to Catherine [Cattie] Caldwell, January 28, 1862.
42. Harriet Caldwell Strother to Julia Caldwell Cozart, August 11, 1853.
43. Harriet Caldwell Strother to Martha Caldwell Cozart, October 30, 1861.
44. Harriet Caldwell Strother to Martha Caldwell Cozart, January [undated], 1856.
45. Mary Caldwell to Martha Caldwell, Julia Caldwell Cozart, and Abram Cozart, March 30, 1853.
46. Martha Caldwell to Julia Caldwell Cozart and Abram Cozart, July [undated], 1853.
47. Listed in a small leather-bound book in the Cozart Collection papers.
48. Mary Caldwell to Martha Caldwell, Julia Caldwell Cozart, and Abram Cozart, March 2, 1853.
49. Mary Caldwell to Martha Caldwell Cozart, November 20, 1863.
50. Harriet Caldwell Strother to Martha Caldwell Cozart and Abram Cozart and their family; Samuel Caldwell and his family; and Mary Ellen Strother Sneed, January 1, 1861.
51. *The Macon Journal and Telegraph*, January 2, 1861, January 9, 1861. The newspaper for January 2 must have been the one Harriet was to see the next day. However, there were also premium lists in the January 9 newspaper, and also in *The Weekly Georgia (Macon) Telegraph*, December 13,

1860, and December 20, 1860. These premium lists give a good idea of the kind of handwork being done in Georgia at that time.

52. See, for example, Robert Manson Myers, ed., The *Children of Pride: a True Story of Georgia and the Civil W* (New Haven: Yale Univ. Press, 1972). In the Jones family letters are several references to the clothing being made for the family.

Quilt Talk: Verbal Performance among a Group of African-American Quilters

JaneE Hindman

In order to offer an alternative to the material culture research model, this essay explores the social and oral context within which African-American women teach and perform quilting. The data were collected over a four-month period during which I was a participant/observer in a racially mixed sewing class sponsored by a neighborhood center in Tucson, Arizona, and predominantly attended and taught by African-American women. First classified according to type of performance and then considered holistically, the data corroborate the notion that from the verbal performances of any group—rather than from the group's material culture alone—emerge the values, beliefs, and notions of order that provide an impetus for the aesthetics informing the traditional material items that a group produces. A narrative account saturated with the dialogue of the African-American women, the essay is organized like a quilt itself: a few scraps of talk are grouped into four blocks, each one representing a particular speaker and a specific type of quilt-talk performance, and then quilted together with the folkloristic and sociolinguistic theory that reveals the patterns not only in these performances but also in their relationship to those in other African-American communities and other quilting environments. The conclusion: it is only by listening to the voices of African-American quilters speaking their subject that quilt researchers can come to understand the complex context of the traditions, beliefs, values, and aesthetics that comprise African-American quilts.

A Few Scraps

"I bring in the quilt to show Miss Jordan and she says 'Oh, I thought you were going to make a *hand*made quilt.' And I tell you I ripped out all those machine stitches. When Miss Jordan says 'by hand' she means by *hand*."... "Now, honey, maybe that's how you want to use a thimble, but you sure ain't sewing with it."... "You know even at the quilt shows where they have the experts, if you look, you'll find mistakes. That makes a quilt like life: it don't always work out just right."... "Taking apart all those blocks in a whole quilt—that's how I got my degree in ripping out. You got to go a long way if you want to catch up with me in that area."... "Didn't nobody teach me how to quilt: I'd sit up with a string and paper and teach myself how to do those patterns before I sewed them."... "Quilting is like cooking: everyone adds a little and takes some away to make it their own."... "If you want to keep quilting, you need to get used to our jokes because you know jokes tell something serious too ... That's what our [quilting] class is good for, teaching communication."

The structure of the essay that follows is meant to emulate that of a quilt. I begin with a few snippets of quilt talk, piece those fragments together into four blocks, and finally quilt the blocks together into a patterned whole. Each block of the essay characterizes the talk of one of the principal African-American women of the classroom, though not all women of the class are represented herein. The metaphorical blocks are modeled on the literal four blocks of the quilt I made during the times I spoke with and listened to these women's quilt talk. Arranged in the Split Nine Patch pattern, each block is pieced from a similar striped bacround material contrasted with some other bright color, one color to a block.

The examples of quilt talk I present here occurred within the context of a sewing class given on Tuesday mornings at the Northwest Neighborhood Center in Tucson, Arizona. Though the class is ongoing and has been meeting for over five years, the data represented here was collected during the September through December session of 1991. Comprised of a mix of Anglo women and women of color, the class is for the most part an exclusively female environment, with only occasional and brief visits by males; the size of the class varies widely with sometimes as many as ten women in attendance, sometimes as few as three. Because the teacher and a majority of the attendees are African-American, because these particular women are older and have been attending the class longer and more regularly than anyone else, and because the Center is located in a predominantly and historically black neighborhood, the sewing class feels as if it is "theirs" to me. Though I recognize that this setting is not exclusively African-American (after all, I am there and so are one, two, sometimes three other Anglo women and occasionally the same number of Hispanic women), I think it nonetheless represents to some extent the context and text of African-American "quilt talk."

Four Blocks

BLOCK ONE: *Lilac*, Vergiree Jordan

The story of this quilt's blocks begins with the lilac one. Because this block is the one I finished first, the one that taught me how to complete the rest, I attribute it to Miss Jordan; she is, after all, the teacher, the one who showed me how to measure the pieces correctly so they'd match each other and produce even edges. But also the tone and construction, the feel of the lilac block seem to suit the "Miss Jordan" that I've constructed: its colors are subtle, soft, subdued, even elegant. Of all the blocks of my first quilt, this has the fewest number of mistakes. Likewise Miss Jordan herself is the most quiet, precise, perhaps even refined of the quilt talkers in the sewing group. Her talk is the most subdued and infrequent; it's also rarely if ever performed for entertainment—though she certainly seems to enjoy being entertained by others—and never, that I have seen, used to assert power or control. Though she never claims expertise for herself, others often attribute it to her. A professional seamstress before her instruction days, Miss Jordan is talked up as *the* expert when it comes to sewing and for letting no shoddy work slip by her: "If Miss Jordan showing you how, you know you're learning it right!"

The quilt talk type most indicative of Miss Jordan is the "teaching how to quilt" performance that primes students for getting it right. Unlike other teaching performances I have given or seen, Miss Jordan's particular version contains as much if not more showing than telling; that is, it demands more watching than listening from the learner, more action than talk from the teacher. Most often the interaction sounds like this: "this goes here this way like this," followed by a long period of silence during which Miss Jordan executes the task being taught while the learner watches. Demonstration, rather than explanation, is privileged. Other quilters' brief teaching performances verify that this particular characteristic of the teaching quilt talk performance holds true across performers. For instance, one quilter's lesson to me on how to tie a quilter's knot was a non-verbal demonstration; another's on using a thimble consisted of watching me work and saying at the appropriate moments, "Yes, honey, that's right; that's how I do" or "Oh, no, honey, I don't do like that." In more collective teaching sessions, the women often tell me, "don't you worry; you'll get the feel of it after a while; you won't even need to look, you'll just feel where the needle goes" whenever I say that I'm not sure how to do something that they have demonstrated.

Miss Jordan's individual style within this form of quilt talk teaching performance is very even, quiet, and softly spoken, one that I've heard the other women call "sweet" even as they are jokingly complaining about the way Miss Jordan demands perfection: "she'll tell you you have to rip that seam out but she'll say it so sweet you'll think ripping out is an honor." Because Miss Jordan certainly has the ability to talk sweet, perhaps the respect that she earns is a result of her type of quilt talk, a type of talk which is helpful and never boastful. And so, I attribute to her that block of my quilt that is the most precise, well-executed, sensible, and lilac-sweet in color and performance.

BLOCK TWO: *Hot Pink,* Lily Bacon

To Mrs. Bacon, I dedicate the "shocking pink" block. Just as the bold, hot pink block jumps out at me, so too does Mrs. Bacon's presence seem to fill the sewing classroom and command attention. Though she's attended infrequently during the months I've been collecting material from the sewing class, her impact has been far-reaching. When she walked in the room, everyone, including Miss Jordan, stopped what she was doing to minister to Mrs. Bacon: someone brought her a chair, another found her a vacant sewing machine, others cleared off table space so she would have room to work. The oldest of any of the women who have attended the class, Mrs. Bacon commands more respect than anyone else.

I perceived almost all of Mrs. Bacon's classroom talk to be a performance of some sort. Just in telling me her name, for instance, she recited a sort of poem: "I'm Lily Bacon, bacon and eggs, eggs and bacon, Lily Bacon. Now don't you forget it." A grand teller of her own tale, Mrs. Bacon gave me her stories of her girlhood, married life, and more recent times; a native of Texas, she became mother at age eleven to nine sisters and brothers when her own mother died. Married at fifteen to "a good husband . . . he raised them kids like they was his own," Mrs. Bacon and her husband adopted her brothers and sisters and eventually had another eleven children of their own.

Not surprisingly, Mrs. Bacon's most prominent form of quilt talk was the quilter's autobiography, wherein the quilter tells the story of when and where she learned to quilt, who taught her, what her first quilts were like, and what current quilting projects she has underway. I learned that for Mrs. Bacon quilting, like cooking and rearing children, was a skill learned not from her mother but out of necessity of circumstance. "I'd sit up with a string and paper and teach myself how to do those patterns before I sewed them."

As you can imagine, it's virtually impossible for me in this article to do Mrs. Bacon's type of quilt talk real justice since *her* wordings are what make her story her own. Wanting to capture that essence, I asked her if she'd mind repeating and letting me tape some of the stories she'd told me about quilting. Her response was "there ain't nothing to tape. I done said it all. That's all there is." I feared that I would forget what she'd told me.

My fears were unfounded, however, as I discovered in the weeks after Mrs. Bacon's visits to the class. Because Mrs. Bacon and I were sitting some distance away from the others while she was telling me her story, I thought our conversation had been private. Yet, time after time, the other women of the group would remind me of what Mrs. Bacon had said, applying her advice or humor to other situations that would crop up. For instance, the week following Mrs. Bacon's last visit, Mrs. Summers took the occasion to say to me, "Why are you standing up when you could be sitting down? You remind me of what my daddy used to say to me: when you're older, it'll still be sitting on the curb waiting for you. That's what Mrs. Bacon was trying to tell you last week. Remember what Mrs. Bacon told you about that?"

In actuality, it seems that *every*one (at least every other African-American woman) was listening to our conversations, mentally recording them for further references and use. This aspect of audience participation in others' conversations is something that I realized only after the fact and which made clear another essential aspect of the group's "quilt talk." It appears that at least to these women, during quilting/sewing classtime, *any* conversation that *anyone* can hear—even if listeners have to strain to hear—seems to be open for report, response, and interpretation from the audience, which includes anyone in the room, not just the person being directly addressed.

Mrs. Bacon is also a performer of the teaching how to quilt version of quilt talk. Like Miss Jordan's, Mrs. Bacon's laissez-faire attitude toward teaching fosters the learner's individual techniques and styles. Her teaching technique was once (in my memory) directed at me: very casually glancing over at me struggling to stitch together pieces while I listened to her stories, Mrs. Bacon said to me "Now maybe that's how you want to use a thimble, but you ain't sewing with it." This comment was one that I could either ignore or capitalize on as an invitation for Mrs. Bacon to show me how to use the thimble properly. Similarly, Mrs. Summers' favorite story about Mrs. Bacon demonstrates the patience and confidence with which the latter instructs apprentices. Rather than asserting authority by telling the then-novice what she had to do, Mrs. Bacon's response to Mrs. Summers' complaints about not liking thimbles and deciding not to use one was (in Mrs. Summers' rendition): "Oh, don't worry, honey, you will, you will." Like Miss Jordan's teacher talk, Mrs. Bacon's too is often re-presented (either through reported speech performances or the sorts of comments mentioned above) to me by the other women. The women's attention to her talk indicates how they value her as an experienced quilter. For instance, in introducing Mrs. Bacon, Mrs. Summers honored her with a very formal introduction: "Now here's the one who taught me everything I know about quilting."

BLOCK THREE: *Blue*, Marion Stevens Turner

Most noteworthy to me about this block is the stretchiness of its work-shirt blue material; it gave me fits at first because it kept stretching out of kilter and thus I couldn't get the pieces to fit together smoothly. However, when I eventually connected this block to the others and quilted the entire construction, the gaps and tightness of the blue cloth worked themselves out for the most part. This experience with the literal cloth brings Marion to mind for me.[1]

For one thing, when I include Marion in this discussion, I'm stretching the definition of quilt talk because she is not a quilter herself. However, she is a regular and integral member of the sewing class and further has played a definite role in the story of my quilt, a part characterized for me by that "stretch-to-fit" aspect of the blue material. Marion's most frequent type of talk in the sewing class deserves attention for what it illuminates about the context of African-American women in the racially mixed sewing class.

Marion's quilt talk expertise is joking. By watching and listening to her, I developed some insight into how to interpret and present jokes in this crowd and thus how to become part of it. This step was an important one for me. One reason is that—up until the point when I first made a joke that she liked—Marion never spoke to me at all; about me, yes, but to me, no. Another reason is that, since this type of joking is very different from the type I'm used to, the shift was a difficult but necessary one: it taught me how to acquire some of the values essential not only to this group but to quilting as an enterprise.

The women's favorite topic for jokes specifically related to sewing and quilting is "ripping out" stitches. I had already heard some such jokes on these topics before I became aware of how Marion had cleverly incorporated me into one of those jokes. The context surrounding her joke began weeks earlier, namely on the first day I actually constructed the first block of my quilt. After cutting out the fabric from a template I had made and sewing (awkwardly) my first two pieces, I showed my product to Mrs. Summers, another woman in the class. Intending to make the same sort of self-deprecating, ironic joke to her that I might make to other friends of mine, I said, "Okay, I've practiced enough at this. Now I'm ready to be an expert." Either Mrs. Summers thought me simply a bad joker or she took me literally; either way, she didn't laugh. Rather, she seemed amazed that I would say such a thing. I heard her repeating my remark in whispers to Marion later that day and then laughing out loud about it as she repeated it more openly to Mrs. Bacon the next week. Soon after these two were laughing at my remark, Marion began a series of jokes about ripping out. The following is a typical opening for such a sequence: Marion (or someone else) says, "Ruth, you awfully quiet over there. You're making me nervous. What you doing?" At this point, everyone looks up and laughs when they see that Ruth is ripping out a seam, and Ruth answers something like "Oh, I'm just doing what I'm good at." More laughter.

During the particular joking exchange made at my expense, Marion added a new dimension: "Maybe I ought to get a Ph.D. in ripping out. Then I could be an expert in *that!*" Her emphasis on the last word "that," the fact that she, like all the African-American women, knew that I was working on a Ph.D., the additional fact that they had apparently found foolish my earlier comments about wanting to be an expert—all these lead me to believe that Marion was having a laugh at my expense. Though I'm not precisely sure, I believe my response won me favor because I refused to take offense: "Well," I said, "at least *that* degree would be a useful one." As I understand the practice of signifying, a unique form of African-American linguistic play that relies on indirection and double entendre for its effect, that sort of response is the preferred one because it allows both parties to avoid direct confrontation and it honors the verbal ability of the signifier.[2]

My attempts to make quilt talk jokes helped me stabilize my own place in the group when one day I added a joke onto one of Marion's statements. In the context of sewing another in a series of clothes for her granddaughter and feeling frustrated about how long it took to finish one project, Marion grumbled, "I'd know I was productive if I came at 9:00 and left at noon [the time the class meets] with something done." I said, "Well, if it was me, I'd have to be coming at 9:00 on Tuesday and leaving at noon on Friday." Speaking to me directly for the first time, Marion said, "Yeah, you got that right. That's me too."

More complete audience acceptance of my performance of jokes came during another class meeting. Miss Jordan had been showing me how to finish the edges on my quilt: "You just pin along here like this, and sew along the pins here. But someday you won't need the pins; you'll just know where to sew." I ruefully said, "Humph, I'll be retirement age by then." Another woman laughed a little and said, "Yeah, you say to yourself I know I'll know it, but when?" I answered, "When I'm wearing wings and playing a harp." This joke earned not just laughter but also some vigorous verbal approval: "You got that right! Hey, she learns fast!"[3]

Perhaps another way to understand the serendipity of my efforts to stretch-to-fit Marion's ways and learn to talk more comfortably with her is to contrast my attempts to befriend her with those of the only other younger-than-forty white woman in the class, Kim. Admiring the couple of projects that Marion had been working on for weeks but happened to be finishing all in one class day, Kim said to Marion "Wow, you sew fast! You must be able to make something in only one day!" Marion—who had never to my knowledge spoken directly to Kim—answered this "compliment" with a huffy and emphatic "I don't sew *nothing* fast!"

In addition, I attribute my eventual acceptance into the group to my completion of a very important initiation rite—a finished quilt. My hunch is verified by a conversation I had with Marion and Mrs. Summer, a conversation that occurred after I had stayed up late several nights in a row sewing and thus had nearly completed my first quilt. I was quite surprised and delighted by the women's response to my work. Marion said, "Well, I'm real proud of you and the work you did because you sure was a novice when you came in here. But you stuck with it." Mrs. Summers added, "Yes, you didn't get frustrated like some people I won't mention." I'm quite sure the latter remark is intended to signify Kim, who had started a quilt much earlier but had abandoned her work. "Well, I had good teachers," was my answer. "But you were intimidated when you first came, weren't you?" Marion asked me. "Weren't you intimidated?" You bet.

BLOCK FOUR: *Green*, Ethyel Summers

Quite simply, this block is my favorite. It boasts work with fewer mistakes and better fit than the pink or blue ones. Though its effect is not quite so bold as that of the shocking pink block, I like the high contrast of the colors of the green block, a contrast that is arresting but somehow soothing too, smooth but resonating. Mrs. Summers herself is vibrant; her contributions to the classroom, vital. An instructor and a joker, Mrs. Summers is also a teller of her own quilt tales and a skillful reader of others' quilt texts; thus, she has introduced me to many other types of quilt talk.

For instance, she's often told me (or anyone else who might ask) the story of her own quilt, the one she is currently working on and that—because it is on display while she works—others ask about. A doubly layered story, this quilt tale involves, on the one hand, the history of the quilt's actual construction. This performance could include items such as an explanation of why the quilter started this particular quilt when she did, intertextual references to other quilts that inform the one being told about, a description of the process by which the quilter acquired the materials (scraps, found objects, patterns, buttons, etc.) for this particular quilt, and so on. On the other hand, telling the story of one's own quilt can also involve telling the narrative that the quilt carries "within itself," a story that explains the referential meaning of the quilt. By "referential meaning" in this case I am indicating the representation that the quilter has of her quilt's meaning, a meaning that perhaps depends on the purpose that the quilter has in making the quilt as well as on her own emotional landscape at the time of the quilt's construction. This meaning of the story of one's own quilt seems to be the least often told; in fact, sometimes the quilter may decide to keep it totally to herself.

Mrs. Summers' most frequently told quilt story is about the second of two quilts she's made for her twin grandsons. Whenever anyone stops to admire her work, which they often do—class members and visitors alike—Mrs. Summers freely explains that these twins are the only family members she's not yet quilted for, that she found in a pattern book the idea for the appliqued boy figures that make up several of the quilt's blocks, that she'd previously made for her grand*daughter* a quilt that was similar but that had bonnets on the figures. She even accounts for the small blood spots on the quilt as reminders of times when she was working too long and not using her thimble properly.

But only once did Mrs. Summers tell me the story of her quilt as it was depicted in the images it displayed; she only told it then because I asked her directly: "But what do these pictures [of animals painted in the material of several large blocks in the quilt] and stitching [of a barn shape around the animal pictures] mean? Who are these figures?" Her answer was a story about a time when her twin grandsons had been younger and had visited a farm. They had liked the freedom and change of this farm; they'd been happy there. She wanted them to be able to remember that time and not the city streets where they lived now. I thought she was making some connection between each of the six or seven differently clothed figures in some of the blocks and the animals or scenes the figures were juxtaposed against: she kept pointing to them during her brief telling. But I couldn't really follow that part of the story; its connections seemed known to Mrs. Summers alone. For every part I heard, my hunch is that there are four or five "meanings" left untold.

Mrs. Summers is also an expert reader of others' quilt texts. Always one to remind me that "quilting is like cooking: everyone adds and takes away to make it their own," Mrs. Summers uses the occasion of reading another quilter's text to infuse it with her own style and interpretations. Her reading of other women's quilts inverts the order of priority of information that she told about her own quilt:

her construction of the meaning of another's quilt involves little discussion of the handiwork or construction of the quilt itself; rather, it emphasizes the emotional landscape of the quilter at the time she pieced her work.

When telling me the story of Rosie Lee Tompkins' quilt *Checkerboard Variations*,[4] for example, Mrs. Summers began her reading on the left hand side of the quilt about midway from the top. Pointing to specific areas of the quilt as she narrated, she told me that the areas where Tompkins had used the tiniest squares showed that when she pieced them she'd had been feeling down and having hard times. "Things got better here near the middle," she said, "but then they got bad again here where the pieces are tight like she can't breathe. That's what we used to call 'lean times.' But then, here at the top [at which point Mrs. Summers made a vertical move up in her reading], that's when they got better and stayed that way." I found this reading remarkable, not only because of its wealth of assumptions about the quilter, but also because of its unique mix of horizontal and vertical reading of the text, a mix that seemed intended to follow some chronological arrangement of the quilter's emotional progress but whose spatial logic I could not otherwise follow. Why, for instance, couldn't the text of the quilter's emotional life have begun at the top of the page/quilt? That is, why didn't she read the quilt as a story about good times that subsequently went sour? Equally interesting to me is the connection Mrs. Summers made between the quilt and another art form: "This quilt, it's like a Negro spiritual." "You mean because sometimes you sing a verse long, like here," I asked her, pointing to a larger square in the quilt, "and sometimes short like here?" "Yes. And it's about feelings and about people, about how they're *feeling*."

In addition to her obvious dexterity at reading another's quilt, Mrs. Summers is quite skillful at telling quilt jokes. Unlike Marion's signifying jokes, Mrs. Summers's humorous narratives rely on reported speech, that is on her retelling of what someone else had said. These reported speech jokes, like signifying, can be at someone else's expense. But, unlike signifying, this version of Mrs. Summers' quilt talk provides another example of her ability to recenter another's "text" for her own purposes. In this latter trait, her jokes (and her skills) are unlike any other woman's in the class.

Here's an example: Mrs. Allen, a local quilter known for her talent as well as her rather cranky disposition, was formerly a member of the sewing class. She had recently been collaborating with the rest of the group in making a friendship quilt which they were going to raffle off in order to buy a serger sewing machine for the class. Mrs. Summers tells a story about a day when Miss Jordan, who had been called out of the classroom for a while, asked the women to work on cutting out the squares for the quilt while she was gone. "Well, Mrs. Allen says [in Mrs. Summers' story] 'I don't want to be sitting in no classroom cutting squares. I'm just gonna tear this material off. Miss Jordan will never know.' So Miss Jordan comes back and takes one look and says 'Oh, you tore it.'" This story sends all the women who hear it (Mrs. Allen not among them) into fits of laughter, presumably because it affirms Miss Jordan's sharp eye for shoddy work and especially because it shows up Mrs. Allen.

Mrs. Summers' repertoire of jokes reappropriating someone else's speech probably has other ends as well. For instance, consider her joke that reports Miss Jordan's appraisal of Mrs. Summer's first quilt: On seeing the completed quilt hung in front of her, Miss Jordan reportedly said " 'Oh, [Mrs. Summers says in a falsetto voice with pursed lips and lots of rapid eye blinking], you've turned the block wrong.' And wouldn't you know," she continues in her natural voice, "that block was right in the middle of the whole quilt. Well, I wasn't about to rip that one out!" As in the former joke/story about ripping out, Mrs. Summers seems to be using reported speech in this example to release tension, to subvert the authority of the teacher who demands the tedious work required to "get it right." This subversion of authority seems pretty good-humored, though. For one thing, Miss Jordan herself (who is always a member of the audience for these jokes) laughs when she hears these renditions of her criticisms. For another, Mrs. Summers does not appear to be any real threat to Miss Jordan's authority as a teacher: in other contexts wherein *she's* functioning as a teacher because Miss Jordan is absent, Mrs. Summers constantly undermines her own authority lest anyone get the idea that she think she's any more "expert" than Miss Jordan. She's quick to remind me of her view of her expertise: "I'm just an old lady telling you my way of how to do it. If you really want to know, you ask Miss Jordan."

And finally, further consideration of the complex context of the joke seems to reveal its main purpose: she told it as I was showing the women the finally-pieced top of my quilt and pointing out the mismatches in the pink block that I said I was considering ripping out. After telling her joke/story about the incorrectly turned block of her first quilt, Mrs. Summers explained that the mistakes were part of the story of any quilt: "Even at the quilt shows where they have the experts, if you look, you'll find mistakes. They're what makes it yours. That makes a quilt like life: it don't always work out just right. It's not perfect. There's always going to be parts that don't work out. . . . Someday you'll look back at this block in your quilt and remember important things about those mistakes. They'll remind you." She continued talking in general about people who had come to the class but hadn't really liked it, who—unlike me, she said—had left after only a little while. "After a while," Mrs. Summers went on, "people get used to our ways. But people like Kim, you know, she's too sensitive. She didn't like our jokes. But you need to get used to our jokes because you know jokes tell something serious too. . . . That's good, you know, because communication is so important. That's what our class is good for, teaching communication." I'd say that I must agree and add that Mrs. Summers' quilt talk has not only taught me about communication but also endeared me to her summer-green fresh humor and heart.

The Quilting

How in the world are all these pieces going to fit together? What pattern is in these blocks, anyway? And what is all this [quilt] talk about? This essay is a new approach to research on the topic of African-American quiltmaking. Like some other researchers interested in this sort of quiltmaking, I am interested in exploring the aesthetics of African-American quilts, in trying to uncover what, if anything, might reveal itself as "that ineffable quality that is curiously black," to borrow Toni Morrison's phrase.[5] Unlike those researchers, however, I am not using African-American quilts themselves as my focal point. Rather, I have chosen to direct attention to the conversations (specifically, the verbal performances) of African-American quilters. Accordingly, I have presented here four portraits of specific African-American women, characterized the ways that each of them talks, and delineated the different types of verbal performances that occurred among them in the context of a class specifically intended to offer instruction in sewing and quilting.

But that still doesn't explain how all these pieces fit together. Why, for instance, have I chosen this method, the "quilt-talk" approach? One very important reason is that African-American quilters themselves have been dissatisfied with others' characterizations of "their" quilts and their quiltmaking practices. For instance, Marie Wilson felt compelled to respond to the legend describing some of the African-American quilts included in the 1990 "Two Centuries of Quilting Traditions" exhibition at The Museums in Stony Brook: "As an African-American who makes quilts, I have often been troubled by the statements that stereotype African-American quilts. In the years that I have been making quilts and enjoying quilts made by others, I have come to know that quilts made by African-Americans are as diverse as the people who make them."[6] Another African-American quilter rejects Eli Leon's theory about the connection between improvisation in jazz and in African-American quilting techniques: "He doesn't understand African-American quilts. He's so interested in his theory he just wants to look at one kind of quilt.... The African-American quilter has yet to answer for herself. But it's like pulling fleas off a dog to find one of them: they just don't want to come out and talk about their work."[7] This latter assessment echoes that of Roger Abrahams, a renowned folklorist and sociolinguist who has studied extensively language use among American blacks: "how women assert their image and values as women is seldom found in the folklore literature. We know even less about the verbal traditions of black women in particular."[8] Foremost authority on African-American quiltmaking, Cuesta Benberry, also recommends work that will "give voice to the quiltmakers themselves. It is important to listen to what African-American quiltmakers say about their work and to give them credence, whether or not their comments coincide with researchers' theories and interpretations."[9] Clearly, these critiques all demonstrate the necessity of work dedicated to considering African-American quiltmakers as a group of women asserting their images and values within their own quiltmaking traditions. My study of this small group of women and their quilt talk is meant to do some of that work.

In making the choice to focus on the verbal behavior relevant to a particular item of folklore rather than on the material item itself, I am participating in what some folklorists call the study of "emergent culture." Unlike some approaches to folklore which spotlight remnants of a lost past and thus on "experiences, meanings, and values which cannot be verified or cannot be expressed in terms of the dominant culture," the study of emergent culture focuses on "new meanings and values, new practices, new significances and experiences [which] are continually being created" and offers "a frame of reference able to comprehend residual forms and items, [as well as] contemporary practice, and emergent structures."[10] In other words, attempts to understand African-American quiltmaking that consider only the history and/or the material items of the practice are likely to uncover meanings, values, experiences that the dominant culture cannot understand or explain. This tendency may account for scholars' (essentialist at worst and simplistic at best) characterizations of African-American quilts and quiltmaking, characterizations built on theories not applicable to large numbers of the quilts made by African-Americans.[11] In her recent book about the contributions of African-American quilts and quiltmakers to American quiltmaking traditions, Benberry describes the inaccuracies and preconceptions of such research that focuses only on the residual forms and items of some quilts; currently in the field, she says, research must address the "need to dispel certain myths that had developed about African-American quilts. . . . It is certainly not useful to view African-American quilts merely as isolated folk art objects, divorced from the lives of blacks and the social, political, and economic conditions under which they have lived."[12]

Much more useful is the approach to folklore studies that prefers *verbal* behavior as its material for study, that considers the verbal performances of a folk group as they emerge in natural contexts; this type of folklore research can give us a different window on the meanings, values, and experiences of a group. Especially if and when a group's values differ widely from those of the dominant group in a society, this new window—called a performance-centered approach to the study of folklore—is less cloudy. In the words of scholar Richard Bauman, "Performance may thus be the cornerstone of a new folkloristics, liberated from its backward-facing perspective and able to comprehend much more of the totality of human experience."[13]

Like others who have undertaken the study of verbal performance, I have interacted with a group in the capacity of participant/observer over a course of time, collected data concerning their face to face interactions,[14] and analyzed the data in an attempt to identify the "learnable and transmittable notions of order through enactment (especially in performance) that provide an impetus for those traditional items"[15] important to the group. In this case the items are those related to African-American quiltmaking. Clearly, this group is a small one; its interactions will not necessarily reflect those of all African-American quiltmakers. Rather than a comprehensive or definitive study, my analysis is an introduction to a different approach to scholarly interest in African-American quiltmaking. What I'm hoping, of course, is that my approach will help us move closer toward answering the question: What, *if anything*, is central and unique to African-American quiltmaking as distinguished from others' quilting practices. I believe that any rewarding answer to that question must address myriad contextual considerations. The verbal performances of the group are only one aspect of this complex context, but one that has not yet, to my knowledge, been considered in the scholarly work dedicated to understanding the history and practices of African-American quiltmaking. If this approach is of value, that value will be in answering questions like these: What, if anything, do these women's performances have in common with performances other scholars have noted among other African-American women? What if anything do the different types of performances in these women's sewing class have in common with each other? What might these commonalities teach us about the values, beliefs, and experiences that African-American quiltmakers present in their art?

Thus, in order to argue for the effectiveness of my approach, the appeal of the essay I am quilting, I need to make some connections between the scraps and blocks you've seen, to provide some answers to these questions. Here then, after the piecing of scraps into the four blocks I've already presented, I am trying to quilt together what I see as the forms of these African-American women's quilt talk: the showing-how-to-do-not-teaching-how-to-say performance of the quilting teacher who insists that students "get it right;" the sometimes cryptic, sometimes historically focused, sometimes intensely personal quilter's autobiography presentation; the signifying and reported speech jokes that release the tension created by having to get it right; the potentially co-optive form that I call telling-the-story-of-another's-quilt; and finally the telling-the-story-of-her-own quilt performance.

Now, on to the question are there any connections between this group's "talk" and that of other groups? Yes, I believe there are. For instance, Miss Jordan's and Lily Bacon's teaching-how-to-quilt-performances are quite similar to those other quilters attribute to their teachers. Pecolia Warner, an African-American quilter, describes the way her mother taught her: "If it wasn't right—if I made a stitch that was too long—she didn't do no laughing and talking!... She'd say to me 'That ain't right. Fix it right or else I'll put a strap on you!'... By me just watching her I learned how to do everything, see."[16]

Miss Jordan's (and other quilt teachers') primary quilt talk performance also reflects the style of teaching that Shirley Brice Heath categorized in her ethnographic study of two rural and poor communities—one black, one white—in North Carolina. Heath describes the black community's doing-rather-than-talking style as follows: "He [Darrett, who is teaching a group of young boys how to do a certain handshake] does not explain verbally how to do it. He says only 'Do it like dis,' as they repeat the interaction again and again.... Watching and feeling how to do something are more important than talking about how to do it."[17]

In addition, I see connections between some of the presentations among the women in the sewing group and what Roger Abrahams characterized as the verbal presentations that negotiate respect among the women of St. Vincent. For instance, it's quite likely that when the women talk about the way Miss Jordan asks them to rip out a seam but "she says it so 'sweet' you'll think ripping out's an honor," they mean "sweet" in the same sense that Abrahams does when he says that ideally an African-American woman "has the ability to *talk sweet* with her infants and peers but *talk smart* or *cold* with anyone who might threaten her self-image."[18] Likewise, Abrahams' discussion of how black women's verbal presentations negotiate their positions in social settings helps explain what I initially thought to be irrelevant material that Mrs. Bacon included in her version of the quilter's autobiography performance. When she was explaining to me how she learned to quilt during her early years spent in Texas, she highlighted how many children—her own as well as her parents'—she had had to raise and how very limited her resources had been. She listed all the good jobs that her children and grandchildren had had, as well as the names of the universities and colleges that some of them had attended. She spoke often and proudly of her grown sons and their offers to help her out financially; because she had refused these offers, they all agreed instead to furnish their mother with a plane ticket whenever she wanted to go visit family who lived out of town. All these details, though not necessarily relevant to the history of Mrs. Bacon's life as a quilter, were nonetheless included in the story she told. In keeping with her standing as a respectable woman, much of Mrs. Bacon's quilter's autobiography evidences "respectability [which] is judged by how effectively her household is run," how well a woman is able to bring her children up right.[19]

Negotiations of respect in quilters' autobiographies and showing-how-to-do presentations in quilters' teacher talk are not the only aspects of quilt talk similar to other patterns in African-American language stylistics. Quilt talk jokes are also very much like other African-American presentations. Like other instances of signifying, Marion's joking—particularly when at my expense—obscured its addressee and relied on double entendre for its effect and on features of the context for interpretation of its meaning. Likewise, her jokes left the addressee and the audience with the responsibility to interpret the message, thus allowing her, the joker, to deny malice if a confrontation were forced.

Mrs. Summers' joking performances are substantively different from Marion's. Examples of reported speech jokes, that is jokes which center on recounts of someone else's speech given on a former occasion, Mrs. Summers' joking presentations demonstrate "the process of rendering discourse extractable, of making a stretch of linguistic production into a unit—a text—that can be lifted out of its interactional setting . . . . [Its subsequent] entextualization may well incorporate aspects of context, such that the resultant text carries elements of its history of use within it."[20] Folklorists define "entextualization" as a transformational operation that emphasizes the emergent structure of new contexts created by the recontextualizing capacity of this feature of verbal performance. So, for instance, Mrs. Summers' joking report of Miss Jordan's response to Georgia Allen's tearing rather than cutting the fabric squares allows the joker (Mrs. Summers) to undermine Mrs. Allen's authority as an elder in the community, to re-assert Miss Jordan's conviction that the patience and commitment necessary to "getting it right" are an important aspect of quiltmaking, and to warn other listeners of the folly in trying to dupe Miss Jordan. Most importantly, perhaps, Mrs. Summers' joke allows her to spotlight her own performance skills, to earn not only laughs but also respect for her creative style at recycling discourse.

The same is true of Mrs. Summers' performances of the telling-the-story-of-another's-quilt version of quilt talk. You may recall her interpretation of the size and spacing of the squares in Rosie Lee Tompkins' quilt, her notion that the quilter had been suffering "lean times" during the piecing of the work. Her reading clearly indicates that a quilt, like other texts, can be subject to the same decentering and recentering of discourse that folklorists Bauman and Briggs discuss. Clear too is the emergent structure of the new context created when Mrs. Summers reads the quilt, a context that may reflect Mrs. Summers' own emotional landscape at the time or that perhaps is intended to explain some lesson to listeners whom she perceives to be suffering from a tight time of life and needing comfort or unaware of what it means to have to undergo "lean times" and in need of understanding.

You may also recall that when Mrs. Summers told the story of her own quilt, her performance was much less interpretive, much more centered on the material construction of the quilt than on its symbolic meaning. Why is this? Why when she reads another quilter's work does she focus on interpreting the "referential" meaning of the quilt whereas when she reads her own, she highlights the actual context? It may well be that Mrs. Summers' reluctance to assign specific meanings to her own quilt, to read hers as closely as she read Tompkins, is intended to leave her quilt open for others' interpretations, to beckon creative recontextualization by some other teller. Art historian Eva Grudin tells us that quilter Lillian Beattie was quite reticent about revealing or assigning meaning to the characters in her narrative quilts; instead, "she set up these active, animated characters for the viewer to 'free associate' with. Once in a while she revealed particulars about one figure or another."[21]

We can see by now that at least some, if not all, of the types of quilt talk performances that I identified among this small group of women occur among other quilters; likewise, some if not all of the characteristics of these women's verbal performances appear in the presentations of other black female speakers. But what, if anything, can this look at quilt talk tell us about African-American quilting? Do we see any patterns here in the ways that these women use folk themes in natural conversations in order to convey culture-specific meanings? If so, what do these patterns tell us about the aesthetics of quiltmaking for African-Americans?

First of all, it seems evident that, at least to some African-American quilters, "getting it right," is very important; at least some African-American quilters are clearly *not* creating broken patterns or multiple rhythms, *not* relying solely on improvisational responses to time or money constraints.[22] Miss Jordan's teaching performances demonstrate a commitment to this value. On the other hand, neither perfection nor claims to expertise seem particularly important either: the group's plethora of jokes about ripping out seams, the women's rejection of my joking wish to be an expert, and Mrs. Summers' condolences when I noted all the mistakes in my first quilt— all these indicate their tolerance of "mistakes" and inexperience. In fact, it seems that boasting about her quilting skills undercuts a quilter's credibility with this group. Rather, the women appreciate modesty, as well as patience and a willingness to make and accept one's mistakes. These values probably explain their penchant for trial and error as a learning and teaching method: practicing and doing are much more important than explaining and being expert.

Finally, all quilt talk presentations that I've noted point to the premium the group places on individual expression: individual style in verbal performances, as well as in material production, are both highly treasured. The teacher's willingness to let students learn how to accomplish techniques in their own way, the quilter's deliberate ambiguity in interpreting the meaning of her quilt so that readers may find their own meanings, the joker's use of other's talk recontextualized to the joker's own ends, the quilt-text reader's interpretations of another's art work in order to accomplish the reader's own rhetorical purpose, the autobiographer's use of her own quilting history as a way to negotiate respect—all of these forms of quilt talk point to the group's reverence for and active demonstration of individual style in expression. Likewise, and not surprisingly, the members of this group honor the act of reappropriation, whether that recentering appears in a reported speech joke, in creative readings of someone else's quilt text, or in objects of beauty and utility created from otherwise "worthless" scraps. Like the art of quiltmaking itself, much of quilt talk—at least in this group—relies on recontextualization, on recycling someone else's speech or situation and infusing it with one's own style. While style is not the sole component of the art form, it is nonetheless the criterion which determines effectiveness and beauty within the use of the form. If and when "getting it right" and individual style compete for prominence among the values of these African-American quilters, style seems to take precedence. Witness Mrs. Summers' comments on the places in my first quilt where I got it wrong: "They're what makes it yours. . . . Someday you'll look back at this block in your quilt and remember important things about those mistakes."

I only hope readers are as generous with the flaws in my quilt essay. Like some African-American quilts, this essay constitutes a departure from previous, more traditional approaches. As such, it needs to be read not for its solid research results but for its implications and suggestions for further research. I am convinced that continued study of the content and context of the verbal performances of African-American quilters will further our understanding of African-American quiltmaking traditions and practices. For now, I must satisfy myself with Mrs. Summers' judgment of my second finished quilt: "I'll tell you one thing she learned: You can make something beautiful out of just scraps."

Notes and References

1. Though all of the African-American women who attend the sewing class are by their own admission "eligible for the senior citizens' ten percent discount" offered by a neighborhood fabric store, Marion is the youngest of the group. I feel certain that this fact explains why she is always addressed by her first name while the other women of the group publicly call each other "Mrs." or "Miss" (both of which are pronounced "Miz"). However, on rare occasion and always in soft tones indicating an intimate and private conversation, Miss Jordan and Mrs. Summers address each other by first name only.
2. Claudia Mitchell-Kernan, "Signifying and Marking: Two Afro-American Speech Acts" in *Directions in Sociolinguistics: The Ethnography of Communication*, eds. John J. Gumperz and Dell Hymes (New York: Holt, Rinehart, and Winston, 1972), 161–79. Also, Marsha Taylor and Andrew Ortony, "Figurative Devices in Black Language: Some Socio-Psycholinguistic Observations," Center for the Study of Reading: Report No. 20. (Urbana: University of Illinois, 1981).
3. Essential influence in my construction of this joke probably came from the book I had been reading the night before: Zora Neale Hurston's *Mules and Men*, in *Zora Neale Hurston*, ed. Henry Louis Gates (New York: Harper & Row, 1990), 207–85.
4. Featured in Eli Leon, *Who'd A Thought It?: Improvisation in African-American Quiltmaking* (San Francisco CA: San Francisco Craft and Folk Art Museum, 1987), 53.
5. Nellie McKay, "An Interview with Toni Morrison" in *Contemporary Literature* 24 (1983): 413–29.
6. *Women of Color Quilt Network Newsletter* 6 (1991).
7. Carolyn Mazloomi, telephone conversation with author, September 14, 1991.
8. Roger Abrahams, "Negotiating Respect: Patterns of Presentation Among Black Women" in *Women in Folklore: Images and Genres*, ed. Claire Farrer (Prospect Heights IL: Waveland Press, 1975), 58.

9. Cuesta Benberry, *Always There: The African American Presence in American Quilts*. (Louisville: The Kentucky Quilt Project, 1992), 16.
10. Richard Bauman, *Verbal Art as Performance* (Prospect Heights IL: Waveland Press, 1977), 47–48.
11. I refer to characterizations given by, for instance, Eli Leon in *Who'd A Thought It* and by Maude Wahlman in "African Symbolism in Afro-American Quilts," *African Arts* 20 (November 1986): 68–76. Also refer to Wahlman's "Religious Symbolism in African-American Quilts," *The Clarion* 14 (Summer 1989): 36–44.
12. Benberry, 16.
13. Bauman, 48.
14. All of my observations and excerpts of talk I represent herein occurred between the dates of September 30 and December 3, 1991 during Tuesday morning sewing class held at the Northwest Neighborhood Center in Tucson, AZ. My records of the classes do *not* include actual transcripts of audio or video tape; rather, they are strictly from memory. After each class, I made copious notes to which I referred when I reconstructed the women's talk herein; hopefully, I am representing my almost immediate memories of the talk in the context of the sewing classroom with as little interference from time lapse and my own memory distortion as possible.
15. Abrahams, 59.
16. William Ferris, ed. *Afro-American Folk Art and Crafts: Perspectives on the Black World* (Boston, G.K. Hall, 1983), 182–83.
17. Shirley Brice Heath, *Ways with Words: Language, Life, and Work in Communities and Classrooms*. (New York: Cambridge University Press, 1983), 85–86.
18. Abrahams, 62.
19. Abrahams, 70.
20. Richard Bauman and Charles Briggs, "Poetics and Performance as Critical Perspectives on Language and Social Life," *Annual Review of Anthropology* 19 (1990), 73.
21. Eva Grudin, *Stitching Memories: African-American Story Quilts*. (Williamstown, MA: Williams College Museum of Art, 1990), 80.
22. Again, I refer to those descriptions, offered by scholars such as Maude Wahlman and Eli Leon, which portray broken patterns and rhythms and improvisation as the definitive characteristics of African-American quilts.

Her Grief in the Quilt

Carolyn H. Krone and Thomas M. Horner

Quiltmaking is a form of indigenous healing facilitating mourning. Through its fabrics and associated activities quilting provides a path toward coming to terms with loss. In the modern era, grief and mourning are often managed by professional grief counselors in packaged formats which emphasize verbalized and interpreted communications. In contrast, indigenous healing emphasizes atheoretical and non-prescriptive approaches to loss.

Drawing from the historical record as well as from contemporary examples arising in clinical practice, the authors present material illustrating five categories of quilting which serve healing purposes: 1) emollient quilting, used by established quilters to work through painful losses, 2) memorializing quilting, which is intended to commemorate specific losses, 3) thematic quilting, which links quilters who share a common cause or concern, 4) therapeutic quilting, used to deal with clinically definable severe ranges of depression arising from loss, and 5) quilt completion, activity aimed toward completing quilts others have begun but been unable to complete. The authors provide examples of each category.

In this paper we present descriptions of indigenous healing arising from the creative and spontaneous forces within several communities. We take as our point of reference the art or craft of quilting, which has been a traditional practice among many women for centuries. We have drawn material from the historical record as well as from our everyday work with bereaved persons where quilting has been a fundamental component of coming to terms with their loss. We shall present experiences and encounters we have had with quilting as facilitators of mourning, both by virtue of the kinds of activities quilting entails, and by virtue of the quilt's symbolic nature vis-à-vis loss itself.

Quilting and Quilters: An Indigenous Healing Setting and Force

Quilting has been traditionally a woman's activity uniquely fitted to women's experience of themselves and others, and this is fundamentally instructive. We focus on quilting, therefore, not only for the creative and self-healing properties it communicates of itself, but for what it might also communicate in relation to other creative, self-healing domains as well.

When quilting was yet a vital domestic art, women would gather to work on each other's quilts. Such groups might consist of relatives, friends or members of, say, a specific religious community. As they quilted they would share their lives and offer nurturance and concrete support to each other. When a member of the family, group, or community died, bereavement would be shared by the quilting group. Quilting was a mode of remembering past events, and a woman looking back on one or another quilt would be able to say that she made this or that quilt when someone married, or was born, or died.

Although quilting during times of loss probably extends far back into history, the terms "mourning quilt",[1] "memorial quilt", or "widow's quilt"[2] have come to designate quilts made specifically in relation to mourning. Examples of such quilts date from the Civil War era.[3] Such quilts were often made from clothing of the deceased or of the mourners themselves.

Deep currents of connectedness with others, as well as the opportunities quilting afforded for deep confrontations with life and death, are integral to quilting. Radka Donnell has commented on the touch-specific meaning and action of quilting for the quilter.

> Visibly and tangibly, quilts show us the innumerable and infinitesimal acts of women, acts we perform to *hold* ourselves together, to *hold* the elements of our lives together, to *hold* fast to the good in life, to celebrate the persons we love and our embeddedness in nature.[4]

The eminently hospitable, comforting, and enveloping nature of cloth and quilts—their purpose and their substance—make the quilt a solacing object.[5]

Echoing these views, Annrae Roberts has observed, "Whether quilting alone or in our groups, we are in that enabling space . . . connected, supported, encouraged by those before us and the act of creating."[6] Carolann Barrett has echoed this in her personal account:

> I realized that the experience is about feeling integrated and whole, both within myself and with another woman. It's a connection to women of other times and ways of life, quilters and non-quilters alike—a primal connection to something's [sic] that important and true. It has been a powerful, satisfying, almost archetypal experience, a knowing of self and other. That wholeness sustains me at a deep level. . . .
> Mind you, that kind of connectedness/wholeness doesn't happen all the time. Sometimes, I feel fragmented, different parts of myself being at odds with each other, or my being at odds with the world. But that experience of wholeness draws me back; . . . It's a reflection of quilts them-selves, pieces stitched together, many disparate patches, held together at the end as a complete integrated work.[7]

Quilts currently occupy the public's consciousness concerning grief. The NAMES quilt, which memorializes victims of AIDS, the Mothers Against Drunk Driving quilt, the Perinatal Bereavement Quilt Project (Pregnancy and Infant Loss Center, Wayzata, Minnesota), exemplify an expanding use of quilting to convey and to participate in the mourning that is stimulated by recurring losses. In each instance, the personal, intimate social contexts that have traditionally been embedded in the quilting activity have been enlarged so as to unite the huge and myriad individual stories underlying the same kinds of losses.

The narratives of two recent literary works, one a novel, the other a play, provide insights into the existential dimensions of quilting. In their play, *Quilters*, whose dialogues are drawn from the edited accounts of actual experiences, Molly Newman and Barbara Damashek portray the many ways in which the strong forces of individual lives converge, therapeutically, within a quilting group.[8] One of the

Quilters' characters, Sarah, tutors a younger member of the quilting group:

> Look, these are all darks. I've always had plenty of darks. I use them if I need a shaded area in a block. . . . Sometimes, I'll set off my bright patterns with a solid dark block of fabric with no design to it at all. Some call it a plain block—I call it a shadow block.[9]

In an explanatory note accompanying their play's text, Newman and Damashek tutor audiences that some quilt components

> are essentially nonverbal representations of the darker side of the women's rites of passage. The events depicted are not always tragic, but we should get a sense of the unspoken fears involved and the presence of Mystery and Death.[10]

In her novel, *How to Make an American Quilt*, Whitney Otto uses the actual as well as metaphorical properties of a quilting group to convey a similar convergence of forces. The lives of her true-to-life characters are related within the context of weekly gatherings over many years. The members of the group, while not always the best of friends, are always connected by what they do and say together as quilters. What affects each affects all, and the quilting itself symbolizes the integrative and at times reparative powers of their felt connectedness.

Ferrero, Hedges, and Silber have referred to several types of quiltmaking activity, and to the quilts that have long been associated with the deeply abiding emotional ties among women. They list children's "nine patch" quilts, the friendship quilts of young women, engagement and bridal quilts, crib quilts, and widow's quilts as familiar pieces that have united women in both creative expression and relationship formation across generations.[11]

Radka Donnell has commented effectively on the power of quilting to bridge the gaps between the quilter and the *other*, whether it be an immediate other (or others), or an other (or others) of the quilter's past. Adopting a feminist perspective, she also conveys an encompassing tone of reconciliation in her commentary. Piecing, Donnell states, is a reparative process, which corrects for the individual's sense of disconnection or, as she puts it, "overseparation".[12] Addressing the dialectic of separation and unity, Donnell states

> Inasmuch as *separation* and *difference* are connected, they both are actively dealt with in quiltmaking. Since no two quilts are alike, difference asserts itself as part and parcel of each quilt and as an act of healing, endowing the maker with a greater sense of identity than she has felt before.[13]

Yet, Donnell continues, quilting serves to build bridges, whether between past and present or between present and present, which grant, then, continuity within the person. Quilts occupy a symbolic position in the quilter's life, epitomizing comfort and the pleasure of closeness and union with the wanted other.

Quilting, Grief, and Mourning

> A few days later our first baby, too soon by many weeks, was stillborn. I blamed myself; I shouldn't have made the long hard buggy trip in the first place, and I shouldn't have treadled a sewing machine all those hours making those little tucks. But I had always done such things, and it hadn't occurred to me that it could hurt me now, or the baby.
> Bert made a coffin from a stout little ammunition box, and I told kind old Grandma Houk where to look in my box cupboard for a lovely little feather-stitched silk doll quilt that Aunt Ollie had given me years before. They wrapped the baby in the little quilt and laid her in the box. And while Bert nailed the lid gently down above her, some lines, learned long ago, came into my mind:
> > You are quiet, and forever
> > Though for us the silence is so loud
> >   with tears.[14]

These words, spoken by Grace Snyder to her daughter, Nellie Snyder Yost, contain but a passing, inconspicuous reference to the quilt in which her baby was wrapped to be buried. Yet, in a subsequent narrative she refers to quilting which is more telling in relation to the topic at hand. Recounting her sister's death in childbirth, Ms. Snyder states:

Stell took the baby back to the Platte with her and Ethel and I went on home with John to help put Florry's [the deceased] things away. Among them I found enough pieces, cut and laid in neat little piles, for a 'wild goose chase' quilt. I told John I'd take them home with me, and when the baby grew up I'd make them up into a quilt for her.[15]

As with so many quilts that have come to occupy the memorial genre, Ms. Snyder's quilt served as a specific artifact of grieving, a remembrance of the deceased.

Quilting as a process facilitating mourning recurs throughout the historical literature that deals with this social craft and art form. Talula Gilbert Bottoms related to her granddaughter, Nancilu Burdick, that quilting was an effective way for her and others to deal with losses to death.[16] Echoing this assertion, again from a literary perspective, Newman and Damashek portray, in *Quilters*, Cassie, pregnant, telling of her being brought the remains of her husband killed suddenly while laying track for the railroad:

> None of 'em could figure out why he didn't hear the train. We never did get a clear reason, but they had to bring him home in that bushel basket. They tell me I didn't cry or say a word. I just sat down on the porch kinda in a little ball and started rockin' back and forth—rockin' and starin', rockin' and starin'. Course I don't remember much now . . . hardly anything in fact. Just what they tell me. I stayed in the back room . . . never came out. I guess it must been my momma came in and set a piecin' bag in front of me, a needle, a spool of thread, a pair of scissors. I didn't know what those things were for. But one morning, my hands reached out . . . my hands remembered . . . they grabbed the top piece and sewed it to the next piece and the next—didn't matter what it looked like. I never laid a cuttin' edge to any of 'em. Four months later I had a whole quilt and the baby was born; and my eyes came clear again.[17]

Quilts made during periods of mourning are common.[18] One quiltmaker, possibly literary in origin, is said to have related:

> Mother had fourteen children, but only my brother and I lived. Some did not live long enough to be named, but there were two, twins, that lived a week, and she named them Rose and Roselle. I think she grieved

for them more than for all the others. They were buried in coffins dug out of pine logs. . . . The field was plowed up the next year, and she lost track of their graves; they didn't have any money for burying stones in those days, you know, and she wanted to keep them in mind somehow, so she made up the pattern of the twin roses. Her stitches are finer on this quilt than on any of the others, and she never let anyone use it or touch a hand to it.[19]

Ferrero, Hedges, and Silber state that since quilts could take many hours to make, a woman could remember, mourn, and eventually find comfort and resolution in her quiltmaking.

The individual character of a mourner would express itself variously within a collective quiltmaking effort. In 1843, Hannah Cranmer in Cranmertown, New Jersey, inked into a quilt top:

Isaiah Cranmer Born Feb. 12, 1816,
died April 15, 1816.

On the same quilt top Louisa Atwood, a friend of Hannah Cranmer, penned for her little deceased boy:

Died, or was drowned, Unionville
July 11th, 1842.[20]

Anna Marie Schmidt Steinbock, in the late 1800s, embroidered the names of three of her siblings into the hands of angels, indicating that they had died.[21] In 1842, the grandmother of twenty-month-old Nancy Butler created a tombstone quilt commemorating Nancy's death:

NANCY♦
A♦BUTL
ER♦DIE
D♦FEB♦3
♣1842♣
AGED 20 mo[22]

Inscriptions such as these are found on many quilts.[23]

In their book based on oral histories of quilters, Cooper and Buford relate the following anecdote given by a woman in the Texas panhandle:

When I was about four years old the neighbor's baby died, and all the women was called in to help. Mama knew what her part was because right away she took some blue silk out of her hope chest. I remember that silk so well because it was special and I got to carry it. When we got to the neighbors some of the women was cooking and the men was making the casket. Mama and three other women set up the frame and quilted all day. First they quilted the lining for the casket, and then they made a tiny quilt out of the blue silk to cover the baby.[24]

In Michigan, Merry Nader, who during her pregnancy created a baby quilt while mourning her recently deceased father, used it to wrap the infant for burial when, tragically, it was stillborn.[25]

Stimulated by her ongoing research into her grandmother's story, which centered in large measure on that woman's quiltmaking, Nancilu Burdick came herself to undertake the making of a quilt in order to deal with the death of her own son some fourteen years earlier. The quilt would come to incorporate one of her grandmother's patterns as well as to reflect the richness and intensity of his short life. Although the quilt was begun long after her son's death (on the anniversary of his birth), Burdick related that the quilt was important to her continuing adaptations to the loss of her son.[26]

Taken by themselves, these historical anecdotes place but a shell around the core themes and imagery that are present during quiltmaking. They convey the psychologically intricate nature of quiltmaking in relation to grief and mourning. Yet, as condensed descriptions of what is in so many respects a collective experience amongst quilters, they highlight the degree to which the routines of everyday life may be taken for granted—or even overlooked—by professionals as means of dealing effectively with every life's burdens.

Consider, therefore, the following more extended accounts given to us by women who have recently dealt with losses through their quiltmaking.

Rachel

Rachel was the thirty-eight-year-old mother of a son, and was active in her community, particularly her church, where she headed a group which made quilts for new mothers in the congregation. For years, she and her husband had sought to enlarge their family, only to experience four miscarriages and three ectopic implantations resulting in irreversible damage to both of her Fallopian tubes. At the outset of each pregnancy she had begun an embroidered block of a particular pattern called "Woodland Animals". Now, after fourteen years, having worked sometimes alone, sometimes with others, she completed her quilt using the small blocks she had made. With other quilts donated by her guild, Rachel gave this to a local Safe House. Neither we nor she had any doubt that her quilting marked the several losses she had endured during her childbearing years, and marked as well her transition from childbearing to non-childbearing womanhood.

Beth

Beth, a forty-one-year-old mother of three children, became pregnant with a fourth child who was born at twenty-four weeks gestation, and who lived for one hour. He was given the name William. Eighteen months later, she turned to making a quilt, which she said, was to represent herself. She chose a round format, which, she said, was a calendar that moves clockwise. The fabrics and forms she selected for the quilt represent the members of her family individually. In the area which corresponds to October, the month in which her deceased baby was born and died, she placed a red and orange motif that she calls "Trial by Fire". The month in which William had originally been due, February, is represented by a small heart sewn next to a big heart, the first representing William, the second her deceased mother, who had also died during a February. Each heart is sewn so that it can hold herbs such as rosemary for remembrance, or sage to mitigate grief.

Hannah

Hannah's first pregnancy at age twenty-four ended at twenty-five weeks with a son who died within a day of being delivered. Her second pregnancy at age twenty-six resulted in the preterm stillbirths of twin girls. Shortly following these births Hannah took up quilting with a quilting teacher who had encountered losses of a similar kind in her quilting community, and who offered quilting as a distraction which, from a clinical perspective, was therapeutic for her. Hannah made crib quilts during each of her next pregnancies, each of which resulted in the birth of a healthy baby. She then undertook to create a memorial quilt in which her first three infants would be memorialized.

Polly

In response to the death of her mother, Polly, age forty, felt a strong urge to undertake the making of a quilt using her mother's clothes. The quilt was to be for her brother. She could, she related, wear her mother's clothes. But her brother, she said, had few of her mother's belongings. This would be her way of giving him something of her mother's that would be comparable to what she felt she had. Included, therefore, was her mother's favorite shirt as well as a shirt which had been worn by their mother for a family portrait presently in her brother's possession. She envisioned the task as a self-occupation, something to which she could return and return.

Having done some hand sewing, Polly had never quilted, and possessed no knowledge of the historical practices associated with making quilts (e.g., the use of the deceased's clothes as fabrics for quiltmaking). Polly nevertheless envisioned quilting as a means of dealing with the loss of her mother, and of sharing her grief with her brother. She turned to a woman who herself was a quilter, and who had often experienced with other women the healing effects of quilting.

Discussion

Quilting brought, and for some continues to bring, the community, and the persons most closely affected, closer to the death of a loved one, and therefore more cognizant of death itself. Ricky Clark, a historian of quiltmaking, has commented that most of the mourning quilts she has encountered from across the generations have been devoted to losses of children. "Surviving one's children must be the most painful bereavement for women; perhaps that has something to do with it."[27] This high proportion of quilts originating from the losses of children has been our experience as well.

Quilting in the service of mourning offers tangible as well as symbolic means of directly dealing with the feelings and adjustment requirements of loss. For some clinicians (e.g., Dunton[28]) it is a staple of occupational therapeutic approaches to mental disorder. Donnell has been most articulate in this regard, bridging both the life-celebrating and death-accepting opportunities afforded by quilting. In particular, psychic shifts which entail individuation and, ultimately, self-affirmation are involved.

> Women not only seek to shelter their children with quilts they make for them. They also use quiltmaking to deal with the dynamics of separation and the boundaries of space and time, as these are significantly changed at critical points in their lives.[29]

As one surveys the history of the many creative outlets women have had as they have dealt with their feelings and experiences, one discovers quilting to be an enduring form, typically blended of practical and expressive art. Its wide appeal no doubt rests in large part with its creators' abilities to draw material and inspiration from the fabrics and tools of everyday life. This we have seen again and again in the individuals who have shared their creations with us.

As we have gathered examples of quilting, both from history and from our work with grieving persons, we have come to define five categories of quilters. These categories distinguish 1) quilters who quilt during periods of loss as an emollient, 2) quilters who quilt for a formal purpose, e.g., memorialization, 3) quilters who are linked by a common cause or theme , 4) quilters who quilt for its distinct and decisive therapeutic effects, and 5) quilt finishers—quilters who complete quilts begun by others who have died.

Quilting as an Emollient

Through its fabrics and associated activities, quilting softens and smooths the rough edges of painful realities. Quilting is an emollient for the bereft quilter. Into this category fall persons who, as day-to-day quilters, use quilting itself to deal with the immediate effects of a loss. The quilts of Talula Bottoms and Grace Snyder were the creations of quilters who quilted in this fashion. Also in this category are individuals who, though they may have taken up quilting only after the death of a loved one, came to discover in it a way of coping with the feelings or unresolved issues that were connected with the death. Hannah in our example above therefore belongs to this category. These quilters drew on established patterns of activity and involvement with their quilting in order to carry on a process of mourning.

In some instances of emollient quilting, the simple distraction of quilting accomplishes the quilter's aims. In others, it is a way to do some serious thinking, which expectably might include reminiscences, atonements, problem-solving in the face of conditions created by the loss, and similar occupations of the mind and heart. The quilts of many such quilters become landmarking devices around which they construct narratives concerning their losses and the effects of their losses over the course of their lives. Thus, as we stated at the outset, like so many artifacts of creative endeavor, quilts constitute a mode of remembrance, an organizer of life's salient losses.

Memorial Quilting

These quilters adopt a deliberate orientation to their quilting when applying it to losses in their lives. Thus, their quilts are intended to commemorate specific losses. The quilts of Anna Marie Steinbock and Nancy Butler belong to this category, as does the quilt made by Polly in our contemporary examples.

Thematic Quilting

From time to time the public becomes aware of the concerns and interests of regional as well as national organizations. Many of these organizations have, as it turns out, used quilts as means of communicating and portraying issues relating to loss. Quilts completed by Mothers Against Drunk Driving (MADD) and the NAMES project (AIDS) are two well known examples belonging to this genre.[30] Such quilts serve the purpose of uniting individuals in a cause, or in the expression of a loss. Thus, Carol Williams Gebel, who has researched quilting in relation to bereavement, and who has identified many such quilts, describes a quilt made by Zelda Fitzgerald in Greenville, North Carolina, which is signed by parents of children they have lost to death.[31]

Therapeutic Quilting

Therapeutic quilting entails quiltmaking that follows a definable and in some instances compelling path toward working through particular impasses or burdens created by the loss of a loved one. While most quilting can be said to fulfill deeply personal aims, therapeutic quilting typically focusses on the deepest and most compelling pain stimulated by loss.

In individuals whom we have encountered in our research, therapeutic quilting has occurred when reactions were, by conventional expectations, extreme. Thus, we encounter therapeutic quilting in individuals who have been paralyzed by their grief. Cassie in *Quilters*, cited above, represents one such person. Drawing from the materials of the California Heritage Quilt Project, Jean Ray Laury has described the catastrophic reaction of Nancy Lusby Washburn at the death of her nephew at the outset of World War II, a death which was one of several she had experienced in her life beginning with her mother's death at age three.

> She was inconsolable.... She declared war on everyone, going window to window looking for enemies and threatening to shoot anyone "who

didn't look right." Her husband, in an attempt to help her, made a quilting frame she had always wanted.

As Nancy Washburn's daughter later recounted, the effect of her mother's quiltmaking was to help her recover from her extremely reactive state of mind.

> I understand how my mother was comforted by the pleasure of her childhood while making the quilt in a world gone mad. It took her mind to something needing her. It saved my mother's reason as well as the reason of the rest of the family. She became normal again after making that quilt.[32]

Quilt Completion

Clark tells of a quilt started by fourteen-year-old Laura Mahan before her death in 1848. Her stepmother, Sarah Mahan, took fragments of Laura's dresses in order to complete the quilt Laura had begun, which she later bequeathed to Laura's sisters according to the will she (Sarah Mahan) wrote upon it.[33] The quilt made by Grace Snyder is another example of a quilt completed not by the deceased but completed by someone close to the deceased. Among quilters and non-quilters alike, it is not unusual for descendants of the deceased to pick up uncompleted quilts in order to finish them. One of the authors completed the quilt of a grandmother, and we are familiar with many others who have done similarly.

Conclusions

Ours is an age of commodotization and professionalization of care. In the modern era one frequently encounters professionalized approaches to grief and mourning, many of which entail standard office visits, prescriptions for medications to treat specific conditions such as psychoses, depressions, manic states, and the like, as well as more traditional forms of psychotherapy or counseling.

Professionalized care tends to reject mutuality/reciprocity in favor of asymmetrical relationships, in which, for example, one individual is defined as an agent of change—e.g., therapeutic change or "working through"—while the another, the mourner, is defined as the object of the change agent's efforts. The means by which this change is effected is predominantly through the displacing modalities of verbalized and interpretive communication.

It is not always easy to verbally address observations and reactions related to the most deeply personal issues and dynamics of individuals facing loss. In the words of Joseph Campbell:

> The best things cannot be told, the second best are misunderstood. After that comes civilized conversation; . . . and so, proceeding, we come to the problem of communication: the opening, that is to say, of one's own truth and depth to the depth and truth of another in such a way as to establish an authentic community of existence.[34]

In our encounters with grieving individuals we have come to an awareness of how much goes on within the bereft that is outside the purview of others. This awareness has led us to the belief that much of grieving is a private process with its own course and dynamics, which may only incidentally reveal themselves as time goes by. Dealing with grief through verbalization is especially difficult when the mourner has lost the person with whom she had felt most free to reveal depths and truths of herself.

Quilting itself provides a means of coping with and expressing grief which can remain, to whatever extent the quilter wishes, outside the verbalizable realms of communication. We have encountered so many instances of quilting, both historically and in our clinical work, in which the quilting itself, not the verbalized accompaniments, served the grief needs of the affected individuals. For example, one woman completed a quilt over a year's time having never communicated to anyone, even those who knew her well, the specific meanings her activity bore in relation to the loss of her husband. As a solitary creative process, quilting affords the opportunity for reflection and reminiscence which remains "just between" the mourner and the loved one she has lost. The quilt thus serves as a link to the memories of the unique and irreplaceable, the aspects of the relationship which were so special that (and because) they will never be shared with anyone else.

The social context of much quilting, on the other hand, provides occasions through sharing for overcoming the emotional and personal impasses created by loss. Quilting groups existed long before the modern re-invention of the "support group", as an intrinsic part of the social-communal landscape. Such groups are media of what we term, following Kleinman,[35] indigenous healing; that is, healing that arises from the inner resources and practices of the communities in which they occur. In contrast to professionalized care, indigenous healing emphasizes creative, spontaneous, atheoretical, and non-prescriptive processes in the context of mutual or reciprocating relationships. Experiential knowledge, relatedness between the healer and the healed, the personal qualities are emphasized over formal training and credentials.

Participation within a quilt group provides a sense of linkage, both locally and universally, to the community of women who have faced similar losses and survived them. The group offers opportunities to share, insofar as sharing is possible and desired, one's own loss, and to turn one's attention from what has been lost toward what can be created. Offering hope for the re-establishment of the "authentic community of existence" to which Campbell, above, has referred, quilt groups provide clinically significant pathways to therapeutic working through and closure in relation to personal loss.

Acknowledgments

The authors gratefully acknowledge the helpful comments of Kathie Albright, John Bennett, Ricky Clark, Susan Darrow, Douglas Davies, and Geoffrey Krone.

Notes and References

1. Gail A. Trechsel, "Mourning Quilts in America," *Uncoverings 1989*, ed. Laurel Horton (San Francisco: American Quilt Study Group, 1990), 139–58.
2. Patsy Orlofsky and Myron Orlofsky, *Quilts in America* (New York: McGraw Hill, 1974), 227.
3. Ricky Clark, "Fragile Families: Quilts as Kinship Bonds," in *The Quilt Digest 5*, ed. Michael M. Kile (San Francisco: Quilt Digest Press, 1987), 4–9;

Jonathan Holstein, *Kentucky Quilts 1800–1900*. (New York: Pantheon Books, 1982); Margaret Horton, "Quilts of the South: Mourning Quilt," *Quilt World Omnibook 1983*, 5, no. 3: 46–47; John R. Irwin, *A People and Their Quilts*. (Exton, PA: Schiffer Publishing, 1984); Trechsel, 143–44.
4. Radka Donnell, *Quilts as Women's Art* (North Vancouver, BC: Gallerie Publications, 1990), 68.
5. *Ibid.*, 117.
6. Annrae Roberts, "Creative Options," *Lady's Circle Patchwork Quilts* 79 (January-February, 1991): 36.
7. Carolann Barrett, "Quiltmaking: Telling the Truth of Women's Lives." *Sojourner: The Women's Forum* (July, 1991): 15.
8. Mollie Newman and Barbara Damashek, *Quilters* (New York: Dramatists Play Service, 1986).
9. *Ibid.*, 16.
10. *Ibid.*, 16.
11. Pat Ferrero, Elaine Hedges, and Julie Silber, *Hearts and Hands: The Influence of Women and Quilts* (San Francisco: Quilt Digest Press, 1987), 11–12; Clark, 5; Trechsel, 139ff.
12. Donnell, 128ff.
13. *Ibid.*, 125.
14. Grace Snyder and Nellie Snyder Yost, *No Time on My Hands* (Lincoln, NE: University of Nebraska Press, 1986), 335–36.
15. Snyder and Yost, 377.
16. Nancilu B. Burdick, *Legacy: The Story of Talula Gilbert Bottoms and Her Quilts* (Nashville: Rutledge Hill, 1988), 80.
17. Newman and Damashek, 51.
18. See again Ferrero, Hedges and Silber.
19. Related by Francis Garside in "Patchwork Romance", *House Beautiful* (January 10, 1919): 24.
20. Linda Otto Lipsett, *Remember Me: Women and Their Friendship Quilts* (San Francisco, Quilt Digest Press, 1985), 24–25.
21. Holstein, 69.
22. Doris M. Bowman, *The Smithsonian Treasury: American Quilts* (Washington, D.C.: Smithsonian Institution Press, 1991), 37.
23. Ricky Clark, George W. Knepper and Ellice Ronsheim, *Quilts in Community: Ohio's Traditions*. (Nashville: Rutledge Hill 1991); See again Ferrero, Hedges, and Silber; See again Irwin.
24. Patricia Cooper, and Norma Bradley Buford, *The Quilters: Women and Domestic Art*. (Garden City, NY: Doubleday, 1977), 49.
25. *Quilt* 7, no. 1 (1985): 41.

26. Nancilu B. Burdick, *Family Ties*. (Nashville: Rutledge Hill Press, 1991).
27. Nancilu Burdick, Personal communication, December 4, 1992.
28. William Rush Dunton, *Old Quilts*. (Published by the author, Catonsville, MD, 1946).
29. Donnell, 124.
30. Lawrence Howe, "A Text of the Times: The NAMES Project.," In *Uncoverings 1991*, ed. Laurel Horton (San Francisco: American Quilt Study Group, 1992), 11–31; Clark, Knepper, and Ronsheim, 156, 159.
31. Carol Williams Gebel, Personal communication, February 2, 1992.
32. Jean Ray Laury, *Ho for California: Pioneer Women and their Quilts* (New York: E.P. Dutton, 1990), 145.
33. Clark, 13–14.
34. Joseph Campbell, *The Masks of God: Creative Mythology*. (New York: Viking Penguin, 1968), 68.
35. Arthur Kleinman, *Patients and Healers in the Context of Culture* (Los Angeles: University of California Press, 1981), 311–74.

Show and Tell
in Contemporary Quiltmaking Culture

Kristin M. Langellier

Although the vitality and significance of Show and Tell is widely known and appreciated within contemporary quiltmaking culture, it has not received systematic scholarly attention. Data on Show and Tell were collected in two years of fieldwork in Maine, including participant-observation in three local quilting groups, interviews with quilters, and a survey of the Maine state quilters' guild. Data were analyzed in a two-part analysis: first, as a performance event with regard to setting, participants, and ground rules for performance; second, as narrative performance, including six narrative strategies for telling quilts' stories and quilters' stories. The study concludes that Show and Tell functions as an oppositional practice under the control of "ordinary" quilters in an egalitarian, embodied, local, and communal event. As oppositional practice, the form and process of Show and Tell resist the hierarchical norms of public cultures of performance and of quilts as art and quilts as commodities separate from their makers' lives. Thus, Show and Tell serves quilters' own multiple and varied interests within the changing quiltmaking culture and social roles for women near the end of the twentieth century.

With expectancy and patience, the women stand in line or await their turns from their seats, each gripping the tote bag—itself often quilted—that holds her latest quilted item: a miniature quilt, a Christmas wall hanging, a bed-size quilt. Singly or in pairs and occasionally in groups of three or four, they take a turn. With each, there is the moment of suspense as the quilt is unfolded and displayed to the audience, whose oohs, aahs, or applause mingle with the quiltmaker's speech—as brief as the pattern's name, as elaborated as the quilt's history—followed perhaps by questions or comments from the audience. To the outsider, the quilters' Show and Tell may appear quite ordinary, somewhat repetitious, even self-indulgent; to the communication scholar, amateurish and flawed according to conventional standards of performance and public speaking. But to quilters, Show and Tell is the highlight of every meeting—local, regional, state—of their groups and guilds. Indeed, some quilters who travel considerable distances to meetings say, "I go for the Show and Tell."

Show and Tell arose as a cultural practice within the recent quiltmaking revival, dated from the 1970s and usually attributed to the resurgence of quiltmaking among middle-class women.[1] The contemporary revival does not signal a simple return to a traditional aspect of women's culture but entails two recent, simultaneous developments: quilts as art and quilts as commodities.[2] Most significantly, quilts have come forth from their situation in the home to enter a variety of public arenas, including a nation-wide network of quilt guilds; museums, galleries, and auctions; and the marketplace of shops, fairs, and shows organized locally and internationally. Within this emergent and changing culture, Show and Tell flourishes as an event initiated, organized, and controlled by quilters, particularly "ordinary" quilters in the network of groups and guilds.

Show and Tell is characterized by its unique combination of visual (the "Show") and verbal (the "Tell") communication. As a part of the contemporary quiltmaking culture, Show and Tell has not received systematic and close attention in either the scholarly or popular press, although its vitality and significance is widely known and appreciated. Because it is oral as well as visual, seemingly unorchestrated, highly contextual, local, and communal, its study presents a challenge to quilt researchers. One way to approach the study of Show and Tell is as a performance event.[3] By "performance" I mean a way of speaking in which one assumes responsibility to an audience for a display of competence, here a display of speaking and quilting competence. By "event" I mean that such speaking is understood to be meaningful with reference to its relevant contexts, including the overall quiltmaking culture a well as the particular social situation and scene of the performance.

Contemporary quiltmaking is itself situated in a particular social and historical context. Traditionally, quilting and needlework have been synonymous with femininity, embodying women's containment in the private sphere and domesticity. At the same time, performance genres and public speaking registers have privileged forms of communication traditionally reserved for men. These forms of public speaking and performance tend to emphasize monologues and competition among speakers which structure hierarchical rankings among participants.[4] The form and process of Show and Tell, however, resist the conventional norms of public speaking. In addition, its meanings may resist the imposition of values from outside the quiltmaking culture, particularly those of the fine arts and marketplace. Perhaps the most vivid and visible example of quilters' resistance to values from the arts and marketplace is their opposition to the Smithsonian Museum's contract to sell traditional American quilt designs to an import company for assembly and hand-quilting in China, then to be sold at low prices from various retail companies in the United States. I return to this controversy briefly in the conclusion of this essay.

Thus, I argue that Show and Tell functions as an "oppositional" practice that allows quilters to maneuver within the constraints of femininity, of public speaking, and of the emergent and changing culture of the contemporary quiltmaking revival. Oppositional practices are linked to a culture's art of adaptability, of survival, of maneuver. Of oppositional practice in women's telling of fairy tales, Maria Maclean writes: "it is not a revolutionary movement, it is not aimed at overthrowing society and it does not operate from a position of strength. Rather it contests, affirms solidarity, gains victories within a society, operating from a position of weakness."[5] As a performance event, Show and Tell constructs an empowering identity for quilters that is creative and independent, egalitarian and collective, and situated between the private sphere of the family and the public sphere of art, the marketplace, and cultural performance. And, as oppositional practice, Show and Tell contributes to an alternative form of communication and community among quilters which effectively serves their own varied and multiple interests within the changing contemporary quiltmaking culture and social roles for women.

Data on Show and Tell were collected in two years of fieldwork in Maine, including participant-observation in three local quilting groups, interviews with quilters, and a survey of the Maine state guild.[6] I first analyze Show and Tell as a performance event with regard to its setting, participants, audience, and ground rules for performance. Second, I analyze the form of Show and Tell as narrative, that is, as storytelling by women that strategically negotiates their meanings for quiltmaking within the current revival and the complex realities of their lives.

Show and Tell as a Performance Event

This study did not attempt to trace the origins of the term "Show and Tell," but some quilters have noted its associations with educational practices in kindergarten and elementary classrooms of the same name. While "Show and Tell" is the name most frequently applied to this activity within quiltmaking culture, other terms do exist, for example, "Show and Share" and "Bring and Brag." Whatever its source or variations, the term "Show and Tell" implies a performance within a group setting of local, regional, and state meetings of quilt guilds, and it is not unusual to hear the expression "That's a hard act to follow" within a Show and Tell event. David Chaney contrasts performance to the spectacles in popular culture which are defined by their status as commodities circulating anonymously among individuals within mass culture and appraised in terms of their market value.[7] By contrast to the spectacles of mass culture, Show and Tell is a personally embodied, local, communal, and gendered performance event.

Regarding gender, Show and Tell is primarily if not exclusively a women's performance practice within the organizational structure of quilters' guilds and groups, although men participate in many other aspects of contemporary quiltmaking culture.[8] Its performance features are most highly articulated at state meetings, where in Maine some two hundred quilters gather in a theater three times a year (September, January, and May). Quilters go on stage, talk into a microphone, and are frequently photographed with their quilts by audience members. Applause acknowledges every performance and, as we shall see, rewards particular performances. Regional meetings mirror the state structure of Show and Tell but with fewer quilters present. Local Show and Tells display the most flexibility and variation. For example, they may occur at any time during a meeting; they may be conducted more informally, with quilters seated in a circle or speaking from tables; or they may offer a "tell" (information or experience) without an accompanying item to show.

Significantly, the local group serves as the foundation for Show and Tell: local group identities and bonds are preserved within the larger meeting structures as groups sit together and line up together for Show and Tell. In a survey of the Pine Tree Quilters' Guild in 1989, 93 percent reported participation in local Show and Tell, 52 percent in a regional Show and Tell, and 46 percent in a state Show and Tell. These percentages suggest at least two conclusions: first, that the local group grounds the practice of Show and Tell for nearly all quilters in Maine; and second, because participation drops dramatically beyond the local level, criteria for self-selection may be different and more stringent. One Michigan quilter, for example, indicated that her Ocean Waves quilt was fine for the local group but not "special" enough for the regional Show and Tell where original artistry is prized.

Whenever Show and Tell occurs, it is keyed as a distinct and special performance event among quilters. If some quilters are restless during other parts of the meeting, they are keenly attentive during Show and Tell. Participants anticipate Show and Tell by bringing their items to share, and, indeed, Show and Tell functions as a deadline to complete projects, as a quilter remarks, "Last night at 11:30 I finished sewing the borders on. I'm sitting back there finishing the binding." Moreover, quilters hold back or take back gift quilts from recipients so they can be presented at Show and Tell, for example, "I told her she couldn't have it until after the meeting" or "the minute she opened the box I took it back." Participation in Show and Tell ("I said if I ever got this finished, I'd show it to you girls") and audience appreciation provide both motivation and reward, which one quilter makes explicit: "I almost went crazy getting this top together. If nobody claps today on this one it's going out." The regulation of quilters' time and the emphasis on the communal nature of quiltmaking lend a seasonal and celebratory character akin to a festival to state guild meetings in particular.

The audience does much more than applaud, enthusiastically or politely, the Show and Tell performances. An active part of the performance event, the audience encourages and regulates particular performances with requests to "show it again," "hold it up," or "slow it down" to presenters, particularly those who may be nervous and self-conscious speakers. Audience members ask questions of information or clarification (for example, "Was each block quilted separately?"). They may urge a performer to elaborate a description by asking her to "tell us more about it" or by waiting for the performer to add on to what she has said. Audience interaction also opens opportunity for humor, as when a quilter tells the story of buying an antique quilt at a rummage sale for fifty cents. An audience member shouts, "I'll give you seventy-five!" In the interactive structure of Show and Tell, audience chatter, questions and quips, and murmurs, while considered rude by middle-class standards of politeness, function as a display of interest in and support for the presenters.

Show and Tell belongs distinctively to the quilters themselves who extend an "open invitation" that theoretically includes any quilter present, regardless of age (quilters as young as eight years old and as old as eighty or ninety), level of activity (the occasional or the obsessive quilter), expertise, or social status. Getting the floor is not contested because turns are given. Self-selection is the norm as each quilter shows her own work, and many are eager to do so, reveling in the spotlight. A quilter may also show the work of an absent quilter. For the quilter who is shy or apprehensive about Show and Tell performance, other strategies are available: one quilter may present for another who is present but too reticent to speak, or simply accompany her for moral support. The invitation to inclusiveness may become obligation to represent a local chapter, as when a quilter says, "I had no intention to show this, but no one from Casco Bay came up." Another quilter reported that Show and Tell is "compulsory" in her group: one has to participate or put money in a pot (used for group activities). Show and Tell thus values participation over virtuoso performance as a quilter or a speaker; and participation marks one as belonging to a community of quilters.

The inclusiveness ground rule is key to Show and Tell and distinguishes it from other more exclusionary practices in contemporary quiltmaking culture. A working-class quilter from Maine, for example, remarked that she could never enter a quilt in a big show nor write for a magazine or research journal, but she delights in participating in Show and Tell. Because the inclusiveness rule democratically invites the participation of all quilters, the size and length of a Show and Tell event can become an issue likewise regulated by local ground rules. Implicit rules for time limits, which may or may not be strictly adhered to, emerge. Organization officers, for example, may take longer speaking turns than other quilters. Rules may even be explicitly codified in order to manage interaction. One quilter outside Maine reported that the "tells" for her group must be written out on a card before the event, to then be read by one narrator for all participants.

The inclusiveness rule for Show and Tell implies a norm of equality among participants. As one quilter notes, "It's a mutual admiration society." "Admiration" suggests a second ground rule: to acknowledge Show and Tell performances with acceptance and positive feedback rather than rejection and criticism. A third performance ground rule, suggested by "mutual," further elaborates the reciprocity characteristic of Show and Tell. Boundaries between performers and audience are permeable and fluid—at one moment one is a performer, the next moment an audience member—and indeed, performers and audience comprise the same group of women. Thus, reciprocity norms refer to both risk-taking and rewards for participation. Such ground rules structure Show and Tell as a performance event to make it "what it is," but ground rules, of course, can be broken. Participation may be exclusionary in some ways, time may not be equally distributed among individual quilters, and particular Show and Tells may not receive support from the audience.

Ground rules about inclusiveness, support, and reciprocity complement each other and converge to create a practice that celebrates both the unity and diversity in quiltmaking. Nonetheless, subtle distinctions are routinely made among quilts and quilters within particular performance events and quilting groups. Not only do presenters openly recognize a display of special competence with "that's a hard act to follow," but the audience also evaluates performances through the amount of applause and interaction. Quilts that garner special applause give clues to the taste and values of particular groups or guilds. A particular group may affirm bedquilts over wallhangings or machine quilting over hand quilting or traditional designs over art quilts. The audience in Maine Show and Tells, for example, extended warm support to particular individuals on the basis of their "tells" as well as the quilts themselves: to the new member who shows seven items, to the member who is leaving the area with the friendship quilt she has received, to the quilter who almost went crazy making her quilt, to the quilter who is soon to be married, to the quilter whose husband helped with the quilt.

The interactional strategies of Show and Tell as a performance event align it quite closely with the norms of women's speech in the private sphere as they have emerged in empirical research, especially its norms of equality and inclusiveness that structure mutual, non-hierarchical relationships of support and appreciation among participants.[9] If another ground rule is to "show but not to show off," Show and Tell provides an opportunity for friendly and acceptable competition among women couched within a supportive, communal activity. The form and content of Show and Tell enable the ordinary quilter—often unaccustomed to public performance yet hardly self-effacing—to display her quiltmaking achievements. Because the quilt, embodied with its maker, remains at the center of the performance, she is not on display—neither her speech-making skills nor her physical appearance. Participation by individual quilters in Show and Tell creates a collective identity for women who quilt without excluding the amateur, the unremarkable, the common quilter, and (ideally, at least) without privileging particular quilters by virtue of their individual talent, performance skills, beauty, or status in the group. As a performance of their collective identity as quilters, Show and Tell simultaneously equalizes individuals within the group of quilters and differentiates quilters from two other groups

—from non-quilters, including family and friends, and from quilt contest judges and art critics. The former group, even if warmly and non-critically prizing quilts, do not have the technical knowledge and experience of another quilter to appreciate the artistry, skill, and labor involved in quiltmaking. The latter possess the expertise but are defined by their critical posture, judging quilts by a particular set of criteria or along a hierarchical scale.

As a performance practice, Show and Tell emerges in the gap between the private sphere of the home and the more public spheres of the quilt competition, the quilt market, and the quilt gallery or museum which privilege a few quilts and quilters as valuable but exclude the rest. Show and Tell surpasses the confines of the private sphere by creating a more public audience *of* quilters *for* quilters, but retains the interactional qualities of women's talk in the private sphere which foster relations of inclusiveness, equality, and support—despite the dynamics of sometimes more than two hundred participants. Show and Tell eschews the hierarchicalizing norms of the public sphere, such as overt competition, conflict, and criticism, while enjoying the benefits of a larger, more knowledgeable and appreciative audience. Local, communal, and embodied, Show and Tell resists the potentially divisive relations of the art world, the increasingly commercialized relations of the marketplace, the male model of public speech-making, and the spectacle of the female model in public beauty culture.

Show and Tell as Narrative Performance

As a space, Show and Tell is distinct from the home of the individual quilter, privatized and personal; from the galleries and museums of quilt artists, publicized and impersonalized; and from the shops and marketplaces of professional quilters, commodified and commercialized. Show and Tell is perhaps best understood as a "live quilt show," for its distinguishing features are not simply the quilts shown but the narratives spoken which frame the quilts within the quiltmakers' lives. Indeed, Show and Tell is a site for the generation of women's stories. Show and Tell constitutes a narrative form of performance where quilters engage in tactics that not only tell the story of a quilt within a single storytelling episode or serially across Show and Tell events, but that also allow quilters to maneuver within contemporary quiltmaking culture and negotiate empowering identities as women at the beginning of the 1990s.

The quilt which speaks for itself. Occasionally a quilter will show her quilt without an accompanying verbal text or with a minimal verbal performance, simply naming its pattern: "It's a log cabin with mitered corners." Although no story is told, the gap between the quilt and its maker creates a potential story which may be developed if audience members request more information immediately or privately after the event concludes. Even so minimal a narrative is a significant performance because it embodies the relationship of the quilt to its maker. The audience responds to the quilter as well as the quilt, whether she is smiling broadly or grimacing with self-consciousness. "The quilt which speaks for itself" casts the quilt in the role of protagonist, downplays the quiltmaker, and relies upon the audience's familiarity with the quiltmaking tradition to contextualize the quilt and fill in its story.

This quilt is for _____. A common narrative tactic specifies for whom the quilt was made—a sister, husband, new grandchild, student, a child leaving for college, a friend who is moving, a wedding, a battered women's shelter, a co-worker, a dog! These accounts show that quilts emerge from and are vitally embedded in quilters' lives and relationships; they reinforce feminine roles within the family and private sphere where women are expected to selflessly nourish and maintain others. Although a considerable number of quilters have sold at least one quilt, rarely are quilts intended to be sold presented at Show and Tell.[10] To make a quilt for someone and "say it with a quilt" embodies an affective and personal relationship. Yet one cannot assume that the narrative tactic transparently communicates a dominant reality of women's nurturing and service to others. In fact, this strategy may function discursively to provide an appropriate rationale or "cover" for the quiltmaker's own pleasure in and passion for quiltmaking.

This quilt is from _____. Rather than (or in addition to) offering for whom a quilt is made, quilters may cite the source for a particular quilt, for example, "This fabric came from my ninety-year-old grandmother," the pattern from a magazine or book, the technique from a class or workshop or quilter, or the idea from a previous Show and Tell ("This quilt was inspired right here in this room. I thought, that's exactly what I want to do"). Quilters also credit others who helped them with design or quilting. The narrative tactic citing influence, indebtedness, or inspiration aligns quiltmaking with communal norms connected to other quilters more than with artistic criteria of individualism and originality. However, a few quilters distinguish themselves as individual artists or original designers.[11] The strategy of making connections positions quilters within the history of quiltmaking and in relation to each other within the contemporary quiltmaking culture.

Quilting qualifications. Many narrative strategies implicitly or more expressly focus on the quiltmaker herself, although always in relationship to the quilt displayed. Most often such strategies define the quilter within the changing and sometimes competing values in contemporary quiltmaking culture. For example, quilters self-identified "cheater quilts" made of pre-printed fabric, adding such justifications as "It's for kids" or "It's for a fair," to which another quilter replied, "I don't think anyone should apologize for cheater quilts. We're busy women and that's how I learned." Such a response not only adheres to the supportive ground rule of Show and Tell but also intimates the multiple reasons women make quilts and the diversity among quiltmakers. These strategies may also indicate the contradictory values of increasingly intricate quilts and techniques at the same time that women make quilts under more time constraints and within more complicated lives. Other quilters demur, "It's nothing really creative; just fun to do." Although such narrative strategies can be construed as simple modesty, true or false, they may also operate as tactics within a changing quilt culture which increasingly values originality and individual creativity from an artistic perspective at the same time that it embraces collective and egalitarian norms.

Other quilters identify their quilts as "first tries" at a particular item, pattern, or technique, indexing their development as quilters. Such designations may be accompanied by disclaimers or apologies, such as "It's just a doll quilt," "It's not very good," or "The pattern isn't right." Self-deprecation, qualifiers, and disclaimers have been observed in other studies of middle-class women's speech;[12] and such strategies result in one of the few occasions when Show and Tell is discussed in a quilting magazine. In *Lady's Circle Patchwork Quilts*, July 1989, a writer admonishes quilters against "should-ing on themselves" in public ("I should have done this" and "I should not have done that"). For Show and Tell, the ground rule to show but not show off, a characteristic likewise associated with middle-class feminine demeanor, has limits. Qualifications and verbal disclaimers seemingly present a contradiction between self-effacing "tells" and often exultant "shows," suggesting another way that quilters maneuver within the contradictory norms of equality on the one hand, and individual pride and recognition, on the other.

Some quilters identify personal styles or preferences to give an account of their quilts: "I'm known for hating tiny calicoes" or "I'm hung up on Cathedral Windows." Claiming a more inclusive identity, an occasional quilter may define her deviance from the "normative" quilter within a particular group or guild: "I'm not a traditional quilter." Another claims a pattern is "completely my own design" and will hang in a show. And one requests that the videorecorder taping Show and Tell be turned off for her presentation of an original design she intends to copyright. Like the previous strategies citing quilting connections, these strategies position quilters within quiltmaking history and in relation to each other, revealing diversity in the contemporary culture and some competition among different meanings and values for quilts and quiltmaking. Presumably, local norms may display a relatively explicit or subtly concealed hierarchy of values, for example, between original designs and traditional patterns.

Finished quilts and UFOs. Because Show and Tell as a performance event structures time and deadlines for quilters, numerous narrative strategies define finished quilts and UFOs—Un-Finished Objects. "This is my first big project. It's simple but it's finished." One quilter showed five items she finished in order to get to the quilt she wanted to work on—suggesting a work ethic in quiltmaking as well as the fun of quiltmaking. Another quilter describes the situation that allows her so much quilting time: "I work in an antique store and quilt all day," while another jokes, "Remember, I work full-time and have a son who is trying to kill me before he graduates." In regard to a group project, still another cheers, "I started stitching on my block today. If I can do it, you can do it." Finished quilts serve as an achievement to their makers and an inspiration to other quilters. But they also expose the constraints under which quilters pursue their practice with so much delight and determination, most notably, the multiple demands on women's time. Whereas the demands of housework, childrearing, and family maintenance may either go unmentioned or are the subject of jokes, work outside the home may be cited in Show and Tell as it either limits or offers time for quiltmaking. One quilter adds that she put too much money into a quilt not to finish it, a criticism of wastefulness, but strategies referencing time constraints appear to unite quilting women and to prevail over financial comments. As in previous strategies, stories addressing finished and unfinished quilts disallow the divorce of quilts from the contexts of their makers' lives. At the same time that Show and Tell displays quilts, it tells stories that stitch these quilts into the time and space of women's lives.

Horror stories and helping. These narrative strategies are the most interactive, calling for specific responses from the audience, and they occur especially at local and regional meetings. Here Show and Tell becomes a site of sharing quiltmaking secrets and collaborative problem-solving, revealing in yet another way the cooperative and communal values of this segment of contemporary quiltmaking culture. Often quilters share "horror stories" of ripping out blocks, fading fabric, and "I'll never work with that again." Quilters may also offer helpful new techniques: "I've got a faster method for doing triangles" or "If you don't want to applique by hand there is another way." Others ask for advice on choosing fabric for borders or repairing a mistake. Occasionally a Show and Tell may become a mini-lesson, for example, in selecting batting. These narrative strategies significantly embody quiltmaking as an oral culture of peers who teach and learn by sharing quiltmaking stories and secrets.

Strategies on the process of quiltmaking highlight the labor of making a quilt rather than rendering this work invisible when quilts are presented only as finished objects separate from their makers. Quilters recount stories of mistakes, adversity, and long hours of quilting, or of innovations, discoveries, and victories large and small— all of which virtually disappear in a quilt show, museum, or shop. Some of these stories recount embarrassing moments, like the time a quilter painstakingly produced a tiny quilt, the size pictured on the instruction sheet, rather than making it to scale; some recount poignant triumphs over the physical limitations of aging or the grief at the loss of a parent, spouse, or child. Such strategies constitute quiltmaking as "embodied labor."[13] Embodied labor captures the sense in which quilts are intimately connected to their makers' lives rather than viewed as autonomous objects. The labor of producing quilts is rendered visible and audible in Show and Tell rather than taken for granted or concealed like so much of women's domestic, relational, and emotional labor to maintain families and homes in the private sphere.

The preceding narrative strategies compose partial or potential stories, such as when a quilter identifies an item as "my hospital quilt," because the audience of quilters can be assumed to understand what quilts mean to quilters, the process of quiltmaking, and the complexities of quilters' lives. In order to produce more fully developed stories, quilters may elaborate one strategy, combine strategies, or respond to audience questions either during or after Show and Tell. For example, one genre of stories recounts a quilter's beginnings. In a dramatic performance, a woman who had been to a previous state show as a guest five months earlier but had never sewn nor quilted before, unveils her first quilt, and then her second, third, fourth, fifth, and sixth to the cheers of her newly acquired peers. Another story begins, "I was brought up with quilts and never enjoyed them. I thought we were poor and couldn't afford blankets. Then I took a class on log cabins and made eight or nine." Such a founding, or "quilting out," story signals a woman's entry into the collective quiltmaking culture at the same time that it exposes the culture's endorsement of productivity and the contemporary revival's alignment with the middle class interests that distinguish it from "the poor."

Another quilter begins her story dramatically by shaking three old quilts from a garbage bag: "This is garbage. I rescued it." The story clarifies that others do not appreciate the artistry and labor of old quilts—as quilters do. Another woman tells a story of how she made dolls for all of her female relatives, after which her mother made doll quilts for each of the dolls. "But no one made me anything, doll or quilt." Such a story suggests how generosity and reciprocity distinguish the quilter. Each of these narrators assumes that the audience of quilters will understand the point of the story simply because they are quilters—and quilters are special people, united in their social differences by their esteem for quilts. In this way, quilters' stories position both narrators and audience in relation to non-quilters, male and female. As a narrative performance event, Show and Tell marks a storytelling ritual which bonds quilters together by celebrating both their diversity and the difference being a quilter makes.

Show and Tell as Oppositional Practice

At first reflection, Show and Tell presents an unlikely candidate for resistance to the norms of public performance, the dominant meanings of femininity, and the diverse shifts within the contemporary quiltmaking culture. It is, after all, just talk by quilters about their quilts; and moreover, it sounds familiarly feminine in its themes (for example, "Say it with a quilt"), its strategies, for example, verbal disclaimers, and its horizontal interaction. But situated as a particular performance practice within the recent quiltmaking revival, a more complex picture emerges, grounded in the fact that quilters themselves control the form and content of Show and Tell in the midst of changing roles for women and changing practices and sites of quiltmaking.

Show and Tell creates an audience *of* quilters *for* quilters' stories in performances that preserve quilts as embodied, local, communal, and gendered phenomena. This performance practice generally excludes men as narrators, although men may appear in quilt stories or be present in the audience as they are in other aspects of the quilt culture and quilters' lives. Show and Tell creates an egalitarian community of women who quilt, a community grounded in local quilting groups but extending beyond these boundaries. Most significantly, Show and Tell participates in an oral culture of peers who perform a live quilt show embodied by their makers—"ordinary women" rather than professional quilters, quilt artists, or professional performers. This live quilt show resists the forces in contemporary society and quiltmaking culture that threaten to aestheticize (make quilts into autonomous art objects) and commodify (make quilts into market objects for their exchange value) quilts, forces that would effectively disconnect quilts from the concrete and complex lives of their makers.

Show and Tell creates a unique space for its participants within the multiple and contradictory threads of contemporary quiltmaking culture. That space exceeds the family and private sphere, and even if family and friends receive quilts as gifts, they are not the audience of Show and Tell. At the same time that Show and Tell expands the boundaries of quilting beyond the private sphere by creating a social community of quilters, it minimizes the divisions and hierarchies of the public art and market worlds which have emerged as part of the recent quiltmaking revival. Show and Tell resists the imposition of criteria external to the participants' values, whether they emanate from the arts, the marketplace, or popular culture. The public cultures of quilt artists, collectors, and professional designers recognize some exceptional quilters, but devalue the ordinary woman who makes quilts for personal and social reasons. Situated between the private sphere of the family and the public sphere of art and performance, Show and Tell equalizes participation to constitute a community of peers who both support and stimulate each other as quiltmakers. Participation in Show and Tell identifies one as belonging to the culture of quilters, no matter what one's expertise or social status.

Whereas narrative strategies foreground middle-class values of family, education, and consumption, as a practice Show and Tell actively maintains access to working class women because it requires no formal education, professional credentials, experience, or expertise in public communication. In fact, Show and Tell is ideally suited to the ordinary quilter—middle or working class, amateur or professional, artist or craftsperson—as a speaker as well as a quilter. Show and Tell preserves the interactional characteristics of women's speech in the private sphere, notably, the egalitarian and horizontal relations between participants which engender participation, support, reciprocity, and knowledgeable appreciation. Show and Tell accomplishes speaking in a public setting without conforming to the male register of speech-making. This process of publication, most often reserved for exceptional quilts in publicly legitimized settings, does not function in a dominating way to silence participants of differing talents, backgrounds, experiences, desires, and dispositions. Indeed, the strategies and structures of Show and Tell provide a safe space for diverse women to present their quilts, for women to support the creative work of other women, and for quilters to celebrate their bonds. Reflecting on the encroaching elitism in contemporary quiltmaking culture, Radka Donnell writes, "Only special quilters' organizations offered members a climate of full acceptance and creative encouragement. At the Quilters Connection in Arlington, Massachusetts, for example, regular 'Show and Tell' evenings are a working model of equality and women's support of each other."[14]

Show and Tell creates a place for quilters to tell their stories. In Show and Tell, quilts are visibly and indivisibly displayed with their makers' stories rather than disembodied, dissolved silently into the home, or divorced from women's lives in museums, galleries, or markets. Narrative strategies engaged in by quilters do not represent women's reality in a simple, unmediated way but rather strategically negotiate an empowering feminine identity for contemporary quilters. The narrative strategies of Show and Tell reveal quiltmaking as an acceptable "cover" for quilters, one that maintains family meanings at the same time that it challenges the limitations of femininity.[15] In Show and Tell, a quilter takes public pleasure in her creativity and accomplishments, performing an identity that is compatible with but exceeds her role as a homemaker or paid worker. Through quiltmaking, she is able to meaningfully order the different demands on her time in ways that support her own creative, personal, and social interests. At the same time that women embody the labor and relationships of quiltmaking in Show and Tell, they downplay the concerns of feminine demeanor and beauty culture.[16] To engage in Show and Tell is to participate in a collective and egalitarian form of communication with other women who quilt. Show and Tell thus unites women-quilters-as-a-group distinct from men and non-quilters. Quilting promotes a shared performance among women who may otherwise differ by individual talent and temperament as well as by social categories of class, race, ethnicity, or religion.

The argument that Show and Tell both performs women's collective identity as quilters and constitutes an oppositional practice within contemporary quiltmaking culture depends upon its particular historical situation—for this study, in Maine at the onset of the 1990s. But such a performance practice is always in danger of cooptation, at risk of being removed from the control and context of ordinary women and put to different ends. In concluding this essay, I briefly mention three possible dangers here. First, the aestheticization of quilts, rendering them art objects, may indeed raise their public status but at the potential cost of ignoring the personal, social, and political meanings of quiltmaking in women's lives. Should quilts become increasingly identified and valued as visual objects of individual artists, Show and Tell's emphasis on the oral, familial, relational, local, and communal embodiment of quilts may become devalued. Bringing quilts to a public audience may risk becoming a more impersonal, institutionalized display of art objects in the absence of their makers within groups and guilds of the revival.[17]

Second, Show and Tell as a performance event may risk becoming one more spectacle of popular culture, for example, another aspect of beauty culture which features quilted clothing on the model of the fashion show. In *Uncoverings 1989*, Jane Przybysz contrasts the lively, embodied Show and Tell performance to the quilted fashion show at Quilt Expo Europa of 1988.[18] She argues that in drawing upon the conventional fashion show, the presentation of quilted clothing reproduces the "male gaze" of modern beauty culture before which women are silent and passive objects. It is worth noting that in major quilt shows in the United States, the Houston Quilt

Festival and American Quilter's Society show in Paducah, Kentucky, the quilted fashion shows have become the most popular events. At these venues, some quilters model their own clothing while others ask friends to model. Chaney also cautions that when popular and commercial interests prevail, performance events featuring amateurs are replaced with professionals and "stars."[19] Is there a danger that future Show and Tells at quilt shows will feature only professional quilters, professional speakers, and professional fashion models? Show and Tell as spectacle would dismiss its key performance ground rules of egalitarianism, inclusiveness, interaction, and mutuality.

And third, Show and Tell may be threatened by the increasing commodification of quilts which sets their value in the competitive marketplace apart from their makers and their makers' lives. The most vocal and visible manifestation of the commodification of quilts is the controversy surrounding the Smithsonian's contract to produce hand-quilted American quilts in China. Although there are many dimensions to this controversy, a major concern is that making hand-quilted traditional quilts available to a mass market devalues them, both as art and as personal expressions. The increasing commodification of quilts that makes them exchangeable within mass culture risks trivializing their artistry but especially their embodied labor and "lived" meanings which emerge so tellingly in Show and Tell. Simultaneously, the commodification of the quilt may have a somewhat contradictory effect, what Chaney terms "bourgeousification," or increasing alignment with middle-class interests. Bourgeousification, which takes the form of excluding working class participants from a practice because of costly materials, access to education, travel to gatherings, and special training or experiences in public or media speaking, could also contribute to changes in Show and Tell, for example, should it require male registers of public speech-making for successful participation in the performance event.

I raise these—at this point hypothetical and fanciful—risks of co-optation for Show and Tell not so much to argue that such dangers are imminent, but because they set in relief the very unique and highly significant place that Show and Tell offers within contemporary quiltmaking culture. Indeed, I argue that Show and Tell operates as an oppositional practice precisely because it rests with quiltmakers themselves and often resists external definitions for quiltmaking, as the Smithsonian episode so clearly demonstrates. In Show and Tell quilters exercise agency and autonomy, negotiate meanings of quiltmaking that serve their own varied and multiple interests, and resist the institutionalization of quilts as art or commodity separated from the fabric of their lives. Show and Tell embodies quilts and creates local communities of storytelling women—creative, independent, egalitarian, and collective—situated outside the private sphere but in opposition to the more individualistic, divisive, and hierarchical norms of the public cultures of quilts as art and quilts as commodities as well as speech-making performance. Certainly, the quilting stories in Show and Tell cannot be construed as the great "cover-up" of a feminist quiltmaking revolution, but Show and Tell does name an oppositional communication practice under the control of ordinary women who live in a complex and changing world of quiltmaking and gender roles.

Notes and References

1. My research on quiltmaking in Maine revealed a somewhat more complex picture of social class participation in the contemporary revival. See Kristin M. Langellier, "Contemporary Quiltmaking in Maine: Re-fashioning Femininity," *Uncoverings 1990*, ed. Laurel Horton (San Francisco, CA: American Quilt Study Group, 1991), especially 33–35.
2. See Kristin M. Langellier, "Contemporary Quiltmaking Discourse," paper presented at the Maine Women's Studies Conference, April 13, 1991, Bowdoin, ME.
3. See Richard Bauman, *Verbal Art as Performance* (Prospect Heights, IL: Waveland, 1977), 3–58; and "American Folklore Studies and Social Transformation: A Performance-centered Approach," *Text and Performance Quarterly* 9 (1989): 175–84.
4. Kristin M. Langellier and Eric E. Peterson, "Spinstorying: An Analysis of Women Storytelling," in *Performance, Culture, and Identity*, ed. Elizabeth C. Fine and Jean H. Speer (Westport, CN: Praeger, 1992): 157–79.
5. Maria Maclean, "Oppositional Practices in Women's Traditional Narrative," *New Literary History* 19 (1987): 40.
6. I have also attended local and regional Show and Tells in Michigan which did not differ significantly from those in Maine. But see note 17 for one variation.

7. David Chaney, *Fictions and Ceremonies: Representation of Popular Experience* (New York: St. Martin's Press, 1979).
8. Men may be present for Show and Tell, though they very rarely were in the groups I observed. When a man designed a block for the Pine Tree Quilters' Guild, the state organization in Maine, the president presented his design in the business portion of the meeting. The man did not speak.
9. For further descriptions of women's speech, see Langellier and Peterson.
10. In the survey of Maine quilters, two-thirds reported never having sold a quilt.
11. Quilters who define themselves as artists may have an ambivalent relationship to the quilting groups and guilds that feature Show and Tell. In the research reported in "Contemporary Quiltmaking in Maine" I encountered some quilters who described themselves as artists but also noted that only one of seven Maine quilters featured as quilt artists in the *Lady's Circle Patchwork Quilts* (January/February 1990) belonged to the state guild.
12. The research literature on the use of disclaimers and qualifiers in women's speech reveals contradictory findings and interpretations, however. See Dale Spender, *Man Made Language* (London: Routledge and Kegan Paul, 1985), 32–35; and Deborah Cameron, *Feminism and Linguistic Theory* (London: Macmillan, 1985), 28–56.
13. I am indebted to Mary Lou Woods (personal communication) for the term *embodied labor*.
14. Radka Donnell, *Quilts as Women's Art* (North Vancouver: Gallerie Publications, 1990), 6.
15. Langellier, "Contemporary Quiltmaking in Maine."
16. Sandra Bartky, "Foucault, Femininity, and the Modernization of Patriarchal Power" in *Femininity and Domination: Studies in the Phenomenology of Oppression* (New York: Routledge, 1990), 63–82. Mary Lou Woods (personal communication) also noticed Show and Tell presenters' lack of self-consciousness with beauty culture, even before large audiences.
17. In Maine Show and Tells at state meetings, participants are often photographed by the guild historian and other interested members during Show and Tell. In a regional Show and Tell in Michigan, however, quilts are photographed after the performance without their makers. These photographs of quilts are displayed in albums at subsequent meetings where members may order copies.
18. Jane Przybysz, "The Body En(w)raptured: Contemporary Quilted Garments," *Uncoverings 1989*, ed. Laurel Horton (San Francisco, CA: American Quilt Study Group, 1990), 102–21.
19. Chaney, *Fictions*.

Ink Damage on Nineteenth Century Cotton Signature Quilts

Margaret T. Ordoñez

Among the most historically significant quilts are those with signatures, but the signatures that make them so valuable also cause them to be more fragile than their contemporaries of other styles. This research investigated permanent nineteenth century inks and the effect that they had on cotton, signature quilts. Special needs related to handling, cleaning, exhibition, and storage were identified for both old and new signature quilts.

Although indelible carbon and silver nitrate inks were used in the last century, most of the permanent inks were made from ferrous sulfate and nutgalls which contained tannic acid. Sulfuric acid often was added to prevent formation of ferric tannate precipitate before the ink was used. Cotton fibers have low resistance to damage from acids. Microphotographs of a signed nineteenth century cotton quilt from the University of Rhode Island Historic Textile and Costume Collection show types of damage acidic ink has caused. Much embrittlement and fiber breakage occurred along the margins of the inked areas due to the migration of the inks when drying. Weakened margins result in total loss of some signatures, especially if located along a fold. Ink sometimes wicked along yarns increasing the damaged area.

Nineteenth century cotton signature quilts may not have visible damage, but fibers may be weak. These quilts should not be wetcleaned and need to be vacuumed carefully. Old and new signature quilts should be handled carefully and stored so that areas with signatures lie flat and are not compressed. Rolling such quilts could be harmful. Vertical exhibition should be avoided if signed areas would be stressed.

Signature quilts have special significance because they carry part of their history stamped, stenciled, or signed on their surface. Their background is not as easily lost as that of other quilts because the identity of the signers might be traceable. When signers can be identified, other information such as the reason for a quilt's creation, the date of construction, the maker(s), and group affiliation of the makers or signers also might be obtainable. But the very thing that makes signature quilts extra special often is detrimental to their surviving in good condition. Some inks used in the past for signatures have damaged fabrics, especially those made of cotton and flax which have a low resistance to damage by acids.

Decisions about handling, vacuuming, wetcleaning, storing, and displaying a cotton signature quilt should come after careful evaluation of the condition of the fibers under and around signatures, stencils, and stamps. The integrity of the fabrics in a signature quilt depends especially on the composition of the ink and the care the quilt received after it was made.

Nineteenth Century Signature Quilts

The advent of signed album quilts in the 1830s coincided with the development of indelible inks that would withstand laundering and not harm fabric.[1] Brackman suggests that the development of safe indelible ink may have contributed to the fad for autograph quilts with signatures, verses, and drawings like those in autograph albums that had been popular since the 1820s.[2]

The format of quilt designs was changing also as a block arrangement rather than successive borders of the medallion style began to be used. Block-style album quilts, both pieced and appliqued, were very popular by the 1840s. Brackman hypothesizes that the album quilt influenced the change from cut-out chintz printed patterns to conventional applique that occurred during this time period.[3] This early part of the nineteenth century was an important time in the evolution of quilts in the United States.

Two types of album quilts flourished in the 1840s and 1850s. In sampler album quilts, all blocks were different, sometimes made by

Figure 1. Album quilt from New Hampshire, ca. 1870s. University of Rhode Island Historic Textile and Costume Collection, #76.07.01. The following close-ups are of this quilt.

different people who signed their own blocks. Single-pattern album quilts, also known as friendship quilts, had all or most blocks of the same design, again with different signatures in each block. (See Figure 1.) Based on extant quilts, this type of album quilt remained popular longer than the sampler style, but post-Civil War friendship quilts most often had only a signature and possibly a town name rather than the verses and inscriptions of earlier times.[4] (See Figure 2.)

Another type of signature quilt was used to raise money. People

Ink Damage

were charged a small sum to write their names on pieces of fabric that were incorporated into a quilt. This distinct style of fundraising quilt began to be made in the 1880s.[5] If the ink used for the signatures was corrosive, these quilts would be degraded more than the album quilts because of the larger number of signatures; if the ink was not permanent, and it faded, a valuable historic resource would be lost. The search for permanent inks that did not damage paper and fabric was ongoing throughout the nineteenth century and into the twentieth century. Problems related to the most popular permanent writing inks' settling and reacting with the substrate have been addressed in the twentieth century without changing the basic components—iron sulfate and gallic and tannic acid.

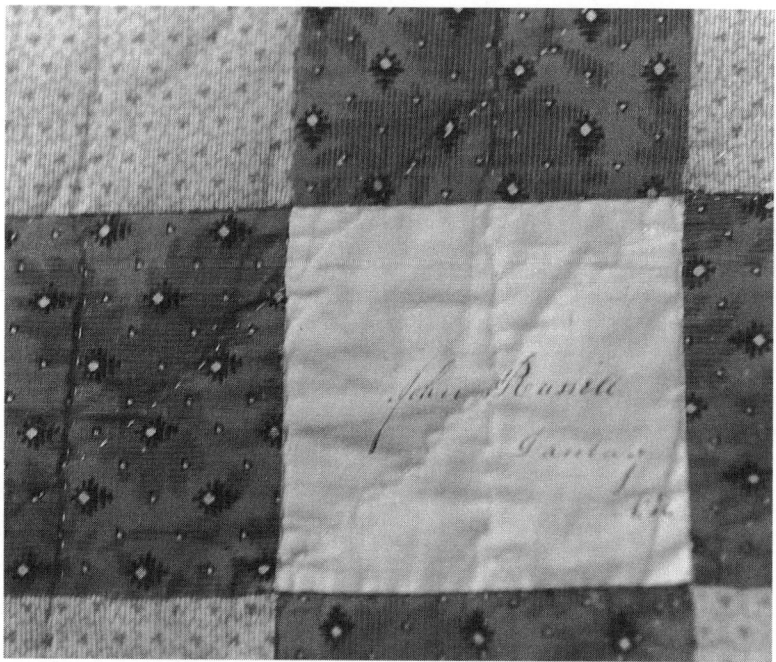

Figure 2. Close-up of signature block in album quilt; John Russell signed this square parallel to the bottom edge, but the square is on point in the quilt so that the signature is at a 45° angle to the edges of the quilt.

Iron Gallotannate Inks

A twelfth century encyclopedia of Christian art written by a monk described a method of preparing writing ink from thorn wood and green vitriol. Literature in following centuries mentioned ink from green vitriol, an iron ink from galls and black ink from galls, and vitriol.[6]

What were these ingredients? Green vitriol is ferrous sulfate ($FeSO_4$) and is also called copperas. Vitriol is sulfuric acid. Galls or nutgalls are nutmeg size swellings on an oak tree formed when a gall wasp punctures the bark and deposits an egg. At that spot the tree produces tannic and gallic acids which serve as food for the developing larva. The methods used to harvest the galls and extract the acids influenced the amount of each acid obtained as did natural variations in the galls. The blue or Aleppo galls from the Middle East had more of the acids than the galls from trees in England and southern Europe and, therefore, were recommended as the best for ink making.[7]

Prior to the nineteenth century iron gallotannate ink was made by dissolving ferrous sulfate in an infusion of nutgalls; fermentation of the mixture was followed by a period during which the liquid was left undisturbed so that the solid impurities could settle out. The ferrous iron (Fe^{++}) reacted with the gallic and tannic acids to form a soluble compound which on exposure to air was oxidized to nearly insoluble ferric compounds (Fe^{+++}) resulting in a murky, black-colored ink. When used for writing, this insoluble component made the ink remain mostly on the surface of the paper. The addition of glue or plant gum to the ink formula kept the solid iron particles suspended and fastened them to the paper. Writing with this ink produced a pale-brown color which turned black over time as further oxidation occurred.[8]

Experimentation at the end of the eighteenth century led to a process that protected the ink from oxidation until it was used. This produced a clear ink, and the oxidation that formed insoluble particles took place within the fibers of the paper producing a more permanent ink. Since the oxidation process occurred over a period of several days, a dye or provisional color was added to the ink to provide temporary color. If the dye were to disappear, black writing would still be visible because of the insoluble ferric compound in the fibers. Over a long period of time, however, the writing would become brownish black due to the formation of ferric oxide.[9]

A U.S. patent was issued in 1856 for this type of unoxidized ink incorporating madder and indigo. Despite the blue-black color of these inks which contained madder and indigo as dyes, they were called alizarin inks, alizarin being the major compound in madder. The maker later omitted the madder, but the name alizarin ink remained into this century. Other ink makers began making this improved type of ink. In 1891, eighty-one German inks were examined, and all were the unoxidized type although the older kind was available from some small makers.[10]

Before the industrial era ink making had been a household art, and although inks were available commercially in the nineteenth century, some were still made at home. Recipes for making one's own ink were published well into this century. A National Bureau of Standards author as late as 1940 wrote: "Anyone who has the ingredients at hand and the necessary facilities can quickly prepare blue-black ink."[11]

Quality control was difficult for both the home and commercial manufacturer of inks. The correct proportions of iron and nut galls were difficult to ascertain because of impurities in the ferrous sulfate and inability to determine the amount of acids in the galls. Achieving a "balanced ink" was difficult.[12] If too few galls and more ferrous sulfate were used, the resulting ink could gradually become rusty brown in color rather than black.[13]

The proportions of iron and nut galls was not the only problem, however. The interaction of iron and acids from the galls produced sulfuric acid. Additional sulfuric acid was added by ink makers to keep inks clear; the more free acid an ink contained, the slower the oxidation process so the ink could be stored without forming an undesirable ferric precipitate and becoming weak. But the acid corroded steel pens and reacted with paper, so the amount of free acid needed to be controlled. Hydrochloric acid was not as successful an addition as the mineral acid because it was volatile; when chlorine gas did not stay in solution, a ferric precipitate formed in the ink, weakening it.[14]

Efforts to filter out free acids resulted in inks that were "rather more prone to precipitate" and adding more gum arabic did not counteract the effect.[15] Other proposed solutions for excess acid included neutralization which rendered the ink too thick and the addition of a few small nails to the ink bottle to provide excess iron to react with the acid. With this last proposal, when pens began to corrode, the user needed to add more nails to the bottle. Whether the nails increased precipitation of solids in the ink or if the color of the ink was affected was not reported.[16]

The balance between iron, tannic and gallic acid, and sulfuric acid was still a problem at the end of the nineteenth century for writing on paper and textiles. One writer reported in 1913 that finally commercial launderers had developed permanent inks that were "free from chemicals which heretofore cut through the fiber, leaving the mark, in the worn linen, like a stencil."[17] Special safety or indelible inks for fabrics received more attention as people increased their use of commercial laundries.

Indelible Carbon Inks

A number of permanent writing inks purported not to fade from light exposure or age had been used on paper and fabric for a number of centuries, but often they did fade and degrade the paper or textiles on which they were used. In 1831 a commission of scientists, including such noted chemists as Gay-Lussac and Chevreul, were appointed by the Paris Académie des Sciences to examine all proposed permanent inks to prevent falsification of documents. The Commission found that all inks prior to 1826 were either too thick, attacked paper, or precipitated too readily. The only two recommended ink formulations contained Indian ink.[18]

Indian or India ink is found on the oldest extant manuscripts. Since ancient times lampblack, fine soot formed by the incomplete combustion of fuel, was made into a paste with glue, gelatin, or plant gum in water, shaped into a mold and dried. In the nineteenth century the solid ink material was traded from China in various shapes including sticks and tablets. The quality of the ink varied considerably with the best being sold in octagonal sticks, called Mandarin, marked with a lion on top and Chinese characters on the sides. Many recipes existed for the formulation of India ink.[19]

One of the two India inks recommended by the Commission contained a number of ingredients, and a document had to be held over ammonia for the ink to become "fixed and rendered indelible." Although cumbersome to use, this formulation had the advantage of containing no free acid. The simpler of the two recipes was India ink mixed with dilute hydrochloric acid.[20]

The formulation of the latter ink was published in the *Journal of the Franklin Institute* in 1837 as the choice indelible ink for writing with quill pens. In the section entitled "Progress of Practical & Theoretical Mechanics & Chemistry, the *Journal* editors stated that the best indelible ink for writing with metallic pens was India ink dissolved in water made alkaline by caustic soda.[21] Two other 1830s inks, called "safety" inks by a twentieth century historian, were (1) a solution of potash and wood tar and (2) a mixture of lampblack with a solution of shellac and borax.[22]

British patents were issued for three indelible carbon inks between 1837 and 1840. The composition of these inks were: (1) carbon in a solution of resinous soap, 1837; (2) lampblack in linseed oil, 1837; (3) gasblack, indigo, and Prussian blue in gall and logwood ink, 1840. This latter indelible ink with a nutgall base posed a threat to paper and textiles when not well balanced.[23]

One of the problems with carbon inks was the difficulty in preparing a permanent suspension of carbon particles in water. Grinding the ink to separate the particles was essential and very difficult to do by hand. If the pH of a carbon ink was lowered, the solids in the ink quickly settled out, but if an alkali was added, the suspension of carbon became more stable. Because of their sensitivity to acids, carbon inks could not be mixed with iron gallotannate inks.[24] One could question if the formulation that mixed gasblack in gall and logwood ink was successful or failed because the carbon precipitated.

Several characteristics of carbon inks favored their use on fabrics.

They were unlikely to contain any substance which would damage the fabric since acid was not a component. Also, carbon writing inks had a high resistance to removal when soaked in water. Soap solutions removed little more ink than the water alone; the carbon particles stayed in place among the fibers.[25]

Indelible Silver Nitrate Inks

An ink utilizing silver nitrate for marking fabrics before laundering was used as early as 1851 when a published recipe was purported to have been used at a District of Columbia institution where the laundering conditions were severe.[26] A 1913 publication states that "The old-fashioned nitrate-of-silver ink is still commonly used for marking linen and for similar purposes."[27] The instructions for making this indelible ink were to dissolve 1 ounce nitrate-of-silver in 2 1/2 ounces of liquid ammonia (ammonium hydroxide); separately a mixture of 1 1/4 ounces of gum arabic and 1 1/2 ounces of carbonate of soda crystals were gently heated and then mixed with the silver nitrate and ammonia; the ink was allowed to stand in a warm place before a few drops of solution of magenta was added.[28]

The 1913 publication also gave directions for putting a mordant on the fabric before the silver nitrate ink was applied. "First moisten the linen with a mordant composed of 9 ounces of baking soda and 1 ounce of gum arabic dissolved with gentle heat in 8 ounces of water. Dry with a warm flatiron, and apply an ink composed of 1 ounce of nitrate of silver, 14 ounces of distilled water, and 1 ounce of sap green. This must be applied with a quill pen, a gold pen, or a brush, as a steel pen will decompose the ink."[29]

After silver nitrate ink writing was dry, it had to be developed. Pressing the fabric with a hot flatiron or placing it in the full sunlight developed a black color. The black marks were resistant to washing but not to chlorine bleach which converted the silver to silver chloride. Silver chloride is slightly more soluble in water and would be lost after a short time. Formulas for silver marking inks colored with dyes had no advantage over the inks without dyes because after use the silver soon turned black, and the dyes washed out.[30]

Ink Damage

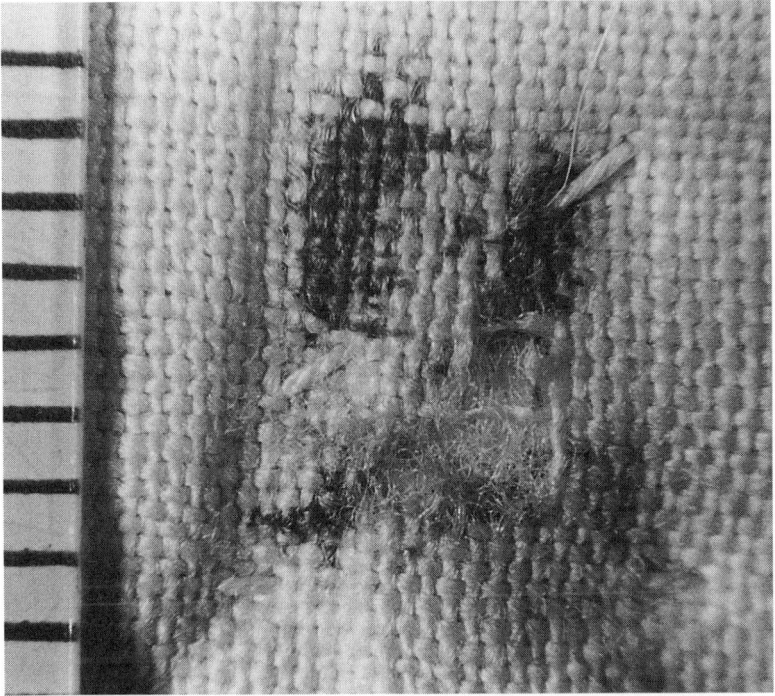

Figure 3. Initial in a signature on a square in the album quilt; cotton fabric with quilting stitches running diagonally across the square; loss of ink-weakened fibers in some of the yarns created a hole in the fabric. Photographed with a stereomicroscope; scale on marker is 1.0 mm per marks.

Degradation of Cotton Fabrics by Ink

Nineteenth and twentieth century literature contains no reports of damage to paper or cotton fabrics from India ink or silver nitrate ink formulations. Frequent references to degradation by iron gallotannate inks exist, however, and signed album and fundraising quilts of the nineteenth century are mute evidence of the presence of free acid in the inks used for signatures. Acids degrade cellulosic materials such as paper, cotton, and linen by a chemical reaction called hydrolysis.

Figure 4. Close-up of fabric in a square that once had a signature inked on it; the area damaged by the ink is so extensive that the name became illegible after fibers in both warp and weft yarns disintegrated.

Ink Damage 159

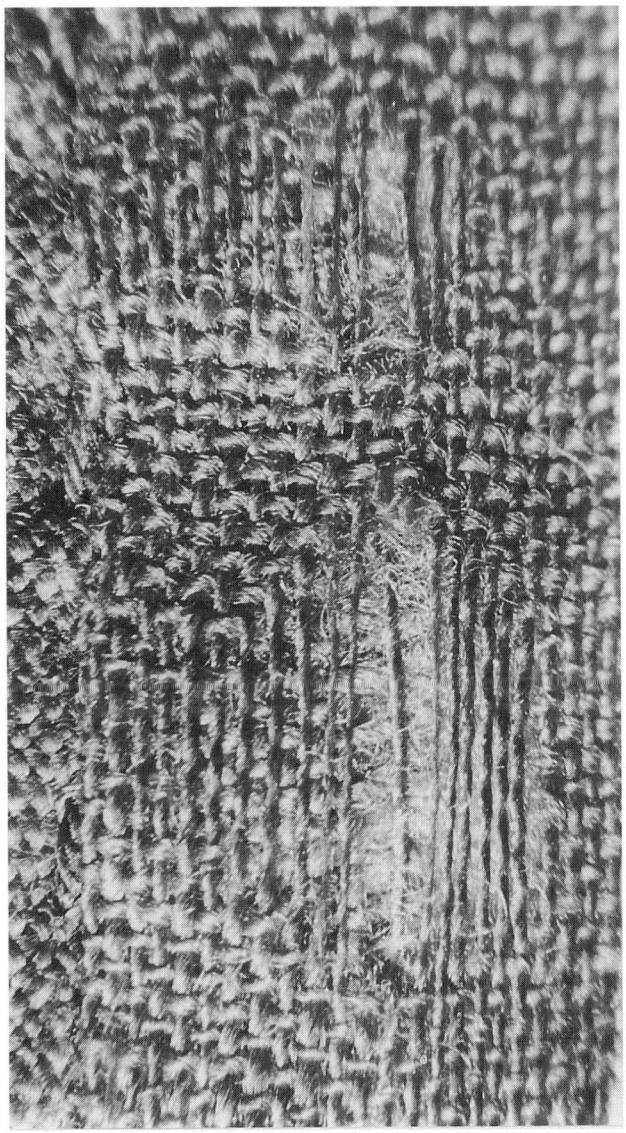

Figure 5. Fibers in warp yarns not weakened by spilled ink as much as those in weft yarns which have disintegrated near the edge of a quilt piece; sizing on the warp yarns may have provided protection to those fibers; yarns in the fabric in the adjacent square and quilting thread sewn along the seamline are still intact but are brittle.

Hydrolysis of cotton fibers by sulfuric acid causes them to lose their flexibility, creating a stiff, plastic-like appearance. Cotton organdy is an example of a crisp fabric made by controlled hydrolysis of cotton by sulfuric acid. Exposure time, concentration of acid, and penetration into fibers is not controlled when inks are put on quilts, so the hydrolysis can be extensive. And the damage does not stop there.

Acid hydrolysis of cellulose produces compounds that are more easily oxidized than undamaged fibers. As signed textiles are used and exposed to oxygen as they age, the degradation continues. The result is stiff, weak fibers that break when movement puts stress on them.

An initial in a signature on the quilt in Figure 1 lies beside creases in a fold where the quilt had been folded exactly the same for one hundred years. (See Figure 3.) The quilting stitches might have stabilized part of the initial, but strain on the fabric caused other acid-damaged fibers to break creating a hole.

Damage can result in both warp and filling yarns breaking, thus creating a hole in the fabric as shown in Figure 4. Only one set of yarns has disappeared in the fabric in Figure 5. The size and amount of twist in both the warp and weft yarns in this fabric are similar, so the question arises as to why one set has broken and the other is intact. Judging by the thread count—usually higher in the warp direction than weft—the intact yarns are warp. One explanation for the warp yarns not breaking is that sizing placed on them prior to weaving limited penetration of the acidic ink.

Often ink components are concentrated along the outer edge of signatures, as in Figure 6. This movement occurs as the ink dries, creating a line of greater deposition like the tideline in water spotting. The acid obviously migrates with the iron compounds because damage along the edges of signatures often is more severe than within the ink areas.

Splits along signature edges are not uncommon, and solidly inked-in areas sometimes fall out because the connecting fibers around the edges are so fragile. Figure 7 shows the edge of a signature that was along a fold line; fibers have broken away completely from the adjoining fabric.

Figure 6. Concentration of ink components at the edge of an ink spill; migration of acid and other compounds to the edges of signatures as the ink dries often results in greater degradation along the perimeters of inked areas.

Figure 7. Fibers damaged by the concentration of acid that migrated to the perimeter of the inked areas broke along the edges of the signature; long breaks such as this obliterate the signature and create the potential for more damage to the surface of the quilt.

Ink Damage 163

Figure 8. Wicking of ink along yarns any from an ink spill; same movement also evident at edges of some signatures but not all; variations in ink composition, yarn construction, or finishes on the fabric may be responsible for different amounts of wicking which carries acids to more fibers, increasing the possibility of degradation.

Figure 8 shows how ink moved along yarns away from an ink spill, and the same happens with some signatures. This migration of ink increases the potential for damage because yarns outside the signature are affected. Usually pieces are signed before a quilt is made so that sewing threads are not exposed to the ink initially, but when ink was spilled on the quilt, it migrated along threads of the quilting stitches as much as one centimeter away from the spill. The sewing threads are larger than the yarns in the fabric and show no damage at this point. They probably are weakened, however.

Damage along signature lines often is very obvious, but a weakened or brittle condition of fibers might not be apparent. Breaks and small holes along signatures are not as easily detected in a quilt as they are in garments and flat textiles because the multilayered construction of quilts prevents light from passing through them. Closely observing the condition of fabric along inked areas is essential in making decisions about the use and handling of a quilt.

Considerations for Care and Use of Signed Quilts

Any decisions about storage, use, and care of a quilt should be based on an evaluation of the makeup and condition of the quilt. Inked areas, purposefully or accidentally made, should be examined closely for broken fibers. Splits in the fabric probably will be obvious. A magnifying glass helps an examiner see if fibers have broken and formed a mustache along the edge of a signature. Look for missing yarns within inked areas. Even if no damage is apparent, one still should be cautious knowing that strength and flexibility of fibers under signatures might be decreased.

If hydrolysis and oxidation have weakened fibers, then obviously stress in handling a quilt could be damaging. Work with the quilt on a large table. Avoid picking it up by an edge or corner. To move it, gently fold along unsigned areas, if possible, and lift it from underneath rather than grasping it along folded edges.

Airing and vacuuming a quilt can be sufficient to clean and freshen it. Do not hang a quilt, signed or unsigned, on a single clothesline to air. Place it flat on a clean sheet in a shaded area. Limit stress on the fabric and friction on the surface when turning the quilt over to air the back side. Use two people to turn it over.

Vacuuming with an upholstery tool and a screen laid over a quilt usually is safe, but brittle fibers along signatures could be broken if pulled against a screen. Vacuum very carefully around squares with signatures or verses and then use a clean, soft brush to gently clean the surface of signed squares. Hold the vacuum attachment near the brush to prevent dust from becoming airborne but not so near that the suction would reach the quilt. If rows of quilt stitches go through or very near signatures, avoid putting stress on the stitches when vacuuming the back of the quilt.

Signature quilts that were laundered soon after signing had the free sulfuric acid neutralized or removed and show no damage along signatures. If the acid stayed on the fabric and caused hydrolysis, the damage is done. Wetcleaning a quilt today to remove the acid is potentially more damaging than doing nothing. If hydrolysis of cellulose fibers has occurred along signatures, just wetting the brittle fibers, which normally would swell as they absorb moisture, further weakens them. Do not wetclean a quilt with signatures possibly made with an iron gallotannate ink. Look for broken fibers along a line of ink or a slight rust or brown color in the ink.

Drycleaning in a drycleaning machine is not a viable alternative, either, because of the stress in the spin cycles and friction during the hot air/tumbling cycle. Cleaning quilts is never a simple matter because of their multilayered structure. Aged soils are difficult to remove from quilts in the best condition; owners can be philosophic and consider soil on signed quilts as part of their history.

Store all quilts with as few folds as possible, changing the placement of folds periodically. Choose fold lines for signature quilts that will stress as few signatures as possible. Fold the signed quilt top to the inside, lining outside, so signatures will be protected. Avoid rolling signature quilts around a tube. The compression that occurs can cause brittle fibers to break.

Protect breaks and holes along signatures by covering them with washed sheer fabric, such as crepeline, cut to the size of the square or piece. Do not use tulle or net; both are very abrasive. Stitch the crepeline through the quilt-top fabric around the perimeter and across the interior of the square on either side of the signature so that the crepeline can reduce both friction and stress of the signed area. Stitches should be at least a half centimeter long so that a number of yarns hold each stitch.

Avoid hanging a signature quilt vertically in an exhibition if gravity will cause stress on signed squares. Use a horizontal or angled support to lessen the gravitational effect. Remember that textiles displayed on an angle or horizontally collect dust more readily, but if dust covers are used, put them off and on carefully. Do not drag them across the quilt surface.

Keep light levels low during exhibition of any quilts, but especially for signature quilts. Damaged cellulose in signatures will oxidize faster than undamaged cellulose.

New Signature Quilts

A few precautions taken by quilters making new quilts that have inked drawings or writing will help prevent the type of damage that has occurred in older quilts. Use inks that are safe for fabrics. Literature has carried this warning for two hundred years, but pens for archival work now are available from conservation supply firms and other outlets. Follow the manufacturer's directions for use. Do not heat set ink in signatures with an iron unless directed to do so for a specific formulation. How permanent the inks are under a variety of conditions is a matter for further study. Prewashing fabric several times to remove sizing might make signatures more permanent. Test inks by writing on a sample of fabric and laundering the sample.

Plan quilting stitch patterns so that you do not quilt through signatures. Also fold quilts so that signatures are not bent. With care, new signature quilts will have fewer problems than their predecessors have had.

Signatures add value to quilts for owners and researchers both today and for the future. Proper care of signature quilts will help preserve these valuable resources and the words that are written on them. Because fibers under signatures may be damaged, special attention to handling, storage, display and cleaning of these quilts is essential.

Acknowledgement

Liisa Kaaret Mobley aided the initial research of ink damage to textiles as a graduate assistant at the University of Rhode Island.

Notes and References

1. Barbara Brackman, *Clues in the Calico: A Guide to Identifying and Dating Antique Quilts* (McLean, VA: EPM Publications, 1989), 118, 179; Schnuppe von Gwinner, *The History of the Patchwork Quilt: Origins, Traditions and Symbols of a Textile Art* (West Chester, PA: Schiffer Publishing, 1987), 115. Brackman cites a Payson's Indelible Ink advertisement promoting Payson's as a household word for over sixty-five years in an 1897 volume of *Home Needlecraft Magazine* (vol.1, no.4). This places Payson's entry on the market as 1832 or earlier; Brackman states 1834 for the first sales of Payson's indelible ink. Gwinner cites an 1899 edition of the magazine with the same advertisement still touting over 65 years of sales two years later, so the longevity of the firm was estimated in the ad. These two authors assumed that indelible ink was an early Payson's product although the ad did not say that specifically. Ink makers were actively testing indelible ink recipes and applying for patents throughout the 1830s as will be discussed later in this paper.
2. Brackman, 20, 118; Jane Bentley Kolter, *Forget Me Not: A Gallery of Friendship and Album Quilts*.(Pittstown, NJ: Main Street Press, 1985), 66.
3. Brackman, 20, 103.
4. Brackman, 26, 118, 147.
5. Brackman, 151.
6. C. Ainsworth Mitchell, *Inks: Their Composition and Manufacture* (London: Charles Griffin & Co., 1937), 8, 9. J. B. Lippincott of Philadelphia also published this book in 1937.
7. William J. Barrow, "Black Writing Ink of the Colonial Period," *American Archivist* 11 (Oct. 1948): 294; C. E. Waters, *Inks* (Washington, DC.: U.S. Department of Commerce, 1940), 4.
8. Waters, 3–4; Mitchell, 14; Sidney Morse, *Household Discoveries and Mrs. Curtis's Cook Book* (Petersburg, NY: 1913), 527.
9. Morse, 527; Mitchell, 14–15; Waters, 22.
10. Mitchell, 14–15. Indigo probably was the only dye available then that did not cause the ferric precipitate to form in the ink, weakening it. The insoluble indigo was converted by a treatment with strong sulfuric acid into

indigodisulfonic acid which dissolved readily and did not combine with other ingredients nor cause the undesirable precipitation. Waters, 4–5.
11. Waters, 20; Morse, 527; Mitchell, 12; C. H. Bloy, *A History of Printing Ink: Balls and Rollers, 1440–1850* (London: Wynkyn DeWorde Society, 1967), 73.
12. Waters, 4.
13. Barrow, *The Barrow Method of Restoring Deteriorated Documents* (Richmond, VA: W. J. Barrow Restoration Shop, 1979), 5.
14. Barrow, *The Barrow Method*, 5; Waters, 4, 11. The use of sulfuric acid continued. In 1940 Waters wrote: "There can be little doubt that nearly all the blue-black writing ink sold contains sulfuric rather than hydrochloric acid. The lower cost of sulfuric acid and its freedom from the fumes which make hydrochloric acid disagreeable to handle would seem to be sufficient reasons for its general use. In addition, it is said that sulfuric acid makes the better ink." Waters, 17.
15. R. Hare, "Process for Ink devoid of free acid," *Journal of the Franklin Institute* 19 (June 1837): 464.
16. Eleanor Celuart, "To prevent Common Ink from attacking metallic Pens," *Journal of the Franklin Institute* 19 (May 1837): 383.
17. L. Ray Balderston, *Lippincott's Home Manuals; Laundering: Home-Institution* (Philadelphia: J. R. Lippincott, 1923), 46.
18. Mitchell, 330–31.
19. Waters, 3; Mitchell, 35.
20. Mitchell, 330–31.
21. *Journal of the Franklin Institute* 20 (Sept. 1837): 184–85.
22. Mitchell, 331.
23. Mitchell, 357.
24. Waters, 34.
25. Waters, 34.
26. Waters, 53.
27. Morse, 530.
28. Morse, 530.
29. Morse, 530.
30. Waters, 53.

Quilting in Webster County, Nebraska, 1880–1920

Kari Ronning

This study examines the kind of quiltmaking activities taking place in a rural, midwestern area in the period 1880–1920. Webster County, Nebraska, was chosen because it is one of the representative sites chosen by the Nebraska Quilt Project; extensive primary sources such as newspapers of the period are available; unique literary materials are available since the area is depicted in many of Willa Cather's novels. The newspapers of the period record quilts, quiltmakers, quilting parties, charitable quilting activities, and county fair results; the newspapers also advertise the goods available to quiltmakers and their prices. The frequency and content of the newspaper records help to document the changes in quilt making fashions, revealing that Webster County followed the eastern, urban fashions in the 1880s when it was still a frontier community; despite the improvements in mass communication which took place in the early years of the twentieth century, the revival of quiltmaking which was taking place in urban centers did not spread so quickly to this community, where quiltmaking was seen as an activity for older women, and quilts were little valued.

In 1849, in a story published in *Godey's Lady's Book*, T. S. Arthur lamented that quiltmaking was a dying craft; other writers in the general women's magazines later in the century spoke of quilting as if it were dead.[1] Yet the great number of quilts that have survived from the last half of the century shows that not only did technical mastery remain, but that design inventiveness, especially in pieced work, was reaching new heights. This discrepancy shows that these writers were out of touch with what was actually being done by women in rural America; by examining quiltmaking activities on a local level, where it was actually practiced, we may be able to get a better idea not only of what quilting was being done at the end of the nineteenth century, but whether and when—perhaps even why—quiltmaking declined in popularity.

We know little as yet of the conditions under which quiltmakers in the nineteenth and early twentieth centuries worked or how their activities were valued by themselves and by the communities in which they lived; often we do not even know who the quiltmakers were. The quilt projects of various states have done valuable work in locating quilts and identifying makers, but the information collected about quiltmaking in the past usually relies on the memories or oral histories of the owners of specific quilts. If we are to get a broader picture of quiltmaking activities in communities in the past, these memories should be supplemented by other sources of information. Ideally, the historian would like to read diaries of quilters which would reflect on quiltmaking activities. But the diaries of women who lived in the nineteenth century and before have not often been preserved; as most quiltmakers were women, quiltmakers' diaries are rare.

Fortunately there is an additional source of information which is available for most communities in this country: the local newspapers. This study uses information on quilts, quiltmakers, and quiltmaking activities found in the newspapers of Webster County, Nebraska, to get a picture of the state of quilting there at the end of the nineteenth century and the beginning of the twentieth. The picture will inevitably be a partial one, since a newspaper presents the public side of life; the quilter working at home for domestic use is usually ignored. However, the attitudes toward quiltmaking presented in the papers would have been part of the influences on the private quilter.

Webster County, in south central Nebraska, was one of the representative areas chosen for the Nebraska Quilt Project's study. Its chief claim to fame is that it was the home of the Pulitzer prize-winning novelist Willa Cather (1873–1947), and its landscape and people are depicted in many of her novels. Webster County is a predominantly rural area of mixed farming and stock raising. The area was used as a hunting ground by native Americans, primarily of the Sioux and Pawnee tribes. The first white settlers, led by Silas Garber (later governor of Nebraska), arrived in 1870. By 1883, when Willa Cather's family came from Virginia to join family members who had pioneered in Webster County, they found a diverse population, with immigrants from abroad who formed well-defined settlements of Czechs, Germans, French-Canadians, Norwegians, and Danes.

In 1880, Webster County was an essentially frontier community. It was connected to the outside world only by the recently arrived links of the railroad and the telegraph lines; both these links were liable to be cut off in times of heavy rain or snow. By 1920, the area was more densely settled than it is today and was near the peak of its prosperity; movies, electricity, telephones, automobiles, rural mail delivery of newspapers and magazines as well as of letters, brought Webster County from the fringes of American society to the heartland.

However, quiltmaking in Webster County, as reflected in the newspapers, did not follow the same lines of progress as other aspects of life. In the 1880s, when life was still comparatively primitive for many of the inhabitants, quiltmakers and newspaper editors were tuned into the prevailing fashions: silk quilts, log cabin quilts, outline embroidered quilts, and above all, crazy quilts. The Webster County *Argus* noted in its report on the 1885 county fair that "Webster County mothers and daughters can make their homes as attractive as any place on the wide earth if their exhibits of silk quilts, worsted work, and needlework of all kinds is a sample of their prowess."[2] The year before, the Red Cloud *Chief* had noted the "handsome quilt" exhibited by Mrs. Douglas Terry of Cowles;[3] I suspect that "handsome" and similiar words in these contexts means silk quilts, as opposed to "plain" cotton ones. Thus, the *Chief* notes that "John Parks was given a handsome quilt for his 50th birthday by his mother in McCook;"[4] in 1887, a "fine quilt" was one of the items to be auctioned off at a church social;[5] and a "handsome log cabin quilt" was offered as a prize to the most popular young lady at a Presbyterian church festival.[6]

The fashion for outline embroidered quilts, whose popularity began in the early 1880s,[7] was apparent in Webster County as early as 1884, when Mrs. Cook and Mrs. Brewer took the first two prizes in this category at the county fair.[8] Outline stitch work was also known as Kensington embroidery; Mrs W. W. Gardner, who ran the second best hotel in Red Cloud, was commended for her Kensington embroidery at the 1886 county fair;[9] Mrs. M. R. Bentley, wife of a local moneylender, gave a Kensington embroidered spread as a wedding present in 1889.[10]

Signature quilts are seldom mentioned in the Webster County newspapers; the few that are mentioned seem to have been presentation quilts to ministers rather than fundraiser quilts, for which people paid a small fee to have their names embroidered in outline stitch on the top. One country correspondent mentioned a quilt presented to Mrs. Wolff, the Methodist minister's wife, which had the names of the donors embroidered on the blocks.[11] Pioneer Methodist minister George Hummel recalled that "many of the quilts [given to him] bear the names of those long departed from this life,"[12] which suggests that such presents were more commonly given than recorded in the papers. However, one or both of the "two fine quilts" which the *Chief* notes were given to Mrs. Hummel in 1892 may have been signature quilts.[13]

Quiltmakers in the late nineteenth century did not have the large network of quilt magazines, newsletters, and quilt art books of a century later to tell them what quilters in other parts of the country were doing. Once in a great while, however, the syndicates which supplied preprinted pages of national news and feature stories to small newspapers would run news stories about notable quilts or quiltmakers. One such story, printed in 1896, describes what seems likely to be an outline embroidered quilt:

A Marvelous Quilt

Mrs. Joshua Biles, of Southington, Conn., has been working on a bedquilt at odd times since 1892, which is a wonder in its way and deserves special notice. The material is a twilled cotton, and is made of forty-one squares, seven squares each way, but the inner square takes up nine of the ordinary ones. On this is inscribed, in blue stitching, which is readily deciphered, the names of all the soldiers that went to the civil war from Southington, together with a picture of the soldiers monument. On the other squares are the pictures of places and persons of local note, such as the pastors of the churches, the postmasters of the three villages, the assessors, the contractors and builders, merchants, etc., the names of the various manufacturing firms, with the list of officers, pictures of various historic buildings, and names of the secret societies represented in the town in 1892. Mrs. Biles has been untiring in her efforts to finish this remarkable work, and it is now stretched upon a frame.[14]

Although it is not a local item, this description can furnish some insight into a number of aspects of quiltmaking, such as the length of time it took to complete a project of this sort, and it may have been a possible source of design ideas for other quilters. Most strikingly, it illustrates some of the qualities a quilt needed to attract the notice of male editors: evidence of great labor, easy decipherability, and celebration of masculine achievements; it seems unlikely that many women's names are included among the soldiers, pastors, contractors, and manufacturers represented in the quilt.

The crazy quilt dominated fashionable quiltmaking in the 1880s; and again, Webster County quiltmakers were right in style. Mrs. Terry and Mrs. Cook took first and second place for crazy quilts in the 1884 county fair.[15] Interestingly, crazy and embroidered quilts were the only categories of quilts for which the names of prizewinners were published; apparently ordinary pieced or applique quilts, if they were entered at all, were not considered worth noting. The prestige of crazy work was such that even a silk crazy work pillow was considered enough of a drawing card to be advertised for a fundraising auction.[16] When Ruby Lafayette's Dramatic Company appeared in Red Cloud, the advertising announced that Miss Lafayette would wear her celebrated crazy quilt dress, composed of over 2,500 pieces of silk and satin.[17] In 1890 a "crazy tea" social was a great success.[18] The prestige of the crazy quilt impressed even the male editors of the newspapers, who almost never mentioned any other work of women's hands; one paper noted that William Letson's birthday present from his mother had been "an elaborate combination of crazy-work."[19] As crazy quilts began to be made in humbler fabrics in the 1890s, they went out of fashion in urban areas, especially in the east; but in Webster County, enough prestige lingered into the twentieth century to make a silk crazy quilt the prize of a drawing held by the Degree of Honor, a women's society, in 1902.[20]

The oddest mention of crazy quilts to be found in the Webster County papers was not, however, a local item. Another syndicated feature told the story of Ada Martin, a Michigan quilter, who had suffered paralysis of the legs and loss of speech some years before. She occupied herself by making crazy quilts with patches which had been autographed by famous people to whom she sent the fabric. When she received a patch signed by President Cleveland, she was so excited that she accidentally knocked over a stand by her couch, which caused a loaded revolver on the stand to fire; the bullet hit her leg, curing her of her paralysis and speech loss.[21]

Clearly silk quilts, crazy quilts, and outline embroidered quilts were the most prized and publicized quilts in Webster County and the nation in the last decades of the nineteenth century. One other kind of quilt has always attracted attention: the quilt of many pieces, which awes quilters and nonquilters alike by the sheer work required to put it together. Virginia Gunn notes this tendency of editors in her study of state and county fairs in Ohio also.[22] As early as 1881, the *Chief* took note of a local woman, "Mrs. Parkes, a lady over 70 years of age [who] has just completed a quilt which contains 4,375 pieces. Any one acquainted with the tedious labor of quilt piecing can form an idea of the magnitude of the task accomplished by this aged lady."[23] The making of this quilt, clearly a show piece, indicates that not all the quilting done in frontier Nebraska was of a utilitarian nature. The news item also shows one male attitude toward quiltmaking: that it is "tedious labor." However, some male quilters have seen the quilt of many pieces as a challenge, and have sought to set records for numbers of pieces in a quilt.[24]

Most of the quilts made in the county were made by the "tedious labor of quilt piecing," a part of women's everyday work. Like many of the *Chief*'s country correspondents, "Betsy" [Elizabeth B. Knight] lamented the difficulty of finding news to send in. She wrote, "I could do as one of your gentlemen correspondents does, write about myself, I could tell how many loaves of bread I had made, the number of pies I had baked, how many quilts I pieced, and when I intend to clean house, etc., etc."[25] The off-handedness of this demonstrates vividly the utilitarian role of much quiltmaking in this period.

It appears that most quiltmaking was done alone. The picture of the quilting bee as a frequent activity in nineteenth century women's lives is not borne out by the Webster County record. It may be that quilting was a part of family gatherings and social events that were not specifically for the purpose of quilting and were not recorded as being quiltings. However, the physical difficulties of gathering people together in the rough and sparsely settled countryside of Webster County in the 1870s and 1880s were great; roads were little more than wagon tracks over the prairie, and horses could not often be spared from farm work. Most of the mentions of quilting bees and quilting parties found in this period date from the 1890s, when the population density was greater, hired help was available for more women, roads had been established and were maintained, and improvement in the means of communication, such as Rural Free Delivery and telephone systems in the mid- and late 1890s made it easier to issue invitations.

The newspaper items concerning quilting parties are especially interesting because they show how quilting was in transition in public opinion. The *Argus* on August 6, 1891, records a quilting bee at the Amack's house in 1891 that was clearly in the established tradition of a social event for various ages and sexes: "the young people in the evening had a good time until early morning." At a similiar quilting in 1893, the correspondent records that twelve young ladies and the men came in the evening.[26]

Only a few months later, however, it is reported that the Albrights have had an old-fashioned quilting, "a pleasant revival of an old time custom."[27] Another report a few years later continues the association of quilting parties with the past: "An old fashioned quilting party was given Thursday by Mrs. Frank Smelser. As in ye olden times the guests were bidden to 'come early and stay all day.' A large number of old friends and neighbors were present and enjoyed of [sic] the hospitalities of the occasion."[28]

At nearly the same time quilting parties began to become parties just for women, especially older women. In 1894, Mrs. Alex Walker of Farmer's Creek invited a few of the "pioneer ladies of this vicinity to a quilting party at her home."[29] Again in 1896, a large crowd came to a quilting at Holsworth's in honor of Mrs. Holsworth's sixtieth birthday.[30] A loss of interest in the quilting itself is perhaps reflected in the activities of a large party in honor of the sixty-third birthday of Mrs. Robert Hicks: "Carpet rags were taken in large bundles and tying quilts was one of the important parts of the day's work, two handsome and substantial quilts being completed."[31] The *Argus* noted that Miss Eva Buker "will entertain the young ladies of the community at a quilting."[32] Her party is exceptional because of the youth of her guests. It should also be noted that most of these events occurred in various rural districts, rather than in Red Cloud, the county seat. Even in an essentially rural area such as Webster County at the turn of the century there may have been differences between rural and "urban" customs.

There is very little evidence in the newspapers of organized, as opposed to social, quilting, especially in the 1880s and 1890s. In 1881, there was a notice that the Methodist Episcopal ladies would be quilting at Mrs. Frisbie's, in Red Cloud.[33] Women's church groups in Red Cloud seem to have preferred to raise money by giving "socials," which they did in great numbers and varieties. A correspondent for the small neighboring town of Guide Rock in the first few years of the twentieth century mentioned the doings of the church societies more often than any other reporters; although quilting is mentioned, it is only one of several activities, such as sewing for the poor, sewing carpet rags, and tying comforters, which these groups undertook. In 1905 the representatives of the three church sewing societies of Guide Rock met and agreed on a price for tying comforters: fifty cents each.[34] But as late as 1912 a correspondent from Batin precinct mentioned that the Ladies Aid had recently completed a quilt.[35]

The lack of notices and announcements may be because the quilting groups met so regularly that the papers felt no more need to announce them than to announce that the stores had opened for business that day. However, when the *Argus* ran a brief story on the Ladies Aid of Harvard, Nebraska, which proclaimed that they had finished their one hundredth quilt and over a period of seven years had earned $1,449.19 by their quilting and by church socials, there was no local followup. Normally the local papers were quick to "boost" Webster County by pointing out similiar feats done locally; this silence suggests that, if there was quilting done by organized groups, their records could not compare with Harvard's. By contrast, a quick scan of the newspapers in the mid-1920s revealed regular announcements of quilting meetings by Ladies Aid and Willing Workers groups.

Women in the towns did organize, particularly as winter drew near, to do sewing for charity which may have included making quilts or comforters. I have found only one record of a meeting where this was done; a correspondent from Inavale, a smaller town west of Red Cloud, reported that "The Ladies Aid Society of this place, Auxiliary to the Home for the Friendless [an orphanage in Lincoln], met one afternoon last week and though there were only eight present they pieced one comforter and tied two and sent them next day to the Home, to keep the children warm these cold winter nights."[36] It is interesting to note that piecing as well as quilting was done by these groups. Not much is known or reported in quilt histories, of group-made quilts other than friendship or presentation quilts, which were usually set together by one person from donated blocks.

Individuals who quilted for others are also hard to find. There are advertisements by women announcing that they would do plain sewing, which may have included some parts of the quiltmaking process. One woman in the town of Bladen in northern Webster County, advertised that "those wishing comforts tied or quilting done, call on Mrs. Mary McCoy."[37] It may be that women who quilted for others were known and had no need to advertise.

Generally we think of quilts as being made by women for themselves and their families. It was therefore surprising to find quilts mentioned occasionally in commercial contexts. A sale of a hotel's furnishings in 1883 listed comforters, quilts, and spreads among the items to be sold;[38] it is possible they were made by the hotel-keeper's wife, but they also may have been bought commercially. In 1895, the sheriff was authorized to buy six quilts for the county jail.[39] During the hard times of the early 1890s, after several years of drought and crop failures and the economic distress following the nationwide Panic of 1893, the *Argus* commended the plan of some merchants in Superior, a town in neighboring Nuckolls County; they proposed to have quilts, comforts, shirts, and other ready-made goods in their stores made by deserving poor families in town, in order to assist the poor and keep the money within the community.[40] This suggests that quilts and comforters had been bought commercially outside the community to be sold retail, but it is unclear whether all commercially sold quilts were factory made. Comforters were sold through the mail order houses also; Sears Roebuck's 1902 catalog carried them at prices ranging from $.47 to $1.98. A dry goods house in Red Cloud offered a line of comforters at prices ranging from $.40 to $1.25. They also advertised "a few home-made knotted comforters, extra large size, equal to two factory ones;"[41] so it may be that someone in Webster County made comforters to sell.

References to outstanding quilts virtually cease by the turn of the century, evidence, perhaps, of the decline in the respect given quilts. On the other hand, references to comforters and bedspreads rise. In the 1890s, quilts were sufficiently valued to make noteworthy gifts; in 1892 the ladies of the Pleasant Grove church gave their minister's wife "an excellent present of two fine quilts;"[42] a correspondent noted that Mrs. McNew of Stillwater precinct gave her daughter Callie a quilt and pillows when she married in 1894.[43] But twelve years later, the parents of Percy Larrick gave their son a pair of blankets and some comforters when he married.[44] What makes this item especially significant is that the Larricks were a quilting family: Mrs Larrick had entertained at a quilting bee in 1899;[45] and her husband, D. H. Larrick, also made quilts.[46] If they did not give quilts it was not because they lacked the ability or desire to make them. It may be that fashion had made comforters more suitable for solemn occasions such as weddings than the everyday quilt.

The idea of comforters having more prestige than quilts seems strange to us now, although Cuesta Benberry has shown that quilting was at a low in prestige and popularity in the first decade of the twentieth century.[47] The advertisements of the dry goods stores in Red Cloud tend to support the idea that comforters may have been more valued than quilts, at least if there is a correlation between the value of an object and the cost of the materials used in making it. Although many comforters were probably made of the same inexpensive calicoes that went into quilts, the materials that were advertised specifically for the making of comforters might cost twice as much as calico and muslin. Standard print calicoes were sold consistently for around 5 cents a yard, with specials bringing the price as low as 2 1/2 cents a yard. In 1885, Ducker's store advertised "Robe prints, nice large patterns for comforts, 5 cts worth 8 cts."[48] In 1898, the Miner Brothers store advertisement suggested "For the Fancy Comforts use . . . Silketene,"[49] though no price was listed. In 1901 Hadell's Cash Bargain House advertised ten cent cretonnes for seven cents a yard.[50]

Comforters needed more batting than quilts, which also increased their cost. Batting came in a wide range of prices and brands, usually from five to twenty cents each.[51] Mrs. Newhouse, who ran a dry goods and notions shop, advertised that she had "Cotton bats at 10 cents—Large Enough for full Comforter, 60 cents."[52]

The decline of interest in quilts has sometimes been attributed to the increased availability of machine-woven blankets. The evidence of the Webster County newspapers, though not conclusive, does not suggest that this was a major factor. Such a theory tends to presume that quilts were made primarily for warmth, and were made obsolete by blankets. Blankets could be cheap: in 1900, some were advertised for forty-seven cents;[53] in 1908, some could be bought for thirty-nine cents.[54] However, these were cotton blankets, usually gray, although some were white or tan, and measured fifty-six inches by seventy-six inches. They probably did not provide as much warmth, and certainly not as much color and decorative value, as quilts. Wool blankets, which would provide more warmth than cotton blankets, were much more expensive, ranging in price from $2.50 (on sale) to $10.00, which put them out of reach for many people.

The decorative function of quilts, however, apparently was being taken over by woven bedspreads. The Miner Brothers store advertised spreads ranging from $ .60 cents to $3.50, adding "See our special No. 6500 Fringed Quilt—a very handsome piece goods."[55] This appears to be a Marseilles-type coverlet, woven in imitation of quilting.[56] Bedspreads seem to have been considered more suitable for gift-giving than blankets, as they show up on lists of wedding presents in the period 1900–1920 more often than blankets—or quilts, for that matter.

Fortunately for the quilt researcher, local advertising during the period 1890–1910 was usually very specific about the goods and prices in the stores. Advertising in the 1880s usually consisted of a standard "card" giving the name of the store and the types of goods sold, sometimes varied by announcements that new goods had arrived. During 1910–1920, illustrations took the place of text. The highly detailed content of the decades surrounding 1900 was probably the local stores' response to the competition of the mail order houses. Many editorial paragraphs exhorting Webster County residents to trade at home, to keep their money within the community, show that local merchants felt the pressure. Local merchants used newspaper advertisements with detailed lists of goods and prices to show their customers that they could compete with mail order house prices. The local ads often read like catalogs.

One ad shows clearly that the advertisements for calicoes were aimed at quilters: "Comforts—The approach of cold weather is nearing us every day. Now is a good time to get your quilts ready. We have both the calico and the cotton bats."[57] Dress goods were always a separate, and much more expensive, category. Calicoes were virtually the cheapest fabrics sold; even unbleached muslin sold consistently at five cents a yard, and apron check ginghams, which Jeannette Lasansky notes were frequently found on quilt backs in Pennsylvania,[58] seldom went below seven cents a yard. Barbara Brackman has called the period from 1890–1925 the era of the dark quilts;[59] over and over the Webster County ads feature "Dark Prints," "Nice Dark Styles," "Standard Prints/Dark Colors." Often the ads are more specific, featuring "indigo calico, black and white calico,. . . . Turkey red black figured calico,"[60] or "blue and white, blue and red, red and white, red and black, dots, stripes, and figures;"[61] the ads even begin to mention brand names such as "Simpson Blacks and Greys, Garner's Red and Garnet."[62]

Once a quilt was completed, what public recognition could the maker expect for an outstanding example? Historians such as Marie

Webster and Patsy and Myron Orlofsky have described the institution of the county fair as a source of honor to the prizewinners, a place to show off skills and see new patterns for entrants and visitors alike.[63] However, the fair records in the newspapers of Webster County were suprisingly scanty; if quiltmakers wanted to see their names in the paper for winning prizes at the fair, they were likely to be disappointed. In the first place, the fair itself was some-what irregular, especially in the hard times of the early 1890s—one year the agricultural society didn't decide until early September that there would be a fair in early October. In the late 1890s, the fair was dropped completely in some years, and other devices such as an inter-state fair (to include neighboring counties in Kansas) and street fairs were adopted. By 1905, the county fair was so dead in Red Cloud that citizens of Bladen in the northwest part of the county formed the Webster County Fair Association. New fairgrounds were built at Bladen, and the fair has been held there ever since.

Even in the 1880s, when the fair was an important event in Red Cloud, there were problems. Apparently a fee was charged to enter an item for exhibit until 1889.[64] That same year the fair board decided not to charge an admission fee to the fairgrounds.[65] These fees may have kept those without much money away from the fair. Even those who did exhibit, however, were irritated by the failure of the fair board to pay the promised premiums to the prize winners; ten years later the *Chief* wrote that the new inter-state fair board had to contend against the reputation of past fairs when only a small percentage of the premiums awarded were paid.[66]

Perhaps even more disappointing than the lack of prize money may have been the lack of public recognition. Although the papers encouraged women to enter their handiwork to make the fair a success, and even though the leading women of Red Cloud were in the Ladies Auxiliary, in charge of Floral Hall where most women's entries were exhibited, often the most that would be said of their work was that Floral Hall was attractive. The papers would frequently promise to publish the lists of winners, but they seldom appeared; occasionally the editor would acknowledge that the premium list had been "crowded out" of the paper;[67] usually the editor made no further mention of the matter. Sometimes just the male-oriented parts of the prize list appeared: the livestock and agricultural lists and the results of the horse racing.

The prize lists that were published, however, do serve to give partial glimpses of what was considered notable at scattered intervals. The crazy quilts and embroidered quilts which won prizes for Mrs. Douglas Terry, Mrs. W. Cook, and Mrs. Brewer, at the fair in 1884, have already been mentioned.[68] In 1894 Mable Bailey won a gingham dress donated by a merchant for the best patchwork by a little girl; according to the 1900 census, Mable would have been about 13 at the time. In 1895 Mrs. E. B. Goble and Mrs. McKeighan (the wife of a former Congressman) took prizes for the best quilt as judged by the quilting; Mrs. M. A. Wolf and Mrs. L. H. Rust won for best pieced worsted quilts.[69] In 1913, Mrs. George Worley, Mrs. Myrtle Cather (wife of Willa Cather's cousin), and Mrs. S. C. True took prizes for patchwork cotton quilts; Mrs. S. C. True also took a first for her silk patchwork quilt; and Ethel Fulton and Lulu Baker won for their patchwork sofa pillows.[70] Although the Bladen paper did not publish any more prize lists before 1920 that include quilts, a later issue does give a rare glimpse of the appearance of quilts at the county fair in 1920, when it mentioned that "Quilts and comforts were suspended from the ceiling."[71]

The decline of quiltmaking in Webster County is most graphically demonstrated in the coverage of a new institution in Webster County, the Farmers Institutes. Beginning as a lecture series on agricultural and domestic issues in 1909, the Institutes quickly came to feature displays of agricultural and domestic products, with prizes, very much in the manner of the fairs. The Red Cloud *Chief* published full page premium lists and reported the names of all winners of prizes: seventy-five cents for first and fifty cents for second place. In addition to a dauntingly long list of other forms of needlework, which shows the fashionable competition for women's time, there were several categories of quilts in 1911: silk pieced quilts, cotton pieced quilts, wool pieced quilts, best display of quilting, and the quilt with the largest number of pieces. The inclusion of silk quilts is interesting; most of the silk quilts found by the Nebraska Quilt

Project are nineteenth century show quilts or crazy quilts; early twentieth century silk quilts are very rare.

A separate division, for women over sixty, had only two categories: log cabin quilts and a prize for the oldest quilt made within the owner's lifetime. The association of log cabin quilts with older women is especially interesting; log cabin quilts would have been popular in the youth of these women, the period 1860–1880. In fact, log cabin quilts remained as part of the premium list for women over sixty through the 1920s.[72] However, there is no mention at all of applique work, which had also been popular in the third quarter of the nineteenth century.

The published lists of winners in all departments make a valuable source of names of quilters active in the county. Recurring names in a category signal women who were especially proficient at certain kinds of work: Sarah Brooks, for example, won prizes for her log cabin quilts in several years. Especially interesting are the names of several Czech women: Mrs. Polnicky, wife of a Red Cloud saloonkeeper, won first prize for the best wool pieced quilt in 1911;[73] Mrs Louis Vavricka took second place for wool pieced quilts in 1913,[74] and Mrs. Kralik took first place in cotton pieced quilts that same year.

Two other categories show additional uses for patchwork. Cuesta Benberry has described the vogue for sofa pillows which arose at the turn of the century.[75] These were still fashionable in Red Cloud in the teens; contestants could enter silk pieced pillows, as well as pillows with cross-stitch, hardanger, embroidery, or novelty decorations. Patchwork was also used to teach young girls how to sew; for several years beginning in 1913, there was a prize for the best quilt patches by a girl under ten years of age.

In 1914, quilts were dropped entirely from the regular needlework department of the Institutes.[76] The association of quiltmaking with older women had been made official. Women over sixty could still enter log cabin quilts, or compete for the prize for the oldest quilt made within the owner's lifetime (although there were few prizes given in this category, suggesting that few quilts were entered). Perhaps there was not enough interest in quilts among younger women to warrant keeping quilts in the regular needlework department; in some years only one prize was awarded in some of the categories, which suggests that there had been only one entry. Or when the same woman took both first and second prizes in a category, one wonders how much competition she actually had. In 1916, the list of categories for women over sixty was expanded to include cotton pieced quilts, although only one prize was given—again, perhaps because there was only one entrant. Not until 1920 did the list expand to include silk and wool quilts again, as well as a prize for best hand-quilted quilt; all, of course, for women over sixty. For a few years there was still a prize for quilt patches by girls under ten, dominated by girls of the Coon family, but that category was dropped in 1917.

The shufflings of premium lists do not, in themselves, prove what the attitudes were toward quiltmaking in this period. Fortunately, Webster County has a unique source of information concerning the lives of its people: the stories of Willa Cather. Cather was a great artist who was also a keen observer; she drew upon her memories of people and events in the Webster County of her girlhood, and her observations of the area as she returned periodically to visit her parents, to create some of her greatest novels.[77] The role which quilts play—or do not play—in her stories serves as a crosscheck to the more impersonal newspaper records, for Cather is concerned with objects as they represent the values and associations of her characters.

In *My Antonia* (1918), for example, the alien nature of Antonia's immigrant family is represented, for their American-born neighbors, by their feather quilt, as Jim Burden, the narrator, calls it; now we would be more likely to call it a comforter or even a feather bed. Used to the thin cotton quilts of nineteenth century America, the billowy feather "quilt" seems as strange to the neighbors as the uses to which Mrs. Shimerda puts it, as a potholder and warming oven to keep coffee cakes and roast goose warm. "The story got about that the Shimerdas kept their food in their feather beds."[78] The achievement of the Czech women who won prizes at the county fair is the more remarkable when placed in this context.

More conventional quilts serve to represent the warmth of home to heroines who must leave home; both Thea Kronberg in *The Song of the Lark* (1915) and Lesley Fergusson in "The Best Years" (1941) sleep in little attic bedrooms (based on Cather's own room in Red Cloud), where they lie snug under heavy quilts as the snow sifts in through gaps between the shingles of the roof.

On the other hand, the absence of conventional quilts underscores the special qualities of heroines such as Nelly Deane in "The Joy of Nelly Deane" (1912) and the fascinating Marian Forrester in *A Lost Lady* (1923). Nelly, a petted only child, is the only girl in town to have a white counterpane and a white fur rug in her bedroom. The prestige of the white bedspread is shown even more clearly in *A Lost Lady*, where a white coverlet graces the bed of Captain and Mrs. Forrester, the wealthiest and most aristocratic residents of Sweet Water, Nebraska. When young Neil Herbert is brought into the room after falling from a tree and breaking his arm, to await the doctor, he contrasts the elegant room with its white bed and walnut furniture with his own shabby home.

O Pioneers! (1913) helps to document the relegation of quiltmaking to the old (and, by extension, the old fashioned). The heroine, Alexandra Bergson, takes charge of the family farm while still in her teens, and makes it a success by her love of the land and her willingness to try new ideas in farming. Independent and progressive as she is, she still values the past. Every winter she invites old Mrs. Lee, her brother's Norwegian mother-in-law, to visit her so that Mrs. Lee can enjoy doing things in the old ways: speaking Norwegian instead of English, wearing nightcaps, taking baths without having to use the new bathtub, and piecing and quilting.[79] Nowhere else in the novel is there any indication that Alexandra makes quilts; it is simply one of the old-fashioned things she does with old Mrs. Lee. The quiltmaking affirms Alexandra's value for the past, but it also affirms that quilts were considered things of the past. Interestingly enough, Mrs. Lee herself values her newly-made cross-stitch apron more, taking it to show off to a neighbor.

One of Ours (1922) reveals most dramatically the attitudes toward quilts in Webster County in the pre-World War I period. The hero, Claude Wheeler, was inspired by Cather's cousin, Grosvenor Cather, who was killed in the war, and many other characters have prototypes among Webster County people. The hired girl in Claude's father's family is old Mahailey, a character based on Marjorie Anderson, who served Cather's parents nearly all her life. Mahailey had brought with her to Nebraska three quilts made by her mother back in Virginia: a log cabin quilt, a Laurel Leaf, and a masterpiece Blazing Star. For years she had hidden them away, knowing that Claude's grasping and up-to-date family would have no use for them except for horse-blankets. Mahailey has been saving the quilts to give to Claude, knowing that he is the only one who cares about her, the only one who is searching for values that are not utterly materialistic.[80] Unfortunately, Claude's wife is the frigid Enid, whose only desire is to be a missionary in China. The fate of the quilts after Claude's death in the war is left untold. The novel thus contains a scathing picture of the greed and materialism, the lack of respect for traditional values and ways of doing things, which Cather saw as pervading American life. The quilts represent a way of creating beauty and order out of the humble materials of life, the beauty and order that Claude tries vainly to find in his life.

Cather's novels help to verify some of the conclusions drawn from the newspapers of Webster County, showing as they do that quiltmaking in this community, in the early twentieth century, was associated with older women and with traditional ways of doing things. Her novels and stories show the greater prestige attached to the white bedspread or coverlet; they also show how quilts, even old family quilts, were of little value to people who considered themselves modern.

The newspapers show what kinds of quilts were valued in the last decades of the nineteenth century, such as the silk and crazy quilts, and quilts with commemorative functions such as some outline embroidered quilts. The records also show how the value was expressed: not only in the fundraising, friendship, and presentation quilts about which much has been written elsewhere, but also in quilts used as prizes and wedding gifts. Reading the matter-of-fact mentions of more everyday quiltmaking also shows how much quilts were part of women's lives: part of their work, part of their philanthropic activities, perhaps even part of their household shopping, as well as part of their recreation and social life. Changes in the participants and nature of the quilting party become apparent, as first the men and then the younger women drop out or are dropped. The newspapers show us the materials quiltmakers had to work with and their costs; they also show us the competition quilts faced as useful objects—from comforts, blankets, and bedspreads—and the competition which quiltmaking faced as an activity from other forms of needlework, as shown in the long lists of needlework premiums at the fair. The newspapers record the names of many quilters, most of them considered outstanding in some way, whose names would have been lost otherwise.

To most appearances, quiltmaking in Webster County in 1920 was a dying craft, practiced only by a few older women, no longer even taught to beginning sewers. Elsewhere the revival of interest in antiques and "Colonial" objects and handicrafts had helped foster a revival of interest in quiltmaking; the national women's magazines in the urban centers of the east had begun to praise "grandmother's quilts."[81] Marie Webster and Carrie Hall agreed that the revival had begun about 1915 or before,[82] about the same time it was discarded from the premium lists in Webster County. Perhaps other local studies will reveal whether the revival came earlier to areas (such as urban centers) where quiltmaking had been old-fashioned long enough to have become quaint rather than dowdy, as it may have become in rural areas.

Clearly the new fashion for quiltmaking came later to Webster County, but when it came, there was no need for revival: quiltmaking had never been dead, just ignored, since it was practiced by the very young and very old. A correspondent from Batin precinct reported that "the Ladies' Aid quilted a quilt for Maudie Duval last Thursday. She says she will have another one ready to quilt on her seventh birthday. She does the sewing herself."[83] Some years later the *Argus* reprinted an article from the *Nebraska State Journal* concerning a Bladen woman, Nancy Garloch, aged ninety-nine; the article ended, "She delights in quilting, and in spite of her failing eyesight, often assists her daughters or granddaughters in their quilting work."[84] Women and girls like these kept quilting alive in Webster County, to flower in the 1920s and 1930s.

Without the newspapers, we should not have known about most of these women. Relatively few of the quilters mentioned in the papers are represented in the Nebraska Quilt Project's Red Cloud survey data. Families move away or die out, quilts wear out, and memories fade. More work needs to be done by researchers in other localities to see how they compare with the patterns which the Webster County records demonstrate. When that is done we may be able to see the ebbs and flows of quiltmaking across the different areas of the country, and understand better what the quiltmakers were doing and why. The records provided by the newspapers, scanty or tantalizing as they sometimes are, preserve for us what may be the only contemporary records of many of the hitherto anonymous quiltmakers of the past.

Notes and References

1. Jeannette Lasansky, *In the Heart of Pennsylvania: 19th and 20th Century Quiltmaking Traditions* (Lewisburg, PA: Oral Traditions Project, 1985), 59.
2. Webster County *Argus* (Red Cloud, NE), October 15, 1885. This paper will be cited as *Argus* hereafter.
3. Red Cloud *Chief* (Red Cloud, NE), Sept 19, 1884. This paper will be cited as *Chief* hereafter.
4. *Chief*, May 8, 1884.
5. *Daily Evening Chief* (Red Cloud, NE), December 29, 1887.
6. *Chief*, February 22, 1884.
7. Virginia Gunn, "Crazy Quilts and Outline Quilts: Popular Responses to the Decorative Art/Art Needlework movement, 1876–1893," *Uncoverings 1984*, ed. Sally Garoutte (Mill Valley, CA: American Quilt Study Group, 1985), 140.
8. *Chief*, September 26, 1884.
9. *Argus*, October 22, 1886.
10. *Argus*, February 7, 1889.
11. *The Nation* (Red Cloud), August 28, 1902.
12. *Nation*, December 29, 1903.
13. *Chief*, September 23, 1892.
14. *Argus*, January 30, 1896.
15. *Chief*, September 26, 1884.
16. *Daily Evening Chief*, December 29, 1887.

17. *Daily Evening Chief*, December 27, 1887.
18. *Argus*, November 20, 1890.
19. *Argus*, May 7, 1885.
20. *Argus*, March 14, 1902.
21. *Argus*, December 23, 1886.
22. Virginia Gunn, "Quilts at Nineteenth Century State and County Fairs: An Ohio Study," *Uncoverings 1988*, ed. Laurel Horton (Mill Valley, CA: American Quilt Study Group, 1989), 117.
23. *Chief*, Sept 22, 1881.
24. See Janet Carruth and Lorene Sinema, "Emma M. Andres and Her Six Grand Old Characters," *Uncoverings 1990*, ed. Laurel Horton (Mill Valley, CA: American Quilt Study Group, 1991), 88–108, for a discussion of some twentieth century male quilters and the challenges they set themselves.
25. *Chief*, January 15, 1880.
26. *Argus*, October 26, 1893.
27. *Argus*, February 1, 1894.
28. *Argus*, August 8, 1896.
29. *Argus*, October 18, 1894.
30. *The Golden Belt* (Red Cloud, NE), March 13, 1896.
31. *Argus*, October 5, 1900.
32. *Argus*, August 3, 1900.
33. *Argus*, December 1, 1881.
34. *Nation*, October 5, 1905.
35. *Argus*, March 29, 1912.
36. *Argus*, January 28, 1886.
37. *The Bladen Enterprise*, November 5, 1915, and subsequent issues for a month.
38. *Argus*, July 5, 1883.
39. *Chief*, December 6, 1895.
40. *Argus*, November 15, 1894.
41. *Argus*, September 21, 1900.
42. *Chief*, September 23, 1892.
43. *Argus*, November 1, 1894.
44. *The Bladen Enterprise*, September 11, 1908.
45. *Argus*, March 3, 1899.
46. See Kari Ronning, " 'Love was in the Work:' Pieced Quilts," in *Nebraska Quilts and Quiltmakers*, ed. Patricia Cox Crews and Ronald C. Naugle (Lincoln: Univ. of Nebraska Press, 1991), 52–53, for a picture of one of the quilts made by D. H. Larrick.

47. Cuesta Benberry, "The 20th Century's First Quilt Revival," *Quilter's Newsletter Magazine* (July/August 1979), 20–22.
48. *Argus*, November 12, 1886.
49. *Chief*, August 19, 1898.
50. *Argus*, June 1, 1900.
51. Miner Brothers' advertisement, *Argus*, October 5, 1900.
52. *Chief*, February 8, 1907.
53. Miner Brothers advertisement, *Argus*, September 21, 1900.
54. New York Store advertisement, *The Commercial Advertiser* (Red Cloud), September 21, 1908.
55. *Argus*, May 19, 1899.
56. The Sears Roebuck Catalog (1902; rpt. New York: Crown, 1969), describes many of its bedspreads as being Marseilles spreads.
57. *Chief*, August 19, 1898.
58. Jeannette Lasansky, "The Typical Versus the Unusual/Distortions of Time," *In the Heart of Pennsylvania: Symposium Papers* (Lewisburg, PA: Oral Traditions Project, 1987), 61.
59. Barbara Brackman, *Clues in the Calico: A Guide to Identifying and Dating Antique Quilts* (McLean VA: EPM Publications, 1989), 159–60.
60. *Argus*, October 25, 1894.
61. *Argus*, May 11, 1900.
62. *Argus*, September 21, 1900.
63. Marie Webster, *Quilts: Their Story and How to Make Them* (1915; New York: Tudor, 1948), 138; Patsy and Myron Orlofsky, *Quilts in America* (New York: McGraw-Hill, 1974), 55–58.
64. *The Republican* (Red Cloud), September 20, 1889.
65. *Argus*, September 12, 1889.
66. *Chief*, September 15, 1899.
67. *Argus*, October 18, 1883.
68. *Chief*, September 25, 1884.
69. *Argus*, October 24, 1895.
70. *Bladen Enterprise*, October 31, 1913; November 7, 1913.
71. *Bladen Enterprise*, September 2, 1920.
72. *Argus*, October 18, 1928.
73. *Chief*, December 28, 1911.
74. *Chief*, November 20, 1913.
75. Benberry, 20.
76. *Chief*, November 5, 1914. The information in this paragraph is drawn from the premium lists published in both the *Chief* and the *Argus*, usually in

November, in the years 1914–1917 and 1919–1920; there was no Farmers Institute in 1918 because of the war.
77. See Mildred Bennett, *The World of Willa Cather* (Lincoln: Univ. of Nebraska Press, 1961); and James Woodress, *Willa Cather: A Literary Life* (Lincoln: Univ. of Nebraska Press, 1987), for discussions of the Nebraska roots of Cather's novels. Evelyn Haller, "Cather and Women's Art," *Nebraska Humanist* 10, (1989): 73–89, discusses quilts in Cather's life and novels in the context of Cather's respect for the way women could make an art out of the activities of everyday life: keeping house, cooking, gardening, needlework.
78. Willa Cather, *My Antonia* (Boston: Houghton Mifflin, 1918), 139.
79. Willa Cather, *O Pioneers!* (Boston: Houghton Mifflin, 1913), 189.
80. Willa Cather, *One of Ours* (New York: Knopf, 1922), 72–73.
81. Jeannette Lasansky, "The Colonial Revival," *Pieced by Mother* (Lewisburg, PA: Oral Traditions Project, 1987), 105.
82. Webster, 8; Carrie Hall and Rose Kretsinger, *Romance of the Patchwork Quilt in America* (1935; New York: Bonanza, n. d.), 17.
83. *Argus*, March 29, 1912.
84. *Argus*, March 10, 1921.

From Myth to Maturity:
The Evolution of Quilt Scholarship

Virginia Gunn

Quilting myths are realities of quilt history. Romantic myths have been combined with historical facts as people interpreted America's quilting past. They continue to be accepted as true even when proven to be inaccurate. Myths survive and thrive because they reflect people's dreams, ideals, and values. They provide images and stories that unite and inspire members of society. Signs of maturity in quilt study, as in other fields of research, include a willingness to revise past scholarship in light of new knowledge, and an ability to recognize and appreciate myths, without letting them impede interpretations based on accurate and documented facts.

The June 12, 1992 issue of the *Wall Street Journal* contained an intriguing front-page story headline: "Tale of Betsy Ross, It Seems, Was Made Out of Whole Cloth." The article goes on to explain that the story of Betsy Ross sewing the first flag for George Washington "is actually—a fabrication," a legend largely invented and embellished by her grandson in the early 1870s, a time when Americans were ready to embrace stories that glorified their "birthright as Americans through their colonial lineages." The tale of Betsy as a founding mother complemented stories about the founding fathers. Artist Charles Weisburger's painting "Birth of the Flag" further immortalized Betsy in the 1890s and her story became an important "part of the nation's fabric."[1] Weisburger and another history enthusiast turned a building near Betsy's original dwelling into her landmark home. Today it is a Philadelphia tourist attraction, almost as popular as the Liberty Bell, and is visited by half a million people each year. While historians note that the legend is factually untrue, most people agree with the director of her home that "some myths are good," and that if people did not believe Betsy Ross actually sewed the first flag, they would need to claim that honor for someone else, a point quilt author Ruth Finley also made in 1928.[2]

Myths, like stereotypes, have some basis in empirical fact. Betsy Ross, for example, did make a pennant for the Pennsylvania Navy in 1777. Myths have to be believable, but they do not have to be historically accurate or based on documented proof in order to be accepted as true and taken to be real. Myths take pieces of the past and hold them together in a colorful mosaic with emotional attachment, which is reinforced by songs, stories, art, nostalgia, and the media.[3]

Myths reflect people's dreams, ideals, and values. They provide unifying images that inspire people and unite them as members of a society. Literary scholar Mark Schorer defines myth as "a controlling image that gives philosophical meaning to the ordinary facts of life."[4] Henry Nash Smith, historian, points out that myth "fuses concept and emotion into an image."[5] Every society perpetuates such images or illusions for they help societies create and maintain order. They are fundamental to the human condition. Myths or stories support the ideals, goals, and values of every society and help make them palatable to the next generation. In times of great movement, myths help unify people from differing backgrounds. They serve as shared truths which help members of society identify with each other and work together for the common good. Little wonder that myths are important to this country. It should be no surprise that "behavior and belief based on myth survives, and in fact thrives, in the contemporary world."[6]

While myths have a positive function, they can also have negative influences. In the practice of history, they can lead to misguided scholarship. Well-entrenched and unrecognized myths long accepted as known facts can interfere with objectivity. As southern historian George B. Tindall points out, they may "predetermine the categories of perception," causing scholars to overlook things that do not fit the established mental images.[7] The created images we call myths can be hard to let go of because they are "emotionally charged mental pictures." If scholars are not careful, and if they do not recognize myths for what they are, the body of "false beliefs" accepted as valid can color historical analysis and interpretation.[8]

Historians cannot simply identify entrenched myths and discard them as useless lies because myths have a "real existence." Myths become true and real in the sense that they are believed and people base action on them. They can be "psychologically true even though factually false."[9] The presence of myths must be dealt with when one attempts to write history of any kind. Myths need to be recognized and valued for what they are, but should not be taken for documented fact. Historians must consider these "public dreams" that help "orchestrate human behavior" and must learn, as Patrick Gerster and Nicolas Cords, experts on American myth, point out, to distinguish "objective reality from perceived reality.[10]

Three steps help one learn to distinguish objective history from perceived history in scholarship. First, scholars need to identify commonly held beliefs which are deficient, romanticized, and inaccurate. They must be willing to reject cherished and relatively unexamined assumptions and be willing to get the facts straight, to be accurate, and to document statements. This may mean, as Kenneth Ames points out, rejecting the "myth-symbol orientation" characteristic of much of the early decorative arts scholarship.[11] After this is done, scholars must consider and determine how and why such errors in understanding came to be part of the literature. Finally, they must understand how myths functioned. They need to identify the values that myths reinforced in order to persist over time. When these steps are accomplished, scholars can accept myths for the positive roles they play in human life without letting them interfere with mature scholarship, which should focus on understanding and telling an interpretation of the past based on careful documentation. This too, hopefully, will be of value to society.

Historians must also recognize that they themselves sometimes contribute to the origin and survival of myth. Creative imagination is an important element in the historical process. Historians must piece together and try to make sense of the clues of the past. History is always a "dual product of documentation and imagination."[12] Despite the illusion of accuracy, historians are often forced to use their imaginations in order to synthesize and make sense of available material. Limited to facts saved and recovered, they never have a complete view of the subject they are working on. As historian William H. McNeill points out in *Mythistory and Other Essays*, arranging facts to create history involves "subjective judgments and intellectual choices."[13] Recognizing this, historians have always considered revision an essential part of the historical process. Those who write history must be willing to revise past assumptions when new facts come to light suggesting new conclusions.

Quilting myths are one of the realities of quilt history. As in most fields of scholarship, romantic myths were often combined with historical facts as people scrutinized and interpreted America's quilting past. Successful quilting myths have been perpetuated because they are satisfying to the American public. The tale of Betsy piecing together bits of red, white, and blue fabric for the father of our country is dear to the hearts of most contemporary quilt lovers, just as it was to past patriots. This excellent example calls attention to the fact that myths are part of culture. Because they may encapsulate a different kind of truth than historical fact, they form a body of beliefs that have a life of their own. They survive and thrive as accepted truth even when proven to be historically inaccurate.

To gain an understanding of how a portion of the "romance" of the patchwork quilt developed and functioned, this presentation will briefly focus on several well-entrenched myths which are offered to explain the origins of American quilts. People are always curious about when and how things began. Early scholars, lacking access to the primary materials we have uncovered today, often guessed at what happened in the seventeenth and eighteenth centuries. They began the intertwined myths which usually identify patchwork quilts as distinctly American textiles which have been important parts of the American scene since the earliest colonial days when women of every class and background pieced together the tiniest fragments of precious scarce textiles by candlelight in order to make warm bedcoverings to protect loved ones. These romantic images were born, embellished, accepted by the general public, and finally questioned by scholars as quilt scholarship passed through three phases: a pioneer period (1890–1930) when interest in colonial-revival decorative arts stimulated quilt study; a practical era (1930–1970) emphasizing patterns and how-to books; and a revival period (1970–1990) characterized by increasingly sophisticated and well-documented interdisciplinary studies.[14]

The roots of quilt study extend back to the interest in collecting colonial artifacts that emerged as a response to the industrialization and urbanization of nineteenth-century America. By the mid-nineteenth century city dwellers began to consider quiltmaking a country craft of nostalgic interest. The women who organized the great Sanitary Fairs in the 1860s to raise money for the war effort presented quilting as a craft of olden times. They arranged rooms of curiosities, precursors to current museums, and included quilts among the antiques, exotic treasures, and battlefield souvenirs put on display. They also gathered antique furnishings and recreated "colonial kitchens" as an attraction of these events, presenting tableaux scenes of women grouped around quilting frames in costumes of days gone by. A New England log house featured at the Philadelphia Centennial Exhibition of 1876 continued these practices.[15] Such events stimulated people's interest in collecting colonial antiques. Ironically, quilts, still being produced in huge numbers, began to be categorized as colonial objects.

As women tired of cluttered Victorian interiors in the late-nineteenth and early twentieth centuries, they often turned to decorating with colonial-revival styles, creating a demand for colonial or colonial-reproduction furniture and textiles. Early twentieth-century tastemakers defined the term "colonial" loosely, so that objects from "early times" could be made anytime in the pre-industrial period from 1620 to 1830.[16] Even with this broad and inclusive definition, quilts did not really qualify as colonial objects, for most of them had actually been made after 1830 when textiles and thread became inexpensive and when middle-class women had more leisure to devote to quilting. Those who liked quilts in their colonial-revival rooms just overlooked this inconsistency.

In the 1890s, expert collectors began to publish books about decorative objects, focusing on colonial furniture, china, pewter, iron, brass, pottery, and eventually textiles. The early authors paid very little attention to quilts for they had begun their collections in the mid-Victorian era when quilts were universally used and not yet forgotten items of the past. Alice Morse Earle, one of the era's most widely consulted authors on antiques, first called attention to quilts in her book *Home Life in Colonial Days* which appeared in 1898, while admitting that quilting was "not an obsolete accomplishment."[17] The same year Eliza Calvert Hall presented her fictional tale *Aunt Jane of Kentucky* with its vivid comments on life and quilts. In 1912, Hall authored the first book devoted exclusively to textile bedcoverings, *A Book of Hand-Woven Coverlets*.[18] The success of this publication undoubtedly encouraged publishers to take risks on other textile topics.

Marie Webster's pioneering book, *Quilts: Their Story and How To Make Them*, appeared in 1915. Following the models for decorative arts historical scholarship, Webster traced the history of quilts in the needlework context from antiquity to the present. Aware that settlers on the western frontier had recycled bits of worn clothing into quilts in the nineteenth century, Webster believed that these pioneers had "passed through the same cycle of development as did their ancestors in the beginnings of the original colonies along the seaboard." Like most people living in an era dominated by interest in colonial-revival styles, Webster expected to find evidence of quilts in the earliest European settlements in the new world. Finding little information on the patchwork quilts which she believed English and Dutch colonists had made, she surmised that quilts were in such general use that authors of that day failed to mention them, a theory later accepted as fact. Webster herself cautioned that much quilt history remained a mystery only "partially revealed" by her study.[19]

The fashion for colonial-revival styles increased in the 1920s. Women who decorated "colonial" bedrooms wanted more information on old quilts, but quilt scholarship had lanquished as women knitted and crocheted in the World War I years. An eager audience read Ruth Finley's *Old Patchwork Quilts and the Women Who Made Them* when it was published in 1929. Finley outlined major areas of study that continued to occupy quilt historians for the next half century.

At the same time Finley, a product of her times, added to the myths about the origin of quilts in a way that made sense to the general public. Following popular Darwinian paradigms, Finley proposed an orderly evolutionary development of quilt designs, working from simple to complex. She began with the random crazy pattern, then progressed logically to hit and miss, Roman Wall, one-patch, two-patch, three-patch, and so on to the more complicated styles. Echoing Darwin's themes, all this took place in the early colonial period, so that by 1750 quiltmaking had became a highly developed and "universal form of needlework" practiced in both mansion and cabin.[20] Unable to document this theory-derived stance with either primary literature or extant objects, Finley suggested that early textiles had worn out in use and in washing, another conjecture often accepted as documented fact.

Like Webster and Finley, most women who liked quilts wanted to believe that they had always been part of American history. Since none remained from the early times, it seemed plausible to believe that they had been in general use and were worn out by hard use, so much a part of everyday life that they were not of particular note to the men who wrote the history of that time. Quilts functioned as symbolic objects. They called attention to women's ability to make things of beauty from small scraps and to do this under difficult circumstances. They testified to women's continuous contributions to their families, homes, and country since the earliest settlements. People accepted imaginative explanations to justify this stance as the truth.

During the second period of quilt scholarship, which extends from 1930 to 1970, interest centered on patterns. The editors, companies, and private entrepreneurs who offered patterns to depression-era quiltmakers quoted and embellished the statements made by Webster and Finley. They used myths as marketing tools to introduce and sell their wares. Advertisements reinforced and glorified romantic myths. Mountain Mist, for example, claimed that the colonial quilt pattern it pictured told "the story of pioneering America."[21]

The tales of early colonial foremothers helping to establish a foothold in a new country by recycling worn textiles into beautiful quilts sustained women making scrap quilts in hard times. They became entrenched in American mythology. Carrie A. Hall and Rose G. Kresinger of Kansas authored the major quilt book of the 1930s which they aptly named *The Romance of the Patchwork Quilt in America*. Hall accompanied the presentation of her valuable collection of midwestern pattern blocks with explanations and folk legends about their names. She accurately placed crazy quilts in the 1870s and 1880s, but continued to believe that early quilts were "strictly utilitarian" and "born of necessity" even though she admitted "no record of them exists."[22] Ruby Short McKim, who turned her quilt pattern catalog into the book *One Hundred and One Patchwork Patterns* in 1931, also stated that "quilts have always been with us" and suggested that a study of quilt names would reveal the course of American history.[23]

Quilt scholars of the 1940s and 1950s made progress at documenting quilts, the first step in good material culture research. Most, however, continued to perpetuate earlier myths.[24] Margaret E. White's *Quilts and Counterpanes in the Newark Museum* (1948) broke ground by documenting a growing museum collection but continued to state that American quiltmaking had "begun in stern necessity."[25] Lilian Baker Carlisle, who documented the well-known Vermont collection in *Pieced Work and Applique Quilts at the Shelburne Museum* (1957), relied heavily on Finley's work but wisely concluded that examples of pre-1776 quilts were too scarce for solid conclusions.[26]

Dr. William Rush Dunton, Jr., a physician whose avocation was quilts, first suggested a more plausible development of quilt designs in 1946. Based on dated quilts examined during his in-depth study of the album styles popular in Maryland in the 1840s and 1850s, Dunton abandoned earlier theories. He suggested a quilt design progression that began with whole cloth quilts, and then led to pieced chintz, to chintz applique, to appliqued calico or whole cloth geometric styles, and finally to the well-known block style of quilt. His worthy analysis had limited impact, however, since *Old Quilts* was privately printed in a limited edition of 2,000 copies during the middle of World War II.[27]

Averil Colby, English quilter and historian, in her 1958 book *Patchwork*, reminded readers that no evidence existed to support seventeeth-century patchwork and that wholecloth quilts had a longer tradition than those pieced or appliqued. Her more global interpretation of quiltmaking stressed important links and differences between American and English styles and called into question the myth of quiltmaking as an indigenous American art. Her work would be more widely appreciated as American scholarship matured in the 1970s and 1980s.[28]

In spite of progress in sorting truth from fiction during the second phase of quilt scholarship, the origin myths, as well as others, persisted, perpetuated as new works appeared. In 1963, Rose Wilder Lane, writing the text for the *Woman's Day Book of American Needlework* continued to report that patchwork originated in "the most extreme poverty" early in the colonial era.[29] A decade later Lenice Ingram Bacon, in *American Patchwork Quilts* (1973), clearly summarized all aspects of the well-entrenched romantic myths surrounding American quiltmaking in masterful fashion; yet her high quality photographs and backgound in oral-history interviews also anticipated new ways of study.[30]

Several books published during the turmoil of the early 1970s pointed the way to the next phase of quilt scholarship. Jonathan Holstein, in *The Pieced Quilt: An American Design Tradition* (1973), continued entrenched myths of anonymous women creating utilitarian pieced covers because of necessity, thereby creating art made out of "useless scraps."[31] At the same time Holstein raised key questions about the romance of quilt history that opened the debate of the next two decades. The exhibit he and Gail van der Hoof had curated for the Whitney Museum of Art in 1972 served as a catalyst for scholarship, inspiring such people as Carleton L. Safford and Robert Bishop as well as Patricia Cooper and Norma Bradley Buferd to initiate important projects.[32] In 1974, Patsy and Myron Orlofsky authored their watershed work, *Quilts in America*. While the Orlofskys questioned numerous myths, they continued the long-accepted conjectures that patchwork quilts originated in colonial necessity and must have been too commonplace for elaborate description in seventeenth-century sources.[33] Their book, however, set a new standard for quilt study for it was done with a careful thoroughness that demanded a higher level of scholarship from works that followed.

The need for in-depth study of primary source material led to the establishment of scholarly works. They began in the private sector at the grassroots level. Pat Almy published *Nimble Needle Treasures* from 1969 to 1976, calling on emerging quilt historians like Cuesta Benberry for articles. Joyce Gross continued the effort, starting the *Quilters' Journal* in 1977. In 1980, Sally Garoutte and a group of California women founded the American Quilt Study Group, dedicated to developing an "accurate body of information" on the "history of quilts, textiles, and the women who made them." *Uncoverings*, AQSG's annual volume of symposium research papers edited by Garoutte and later Laurel Horton, presented a growing body of well-documented and clearly written research, widely cited by others studying quilts. Garoutte's own research set the pace, focusing on questioning the well-established myths, especially those dealing with the origin and progression of quiltmaking in America. For the first time, people began to understand that seventeenth-century quilts were rare and unusual, originating in wealth and leisure rather than necessity, and in the form of whole cloth rather than crazy or pieced styles.[34]

By the 1980s, Americans began to find these new truths easier to swallow for they now had a growing abundance of wonderful quilt stories, based on documented research, to replace well-worn myths. Facts proved to be as interesting as fiction. International scholarship put quilting in global perspective. State quilt projects helped people celebrate regional accomplishments and contributions. Studies of particular types of quilts provided in-depth analysis of design development. Folklorists and oral historians recorded the wealth of information possessed by living quiltmakers. Social-cultural historians and material culture specialists helped set quilts in the social and cultural context. Outstanding exhibition catalogs set standards of aesthetic excellence. The list could go on and on.[35] Quilt scholarship produced a wealth of real-life stories to serve as worthy symbols of women's (and men's) contributions to American history as well as to world history and to provide inspiration in times of the increasing stress characteristic of the so-called post-modern era of the 1980s and 1990s.

Interestingly, the old myths persist for they contain implied or explicit morals or messages still considered pertinent today. Like the myth that George Washington could not lie to his father when asked if he chopped down the cherry tree, quilt myths persist because they fulfill important functions in society. Americans want honest children who will not lie to them. Americans also want to believe that in times of hardship, they can, like their forebears, sustain life and values by creating the best from the scraps alloted to them. The legend of the earliest colonial ladies on the wilderness frontier carefully fashioning quilts of beauty and warmth from scraps graphically symbolizes this important belief. It is a tale that will continue to be told and retold, for as William H. McNeill points out, myths or "shared truths that provide a sanction for common effort have obvious survival value."[36]

Signs of maturity in quilt study, as in other fields of research, include a willingness to revise past scholarship in light of new knowledge, and an ability to recognize and appreciate myths, without letting them impede interpretations based on accurate and documented facts. This presentation contends that history and myth both play important roles in culture, but that their contributions are most positive when clearly distinguished. Well-documented history is often as fascinating as legend. It reveals the solid ground on which further progress in historical scholarship can be built.

Notes and References

1. Valerie Reitman, "Tale of Betsy Ross, It Seems, Was Made Out of Whole Cloth," *The Wall Street Journal*, (June 12, 1992): A1, A6.
2. Ibid.; Ruth E. Finley, *Old Patchwork Quilts and the Women Who Made Them* (Philadelphia: J. B. Lippincott, 1929), 19.
3. Patrick Gerster and Nicholas Cords, *Myth in American History* (Encino, CA: Glencoe, 1977), xiii.
4. Mark Schorer, "The Necessity of Myth," in *Myth and Mythmaking*, ed. Henry A. Murray (New York: George Braziller, 1960), 354–65, esp. 355.
5. Henry Nash Smith, *Virgin Land: The American West as Symbol and Myth* (Cambridge, MA: Harvard Univ. Press, 1950; reissued with new preface, 1970), xi, ix.
6. Patrick Gerster and Nicholas Cords, eds., *Myth and Southern History* (Chicago: Rand McNally College Publ., 1974), xiv.

7. George B. Tindall, "Mythology: A New Frontier in Southern History," in *The Idea of the South: Pursuit of a Central Theme*, ed. Frank E. Vandiver (Chicago, 1964); reprinted in *Myth and Southern History*, eds. Patrick Gerster and Nicolas Cords (Chicago: Rand McNally College Publ., 1974), 1–15, esp. 2.
8. Gerster and Cords, *Myth in American History*, xiii.
9. Ibid., xiii-xiv.
10. Gerster and Cords, *Myth and Southern History*, 1, also xiv.
11. Kenneth L. Ames, "American Decorative Arts/Household Furnishingsj" *American Quarterly* 35, no. 3 (Bibliography 1983): 280–303, esp. 285. Also see Kenneth L. Ames, "The Stuff of Everyday Life: American Decorative Arts and Household Furnishing," in *Material Culture: A Research Guide*, ed. Thomas J. Schlereth (Lawrence: Univ. Press of Kansas, 1985), 79–112.
12. Gerster and Cords, *Myth and Southern History*, xv.
13. William H. McNeill, *Mythistory and Other Essays* (Chicago: Univ. of Chicago Press, 1986), 4.
14. These phases were laid out and discussed in depth as a presentation by author Virginia Gunn entitled "Romance and Reality: A Century of Quilt Scholarship" which was presented at "Directions in Quilt Scholarship" Conference held on February 7, 1992 in conjunction with "Louisville Celebrates The American Quilt" Exhibit (November 22, 1991–March 29, 1992), sponsored by The Kentucky Quilt Project, Inc., P. O. Box 6351, Louisville, KY 40206–0251. [Proceedings of conference, in press.]
15. For further information, see Rodris Roth, "The New England, or 'Olde Tyme,' Kitchen Exhibit at Nineteenth-Century Fairs," in *The Colonial Revival in America*, ed. Alan Axelrod (New York: W. W. Norton for The Henry Francis du Pont Winterthur Museum, 1985), 159–83.
16. See Virginia Robie, "Colonial Furniture," *House Beautiful* 12 (October 1902); Robert and Elizabeth Shackleton, *The Quest of the Colonial* (New York: Century, 1907), 14.
17. Alice Morse Earle, *Home Life in Colonial Days* (New York: Macmillan, 1898), 270–76, esp. 276. For information on Earle, see Wendell D. Garrett "Alice Morse Earle," in *Notable American Women 1607–1950: A Biographical Dictionary* Vol. 1, eds. Edward T. James, Janet Wilson James, and Paul S. Boyer (Cambridge, MA: Belknap Press of Harvard Univ. Press, 1971), 541–42. For fascinating stories about early collectors, see Elizabeth Stillinger, *The Antiquers* (New York: Alfred A. Knopf, 1980).
18. Eliza Calvert Hall, *Aunt Jane of Kentucky* (Boston: Little, Brown, 1898;

reprint, 1907); Eliza Calvert Hall, *A Book of Hand-Woven Coverlets* (Boston: Little, Brown, 1912; reprint, 1914).
19. Marie D. Webster, *Quilts: Their Story and How to Make Them* (Garden City, NY: Doubleday, Page, 1915; reprint, 1926), 60–88, esp. 78; xv-xviii, esp. xv.
20. Finley, *Old Patchwork Quilts and the Women Who Made Them*, 19–29, 48–54, esp. 21.
21. "In this quilt is the story of pioneering America," Mountain Mist Advertisement by Stearns & Foster Co., *Needlecraft* (May 1932): 13.
22. Carrie A. Hall and Rose G. Kretsinger, *The Romance of the Patchwork Quilt in America* (Caldwell, ID: Caxton, 1935; reprint, 1947), 13.
23. Ruby Short McKim, *One Hundred and One Patchwork Patterns* (Independence, MO: McKim Studios, 1931), 3.
24. Florence Peto pioneered in documenting quilts. See her books *American Quilts and Coverlets* (New York: Chanticleer, 1949) and *Historic Quilts* (New York: American Historical Co., 1939). For importance of documentation in material-culture research, see E. McClung Fleming, "Artifact Study: A Proposed Model." *Winterthur Portfolio 9* (Charlottesville: Univ. Press of Virginia, 1974), 153–73. For examples of continued use of myth, see Elizabeth Wells Robertson, *American Quilts* (New York: Studio Publications, 1948), 13–14; Marguerite Ickis, *The Standard Book of Quilt Making and Collecting* (New York: Graystone, 1949; reprint, New York: Dover, 1959), 253–70.
25. Margaret E. White, *Quilts and Counterpanes in the Newark Museum* (Newark, NJ: Newark Museum, 1948), 5.
26. Lilian Baker Carlisle, *Pieced Work and Applique Quilts at Shelburne Museum* (Shelburne, VT: Shelburne Museum, 1957), esp. iii–v.
27. William Rush Dunton, Jr., *Old Quilts*. (Catonsville, MD: published by author, 1946), esp. 16.
28. Averil Colby, *Patchwork* (New York: B. T. Batsford, 1958), 19–25.
29. Rose Wilder Lane, *Woman's Day Book of American Needlework* (New York: Simon and Schuster, 1963), 78–85, esp. 78.
30. Lenice Ingram Bacon, *American Patchwork Quilts* (New York: William Morrow, 1973), 63–109.
31. Jonathan Holstein, *The Pieced Quilt: an American Design Tradition*. (New York: Galahad Books, 1973), 49–50.
32. Carleton L. Safford and Robert Bishop, *America's Quilts and Coverlets* (New York: Weathervane Books, 1974), dust jacket script; Patricia Cooper and Norma Bradley Buferd, *The Quilters: Women and Domestic Art* (Garden City, NY: Doubleday, 1977), 15–25.

33. Patsy and Myron Orlofsky, *Quilts in America* (New York: McGraw-Hill, 1974), 8–18.
34. For examples of Garoutte's work, see Sally Garoutte, "Early Colonial Quilts in a Bedding Context," in *Uncoverings 1980*, ed. Garoutte (Mill Valley, CA: American Quilt Study Group, 1981), 18–27; also Sally Garoutte, "The Development of Crazy Quilts," *Quilter's Journal* (Fall 1978): 13–15.
35. For a succinct summary of this movement, see Marsha MacDowell, "The Study of Quilts Comes of Age: Reflections on its Growth and Observations on New Directions," *Lady's Circle Patchwork Quilts*, No. 62 (Feb/Mar 1989): 49, 51, 53.
36. MacNeill, 7.

Contributors

Nancy Cameron Armstrong is an Associate Professor Emerita from the University of British Columbia. She is Chairperson of the Canadian Quilt Study Group and editor of the CQSG newsletter, *Cover Stories*. She coordinates the B.C. Heritage Quilt Project and has catholic interests in quilt research. 143 16335 14th Avenue, White Rock, BC V4A 1H2, Canada.

Barbara Brackman is a free-lance writer and curator who specializes in the history of quiltmaking. She is a former board member of the American Quilt Study Group and currently on the board of the Kansas Quilt Project.

Dorothy Cozart is a retired teacher. This article, her fourth contribution to *Uncoverings*, combines her interest in family genealogy with her continuing research of American textiles and their makers. She is currently researching the separate significant accomplishments of two early twentieth-century Oklahoma quiltmakers. Rt. 1, Box 93, Waukomis, OK 73773.

Virginia Gunn is an Associate Professor of clothing, textiles, and interiors in the School of Home Economics and Family Ecology at the University of Akron in Ohio. She teaches courses in historic costume, history of interiors, textile conservation, and material culture methods. She is currently serving as President of the American Quilt Study Group Board of Directors. 215 Schrank Hall, University of Akron, Akron, OH 44325-6103.

JaneE Hindman is a graduate student at the University of Arizona and teaches undergraduate composition and literature classes. In addition to African-American quiltmaking, her research interests include basic writing pedagogy, the fiction of black women writers, and African-American sociolinguistics. Department of English, 445 Modern Languages Building, University of Arizona, Tucson, AZ 85721.

Thomas M. Horner is a Clinical Assistant Professor of psychology in the Department of Psychiatry, University of Michigan, and he is also the Director of the Infancy and Early Childhood Clinic in that Department. 3055 Taubman Building, Maternal and Child Health Care Center, University of Michigan, Ann Arbor, Michigan, 48109-0390.

Carolyn H. Krone is a mental health nurse with the Lamaze Childbirth Prepartion Association of Ann Arbor, and she is a lecturer in the Psychiatric Nursing Division of the Department of Nursing, Eastern Michigan University. She enjoys quiltmaking as well as quilt study. 3098 Lakeview Drive, Ann Arbor, Michigan, 48103.

Kristin M. Langellier is Associate Professor of speech communication at the University of Maine where she teaches courses in performance studies, women and communication, and communication theory. In addition to studying quiltmaking as women's discourse, her research interests include family storytelling and women's personal narratives. Department of Speech Communication, University of Maine, 5774 Stevens Hall, Orono, ME 04469-5774.

Margaret T. Ordoñez, Ph.D., teaches textile conservation and the history of textiles and costume at the University of Rhode Island. Her research includes studies of archaeological textiles and problems related to the conservation of textiles. Department of Textiles, Fashion Merchandising and Design, University of Rhode Island, Kingston, RI 02881. 401-792-5481.

Kari Ronning took her Ph.D. in English from the University of Nebraska in 1980. She is a quiltmaker who is interested in the history of quilts and quiltmaking. She works on the editorial team of the Willa Cather Scholarly Edition. 2860 R St., Lincoln, NE 68503.

Index

Page numbers in **boldface** refer to illustrations.

Abendroth, Dottie, 14, 26
Abrahams, Roger, 99, 102–3
African-American quiltmakers, 85–107
African-American quilts: aesthetics, 98–99, 105–6
Alizarin, 153
Allen, Mrs., 97
Almy, Pat, 201
American Quilt Study Group, 10, 201
American Quilter's Society, 145
American Patchwork Quilts, 200
Ames, Kenneth, 194
Andersen, Patricia, 27
Anderson, Marjorie, 186
Andreasen, Karen, 38–39
Andrews, Mary, 14
Arthur, T. S., 170
Atwood, Louisa, 115
Aunt Jane of Kentucky, 197

Bacon, Lenice Ingram, 200
Bacon, Lily, 88–91, 102, 103
Bailey, Mable, 182
Baker, Lulu, 182
Barrett, Carolann, 111
Bauman, Richard, 101, 104
Beaded bag, 67, **68**
Beattie, Lillian, 105

Bedspreads, 179–80
Beeching, Robert, 52
Benberry, Cuesta, 10, 12, 99–100, 178, 183, 201
Benson, Jeanne, 19
"The Best Years," 185
Biles, Mrs. Joshua, 172
Bishop, Robert, 200
Black, Mary Louisa, 51
Blankets, 178, 179
Blaylock, Emma Tyler, 74
Book of Handwoven Coverlets, A, 197
Bottoms, Talula Gilbert, 114, 120
Bovard, Karen, 33, 35
Brackman, Barbara, 149
Broderie anglaise, 75, **76**
Brooks, Sarah, 183
Brewer, Mrs., 172, 182
Buferd, Norma Bradley, 200
Buker, Miss Eva, 176
Burdick, Nancilu, 114, 116
Burns, Mary Cozart, 62, 65
Butler, Nancy, 115, 120
Butterfield Overland Mail Route, 55

Caldwell Family, 61–81, **64**
California Heritage Quilt Project, 48, 121
Campbell, Joseph, 123
Candlewicking, 65

Carlisle, Lilian Baker, 199
Carpenter, Helen, 49, 52
Carr, Helen, 20
Cather, Grosvenor, 185
Cather, Mrs. Myrtle, 182
Cather, Willa, 170, 184–86
Chaney, David, 130, 145
Civil War, 10, 22, 71, 73, 80, 110, 150, 196
Clark, Ricky, 118, 122
Cleveland, (President) Grover, 174
Clinton-Moynihan, Nell, 18, 38
Cockrell, Linda, 21, 27
Coe, Norma, 15
Colby, Averil, 199
Colby, Mary M., 46
Colonial Revival, 187, 196–99, 200
Comforters, 177, 178–79, 180, 182, 184
Conklin, Lee, 39
Conroy, Mary, 10
Cook, Mrs. W., 172, 182
Cooke, Lucy Rutledge, 49–51, 52, 57
Cooper, Patricia, 200
Cooper, Stephanie Randall, 16
Copperas, 152
Cords, Nicholas, 194
Cotton Planters Convention, 80
Counterpanes, 70, 71
Covered Wagon Women series, 49
Cozart Family, 61–80
Cozart, Dorothy, 10
Coverlets, woven, 70; patterns: Double Bow Knot, 70; Nine Snowballs, 70; Orange Quarter, 70; Virginia Beauty, 70
Cranmer, Hannah, 115
Crazy quilt dress, 173
Crazy quilts, 171, 173–74, 183, 198
"Crazy tea," 173

Crocheting, 65
Crockett, Ellen, 36
Currier, Elizabeth, 48
Czarnecki, Elinor, 34

Damashek, Barbara, 111–12, 114
Davies, Marca, 29
Davis, Deanna, 39
Davis, Sarah, 51
Diaries, letters, memoirs, 45–57
Dolan, Pam, 28
Donabed, Sandra, 16, 30
Donnell, Radka, 110, 112–13, 119, 143
Donner, Tamsen, 51
Duncan, Oilen, 266–27
Dunton, Dr. William Rush, Jr., 199
Duval, Maudie, 187

Earle, Alice Morse, 197
Edwards, Mildred, 20
Eikmeier, Barb, 36
Embroidery, 72–73, 77, 183

Fabric: access to, 52–54; camouflage, 18; jaconette, 75; linsey, 71; for quilts, 179, 180
Fair: county, 171, 172, 173, 174, 181–82; Cotton Planters, 80; Sanitary Commission, 32, 196
Faragher, John Mark, 49
Farmers Institutes, 182–84
Fashion magazines, 74
Feather bed, 184
Ficarra, Mary Lou, 39–40
Finley, Ruth, 193, 197–98, 199
Fitch, Michelle, 22, 23
Fitzgerald, Zelda, 121
Francis, Kathleen, 18
Frink, Margaret, 52

Index

Frisbie, Mrs., 176
Fulton, Ethel, 182

Garber, Silas, 171
Garloch, Nancy, 187
Garoutte, Sally, 201
Gates, Hattie Cozart, 61–62, 76–77, 80
Gaubatz, Caryl, 29
Gebel, Carol Williams, 121
GEnie Online Quilters, 36
Gerster, Patrick, 194
Goble, Mrs. E. B., 182
Godey's Lady's Book, 170
Grear, Shirley, 22
Great Platte River Road, 45
Green Quilt Project, 15
Gross, Joyce, 201
Grudin, Eva, 105
Gunn, Virginia, 10, 174

Hall, Carrie, 187, 199
Hall, Debbie, 12
Hall, Eliza Calvert, 197
Harries, Gloria, 37
Haun, Catherine, 51
Heath, Shirley Brice, 102
Henley, Bryding Adams, 12
Hicks, Mrs. Robert, 176
Holmes, Kenneth L., 49
Holstein, Jonathan, 200
Holsworth, Mrs., 176
Home Life in Colonial Days, 197
Horton, Laurel, 10, 201
Houston International Quilt Festival, 40, 144–45
How to Make and American Quilt, 112
Hummel, George, 172

Ide, Lois, 22
Indian Territory, 45–46
Indigo, 70, 153
Inks: carbon, 154–56; damage to quilts, 149, 151, 157–64, **157, 158, 159, 161, 162, 163**; indian (india), 155; iron gallotannate, 152–54; on new quilts, 166; safety, 155; search for permanent, 151; on signature quilts, 149; silver nitrate, 156

Jacobs, Nancy Osborne, 47
Jacobs, Teresa Cooper, 5–6, 31, 32
Jewell, Trudy, 15
Johnson, Carol, 33
Jolly, Judy, 25–26
Jordan, Vergiree, 87–88, 93, 97, 1022, 103, 105
Josefina Story Quilt, The, 48
Journal of the Franklin Institute, 155
"The Joy of Nelly Deane," 185

Kensington embroidery, 172
Ketcham, Rebecca, 54
Knight, Elizabeth B., 174
Knitting, 49, 51, 71, 73–74
Kralik, Mrs., 183
Kretsinger, Rose, 199
Knauer, Katherine, 16

Lady's Circle Patchwork Quilts, 138
Lafayette, Ruby, 173
Lane, Rose Wilder, 200
Langellier, Kristin, 13, 24, 30, 38
Langeloh, Mary, 18
Larrick, D. H., 178
Larrick, Percy, 178
Larrick, Mrs., 178
Laury, Jean Ray, 121

Lehner, Eileen Thompson, 17
Leon, Eli, 99
Letson, William, 173
Lewington-Coulter, Wendy, 26
A Lost Lady, 185
Lyman, Sharon K., 27

Madder, 153
Magoffin, Susan Shelby, 51
Mahan, Laura, 122
Mahan, Sarah, 122
Maines, Rachel, 57
Mangat, Terrie, 16
Marcy, Rudolph B., 46
Marseilles-type coverlets, 179
Martin, Ada, 174
Mashuta, Mary, 24–25, 39
Mattes, Merrill J., 45
McCoy, Mrs. Mary, 177
McFarland, Linda, 23
McGee, Maureen, 36
McKeighan, Mrs., 182
McKim, Ruby Short, 199
McKinney, Betty, 15, 23
McNeill, William H., 195, 202
McNew, Callie, 178
McNew, Mrs., 178
Modern Priscilla, 38
Morrison, Toni, 99
Mountain Mist, 11, 198
Mothers Against Drunk Driving quilt, 111, 121
My Antonia, 184
Myres, Sandra, 49

Nader, Mary, 116
NAMES Project, 18, 111, 121
Native Americans, 54, 55, 171
Nebraska Quilt Project, 170–71, 182, 188

Needlework, 74, 182, 183
Nelson, Cheryl, 39
Nelson, Robert, 63, 65
Netting, 65, 72
Newhouse, Mrs., 179
Newman, Molly, 111–12, 114
Nielsen, Linnea, 15
Nimble Needle Treasures, 10, 201

O Pioneers!, 185
Old Patchwork Quilts and the Women Who Made Them, 197
Old Quilts, 199
One Hundred and One Patchwork Patterns, 199
One of Ours, 185–86
Oregon/California Trails, 45–57, **47**; bedding, 47, 54; camps, 51–52; covered wagons, 46, 47, 49, **50**, **53**, **56**; guidebooks, 46; narratives, 45; preparation, 46; sewing, 48–52, 55–57
Orlofsky, Patsy and Myron, 181, 200
Otto, Whitney, 112
Owens, Emily, 23
Owsley, Robert, 63

Paris Académie des Sciences, 154
Parkes, Mrs., 174
Parks, John, 171
Patchwork Quilts in Australia, 10
Perinatal Bereavement Quilt Project, 111
Peterson's magazine, 74
Philadelphia Centennial Exhibition, 196
Pieced Quilt: An American Design Tradition, The, 200
Pieced Work and Applique Quilts at the Shelburne Museum, 199

Index

Pine Tree Quilters Guild (Maine), 131
Play parties, 69
Polnicky, Mrs., 183
Porcella, Yvonne, 21–22
Point Bonita, 15
Powell, Gen. Colin, 18
Przybysz, Jane, 144

Quilt Expo Europa, 144
Quilt mythology, 45, 48, 49, 57, 192–202
Quilt stories, 94–96, 104–5, 134, 135–41, 143–44
Quilting: by church groups, 176–77; in groups, 175–77, 187; for hire, 177
Quilters, The (play), 111–12, 114, 121
Quilters Connection, 143
Quilters' Journal, 10, 201
Quiltmaking: in healing, 109–24; in letters, 68–69; revival, 128
Quilts: Their Story and How to Make Them, 197
Quilts and Counterpanes in the Newark Museum, 199
Quilts: album, 199; applique, 48; care of, 164–66; chintz, 57–58; color choice in, 17, 20, 22, 23–24; friendship, 112; function of, 54; fundraiser, 18, 150–51; made during Gulf War, 9–40; log cabin, 171, 183, 186; of many pieces, 174, 182; memorial, 110; given to ministers, 172,178; mourning, 18, 110, 110–124; outline-embroidered, 171, 172–73; photo-transfers on, 18; for sale, 177–78; silk, 171, 182–83, 184; symbolism in, 18–24; tied, 176, 177; wholecloth, 199–200; wool, 182, 184
Quilts in America, 200
Quilts or quilt patterns, named:
A Time For . . . , **19**
Arab Tent, 18
Arabic Lattice, 18
Bits and Pieces of America, 22
Blazing Star, 196
Blue Rituals 2, the Gulf, 30
Bows and Glory: a Mourning Quilt, 22
Cathedral Windows, 138
Checkerboard Variations, 96
Consumed by CNN, 18
Desert Storm (Johnson), 33
Desert Storm (McGee), 36
Desert Storm Double Irish Chain, **20**
Desert Storm, A Mother's Reflections, 39
Desert Stormy Weather, 16
Don't Make the War So Beautiful, 32
During the Storm, 29
Eagle Quilt, 36
February, **21**, 21–22
Flower That Shattered the Stone, The, 19
From Sea to Shining Sea, 23
Goodbye Cruel World, I'm Off to Join the Circus, or the Gulf War from the Camel's Point of View, 23
Hands Across the Sea—A Tribute to Friendship, Love and the U. S. Postal Service, 15
Hope, 15
I Love America, 22

Quilts or quilt patterns, *continued*
Inaction, 16
Iraqi Woman Buying Vegetables, **28**
Judy in Arabia, 18
Kevin's Yellow Ribbon Quilt, 15
Laurel Leaf, 186
Lessons Learned, 39
Letters in the Sand, 18
New World Order?, 17
News Reports, 5–6, **31**, 32
Nine Patch, 112
Non incende signum nostrum, Burn Not Our Flag, 22, **23**
Ocean Waves, 131
Peace is Patriotic, 39
Peace Quilts, 15
Poppies in the Sand, 19
Purple Hearts, Broken Hearts, 16, 30
Quilt for the Unknown Civilians, 33, **35**
Rally Quilt, 13
Roman Wall, 198
Salute to America, 34
Salute to Operation Desert Storm, 14
Split Nine Patch, 86
Stars and Pride Forever, 14
Storm at Sea, 18
Storm Windows, 29
Thanks to and in Honor of . . . , 22
Time of War, 22
Tulip, 69
Victory Quilt, 10
War and Peace in the Middle East, 23
War is Hell, Man, **27**
Washington's Puzzle, 18
Watch It, 26
Wedding Quilt, 12
Welcome Home American Heroes . . . who fought in the desert **and** in the jungle, 21
Where Have All the Flowers Gone?, 18
Windblown Tulips, 15
Wings Over All, **11**
With a Little Help from my Friends, 36
Yellow Ribbons, 20

Railroad stitch, 74
Red Cross quilts, 32
Rentzel, Roxanne, 20
Ringo, Mary, 52
Roberts, Annrae, 111
Rolfe, Margaret, 12
Romance of the Patchwork Quilt in America, The, 199
Ross, Betsy, 192, 193, 195
Rowley, Nancy, 10
Rust, Mrs. L. H., 182

Safford, Carleton, 200
Samplers, **66**, 67
Sampson, Betty, 30
Santa Fe Trail, 51
Schorer, Mark, 193
Schwarzkopf, Gen. Norman, 18, 24
Scissors, 78–79
Sears, Roebuck and Co., 178
Sengstacken, Agnes, 51
Sewing case, 79, **79**
Sewing machine, 76, 77, 86
Shackleford, Ruth, 55–57
Shefrin, Sima Elizabeth, 28
Shie, Susan, 15
Show and Tell, 127–46
Signature quilts, 149, **150**, **151**, 172
Sims, Lydia, 48

Index

Sisto, Penny, 30
Smelser, Mrs. Frank, 175
Smith, Henry Nash, 193
Smithsonian Institution, 129, 145–46
Sneed, Dr. Cyrus, 74
Sneed, Mary Ellen Strother, 63, 69, 73, 74, 75, 77
Snyder, Grace, 113–14, 120, 122
Solberg, Winton U., 51
Soles, Gayle, 22, 30
Song of the Lark, The, 184–85
Spinning, 70–71
Steinbock, Anna Marie Schmidt, 115, 120
Steiner, Carol, 22
Strother, Dr. John, 63
Sullivan, Mrs., 16
Summers, Ethyel, 90–91, 92, 93, 94, 104, 105, 107

Teneriffe lace, 65
Terry, Mrs. Douglas, 171, 182
Theorem paintings, 63–64
Thimble, 80
300 Years of Canada's Quilts, 10
Tindall, George B., 193–94
Tompkins, Rosie Lee, 96–104
Tootle, Ellen, 52
Trechsel, Gail, 18
True, Mrs. S. C., 182
Turner, Marion Stevens, 91–94, 103
"Two Centuries of Quilting Traditions," 99

UFOs (unfinished objects), 138
Uncoverings, 201
Urquhart, Heather, 32

Van der Hoof, Gail, 200
Vase, Nancy, 37
Vavloukis, Janet, 22, 26, 27
Vavricka, Mrs. Louis, 183

Walker, Mrs. Alex, 176
Wareham, Pam, 24
Warner, Pecolia, 102
Washburn, Nancy Lusby, 121–22
Washington, George, 192, 202
Weaving, 69–70, **71**, 71, 160
Webster County, Nebraska, 170–88
Webster, Marie, 180–81, 187, 197, 198
Weisburger, Charles, 192
Wesleyan Alumnae, The, 62, 65
Wesleyan College (Macon GA), 62–63
White, Margaret E., 199
Whitney Museum of Art, 200
Wilcox, Margarita, 19
Williams, Lynn, 24
Wilson, Marie, 99
Wolf, Mrs. M. A., 182
Wolff, Mrs., 172
Woman's Day Book of American Needlework, 200
"Women in the Eye of the Storm," 40
Woods, Mary Lou, 24, 30, 38
World War II, 11, 26, 121, 199
Worley, Mrs. George, 182

Yde, Charlotte, 30
Yost, Nellie Snyder, 113

The American Quilt Study Group is a nonprofit organization devoted to uncovering and disseminating the history of quiltmaking as a significant part of American art and culture. AQSG encourages and supports research on quilts, quiltmaking, quiltmakers, and the textiles and materials of quilts. Membership and participation are open to all interested persons. For further information, contact the American Quilt Study Group, 660 Mission Street, Suite 400, San Francisco, CA 94105.